THE SOUL OF A LION

THE SOUL OF A LION:
DIETRICH VON HILDEBRAND

A Biography by

ALICE VON HILDEBRAND

IGNATIUS PRESS   SAN FRANCISCO

Cover design by Roxanne Mei Lum

In dulcem memoriam

Dietrich von Hildebrand

CONTENTS

FOREWORD

Joseph Cardinal Ratzinger

When I was asked by Alice von Hildebrand to contribute a foreword to her biography of her late husband, I was happy to accept, as I was sure that her work would be of considerable benefit to readers in the English-speaking world. While a significant number of the books written by Dietrich von Hildebrand have been translated into English—and are still in print—unfortunately not as much is known about his remarkable and inspiring life. I was thus deeply honored by her request, but at the same time not a little apprehensive at the thought. How could I in a few lines do justice to a man whose life and work have left such an indelible mark on the history of the Church in this century of tragedies and triumphs?

Dietrich von Hildebrand was exceptional in many ways. His extensive writings on Christian philosophy, spiritual theology, and in defense of the Church's teaching, place him among the great thinkers of the twentieth century. His steadfast and determined opposition to totalitarianism, whether in the form of National Socialism or Marxist Leninism, a conviction that would cost him greatly during his life, illustrates the profound clarity of his moral vision and his willingness to suffer for what he knew was true.

In every life there are epiphanous moments, incidents or encounters that disclose something of the person's inner character, moments in which some special quality of the person shines through. When we read Alice von Hildebrand's life of her husband, we cannot but notice that she has discerned these moments with a profound intuition. She presents them to us with sensitivity and liveliness. One such moment, for example, takes place when von Hildebrand is fourteen years old. In the course of a long walk with his older sister, she tries—with increasing exasperation—to explain to him that all moral values are relative; they are completely determined by our circumstances, by our particular time and place. Young von Hildebrand reacts instinctively against such a view and argues forcefully that such cannot be the case. Upon returning home, his sister enlists the support of their father on her behalf, who somewhat dismissively says that it is only because Dietrich is fourteen years old that he could hold such a view, and Dietrich is forced to defend himself by pointing out that his age is not really relevant to the discussion. This small incident, perhaps not uncommon in every family, reveals something fundamental about the character of the man whose life is recounted in the following pages. (It tells us also something about the way in which moral relativism must appeal to the force of authority in order to triumph; in a word, how moral relativism ends in totalitarianism.) In this incident, however, we see how, from his earliest years, Dietrich von Hildebrand was a man captivated by the splendor of truth, by the radiance of a truth that attracts and unites precisely because it lies beyond the subjectivity of each of us. It would be this same fundamental attraction for what is true that more than a decade later, on the eve of the First World War, would bring Dietrich von Hildebrand and his wife into the Catholic Church.

Together with his passion for truth, von Hildebrand also possessed from his earliest years a deep appreciation and love for beauty. Undoubtedly, the artistic vocation of his father, his youth spent in Florence, and his education in music con-

tributed to this aesthetic sensitivity. It was the experience of
God's grace, however, that led him to the fundamental recognition that truth and beauty are not unrelated. They con-
verge. They are one and the same in the Person of Jesus
Christ. This convergence means that love for truth and beauty
leads to authentic communion with others and toward the
overcoming of every form of selfishness and solipsism. In
1933, he expressed this thought with characteristic clarity
when he wrote:

> Every true value, such as the beauty of nature or of a
> masterpiece of art like Beethoven's Ninth Symphony, or
> the moral light of a generous act of forgiveness, or of an
> immovable fidelity, all these values that speak to us of
> God and touch our hearts, draw our spirit towards the
> true world of God, lead us before the face of God, and
> thanks to them, the barriers of pride, egotism, and self-
> assertion, which isolate us and make us look upon our
> fellow-men from the outside as adversaries and competi-
> tors, fall away.[1]

It was his sense of truth, his sensitivity to moral and physical beauty, his immovable fidelity that characterized his entire life and work. I remember so well when, as a young
priest in the early 1950s, I was invited to a house owned by
the von Hildebrand family, which lay within the boundaries
of the parish where I was assigned, to attend one of the
conferences he was accustomed to give during his summer
visits to Europe. Not surprisingly his theme was "beauty",
and with great eloquence and enthusiasm he spoke of its
philosophical and spiritual importance. The joy and freshness

---

[1] Dietrich von Hildebrand, *Liturgy and Personality* (New York: Longmans,
Green and Co., 1943), pp. 42–43.

of his understanding of Catholic doctrine were contagious and stood in marked contrast to the dryness of a type of scholasticism that seemed then to have become stale and brittle. Listening to him, one recognized that it was the transcendent beauty of truth that had captured his heart and his mind, a beauty he found expressed in its highest possible form in the living Liturgy of the Church, most centrally in the Holy Sacrifice of the Mass. In a certain sense, it was this same love for the beauty of truth that led him, many years later, in the midst of the crisis that shook the Church after the publication of the encyclical *Humanae vitae*, to remain ever faithful, defending the teaching of the Magisterium in a small book published very soon after the encyclical was issued.

As these brief reflections show, I am personally convinced that, when, at some time in the future, the intellectual history of the Catholic Church in the twentieth century is written, the name of Dietrich von Hildebrand will be most prominent among the figures of our time. We can therefore be profoundly thankful to Alice von Hildebrand, who has done a great service in giving us this fascinating portrait of his extraordinary and inspiring life.

INTRODUCTION

The LORD loves those who hate evil.
—Psalm 97:10

Saddened by the thought that, because of the difference in age between my husband and myself, there was a large segment of his life that I had not shared with him, I asked him to write his biography. With his usual ardor, he grabbed his pen and *currente calamo* embarked on this task of love. He wrote only in his free time, that is, in the evening when he was alone, waiting for me to come back from my classes at Hunter College. (I had been barred from teaching during the day because I had acquired a bad reputation for confusing philosophy and religion, but I was considered acceptable for teaching after sundown.) When I came home, he would read to me the pages he had added to the manuscript that day.

This book narrates my husband's life from his earliest youth to his arrival in the United States in 1940. He ended his manuscript with the fall of 1937, but I was able to complete it thanks to the wealth of information I had collected through the years. My husband was endowed with a phenomenal memory; after sixty years, he could remember the exact day, month, and year of particular events. He etched for me a most detailed history of his life, from crucial events to small details, knowing that everything is of interest to someone who loves.

The manuscript was not intended for publication, but friends who heard that my husband was engaged in this gigantic project begged him to read the parts of general interest. Their enthusiastic response convinced me, years after my husband's death, to share some of this precious work. It was no small task to decide what to select in this forest of information, handwritten in German and amounting to five thousand pages. I left out what he had shared with me alone, beautiful or sorrowful as it might be, because it was intimate. Cardinal Newman had a keen sense for the respect owed to intimacy. "At this day surely there is a special need of this warning [to be discreet]," he wrote, "for this is a day when nothing is not pried into, nothing is not published, nothing is not laid before all men." [1] Other passages I omitted because the moment was not opportune. Some that were very detailed I shortened, while those that were very condensed I enlarged.

After editing the manuscript, I needed to find a title. Because it was written for me, at my request, I was inclined to call this book "The Longest Letter Ever Written", but the title failed to convey the breadth and depth of Dietrich von Hildebrand's life. Another title had to be found. None that came to my mind and none suggested by my friends were satisfactory, either, until recently, when I was telling my dear friends the Healys about my husband's last days. Because he had been born and raised in Italy, Italian was his first language, and, when he was close to death, he spoke to me in the beautiful tongue of Dante. His voice had become a whisper, but I distinctly heard him say, "I used to be a lion; now I am but a helpless little thing." Then he took a deep breath and added, *"Ma sai, sai, la mia anima è ancora un leone"* (But you know, you know, my soul is still a lion). Upon hearing of

[1] John Henry Newman, "Ignorance of Evil", in *Parochial and Plain Sermons*, vol. 8, sermon 18 (San Francisco: Ignatius Press, 1997), 1716.

these words, my friends exclaimed, "There is your title. It covers the whole span of your husband's life."

In spite of omissions, to which I have referred, this book gives the reader an opportunity to make the acquaintance of a man with the soul of a lion. Dietrich von Hildebrand loved truth and hated iniquity. He was a faithful and devoted son of the Catholic Church and a relentless fighter against injustice. He had a glorious youth, with an intellectual and cultural formation that can truly be called unique. He was protected by grace when he did not know that grace existed, and his conversion while yet a young man was so profound that from 1914 onward his burning concern was to place all of his effort and energy at the service of the Church, which, as he frequently told me, he loved "as a bride".

When Nazism raised its ugly head, he was one of the rare persons in Germany who immediately detected the evil of its philosophy. From the early 1920s, he followed the call of God to fight against Hitler and National Socialism, at great cost to himself. He chose exile in Austria, and consequent poverty and radical insecurity, rather than compromise with the detestable political system in Germany. In Vienna, continuing his opposition to Hitler, he became a marked man and miraculously escaped death at the moment of the Anschluß. He became a refugee in France, where his family was constantly exposed to deprivation and danger, and, when the Nazis invaded in 1940, the von Hildebrands were forced into hiding. Protected by Providence, they arrived in the United States shortly before Christmas that same year.

Now that he is hidden in the mystery of eternity and cannot be tempted by the appeal of human glory, I hope this testimony will gain for Dietrich von Hildebrand the recognition that he deserves. He fought, not for a human crown, but for the glory of God.

PART ONE

CHAPTER 1

Childhood and Adolescence
1889–1906

On Friday, October 11, 1889, a young man by the name of Richard Strauss rang the old-fashioned bell at 3 Piazza San Francesco di Paola in Florence, the villa of the sculptor Adolf Hildebrand. He arrived with a letter of recommendation from a great friend of the Hildebrands, the famous conductor Hermann Levi. The promising young musician was warmly received, and soon a lively discussion on artistic themes developed. But, in the course of the evening, Adolf Hildebrand's wife, Irene, who was pregnant, had to excuse herself. The birth of her child was imminent, and she retired to her bedroom. The next day, about nine o'clock in the morning, she gave birth to her last child and her only son by Adolf Hildebrand. His parents named him Dietrich Richard Alfred. He was born under the aegis of music, and music was to play a prominent role in his life.

What was the background of this little boy who, some forty-five years later, had the singular honor of being called the "enemy number one" of National Socialism by the German ambassador in Vienna, Franz von Papen?

Dietrich von Hildebrand begins the voluminous epistle he wrote me with a hymn of gratitude to God, who had given him existence through his parents, Adolf and Irene Hildebrand.[1] Irene especially gave their last child much love and the happiest youth one can imagine.

Dietrich von Hildebrand's grandfather, Bruno Hildebrand, was a prominent professor of economics in Marburg. It was he who first exposed the fallacious nature of Karl Marx's economic theories.[2] He was deeply involved in political life and became embroiled in the turmoil of 1848; having been accused of high treason for his convictions, he was condemned to death.[3] But he managed to escape to Switzerland; he sacrificed his position to his political convictions.[4] Because of his well-established reputation as an economist, Bruno Hildebrand became associate professor at the University of Zurich. He founded, with an acquaintance, the Nordostbahn (the northeast railway)—already in Germany he had shown a lively interest in the development of railways—and became its successful director. Because of his valuable contributions in this field, the Swiss government granted him an honorary citizenship, and his seven children became Swiss citizens.[5] Swiss citizenship is hereditary. This fact was to save his grandson's life in 1938.

Bruno then obtained a professorship at the University of Bern, and Adolf, Dietrich von Hildebrand's father—born in

[1] Fifteen years later, in 1904, Adolf Hildebrand was knighted by the King of Bavaria, and had the aristocratic "von" prefixed to his name. In 1913, this title became hereditary; in 1917, Adolf received the title of Excellency.

[2] See Paul Johnson, *Intellectuals* (New York: Harper and Row, 1988), p. 66.

[3] See Bernhard Sattler, ed., *Adolf von Hildebrand und seine Welt* (Munich: Verlag Georg Callwey), pp. 771–74.

[4] Eighty-five years later, his grandson did the same, and he too was condemned to death.

[5] Bruno and his wife had seven children, four boys and three girls: Richard, Bertele, Emmi, Adolf, Bruno, Sophie, and Otto.

Marburg on October 6, 1847—lived in the Swiss capital until he was a teenager. The family later moved back to Germany, where Bruno, politically rehabilitated, became professor at the University of Jena.

At a very young age, Adolf proved to have outstanding artistic talents. His drawings were remarkable. He loved nature and was fascinated by its dazzling variety. He was surprisingly naïve, a trait that he manifested throughout his life, as a story from his early childhood will illustrate. When Adolf was five years old, his parents took him to the zoo, and, for the first time, the child saw monkeys. He was struck by their agility and captivated by their acrobatics, and he observed them with passionate interest. Upon coming home, he decided that these lovable animals deserved to be imitated. He stripped himself of his clothing, climbed up a tree facing his parents' house, and tried to balance himself on a branch, in an attempt at impersonating the monkeys he had seen. A Swiss child passing by, seeing little Adolf naked and climbing from branch to branch, gave expression to his puritanical disgust by shouting, *"Du, Schwein"* (You, swine). At this, little Adolf began to cry, and he ran to his mother. "Mama, Mama," he sobbed, "a boy on the street called me 'swine', but I was not imitating a pig; I was trying to be a monkey." The thought that his performance had fallen so far short of the mark was an aesthetic failure that caused him deep grief!

Given his artistic leanings, it is hardly surprising that at the age of nineteen young Adolf moved to Italy, the homeland of artistic beauty. After spending time in Rome, he settled in Florence, which was to become his home for some forty years. In 1873, he bought a sixteenth-century monastery, San Francesco. The house was located on Piazza San Francesco di Paola, close to the Porta Romana, and lay at the foot of the Bellosguardo hills. It was an old monastery of the *Fratres*

Minimi. It had been secularized by Napoleon in the nineteenth century and had become city property. Even though it
was dilapidated, it was ideal both in its location and as a
studio. The house was huge (it still stands today) and had a
double façade, one facing the campo, the other facing a garden that used to belong to the monks. Adjacent was a church,
also named San Francesco. It was in this house that Adolf's six
children were born—five girls, followed by his only male
child.

Conrad Fiedler,[6] an art lover and a very rich man, discovered Adolf's budding talent as a sculptor and decided to become the patron of this promising young artist. He offered to
support Adolf financially on condition that all of the young
man's works would become his personal property. This felicitous arrangement permitted Adolf to live free of care, following the bent of his genius. For a while, he was joined by the
great German painter Hans von Marées (1837–1887), and the
two bachelors spent their time painting, sculpting, and discussing theories of art.

Adolf Hildebrand was blessed with a sunny disposition.
He was one of those rare persons who by their very nature
are free from meanness or pettiness. One of his son's tutors,
Alois Fischer, wrote in his diary that Adolf was the happiest
man he had met in his life; and not only was he happy, but
he radiated happiness to those around him.[7] The British musician Ethel Smythe, who knew him well, wrote: "He was of
a serene gay temperament, absolutely natural, and I think
'amoral' is the term to express his complete detachment, in

---

[6] Conrad Fiedler (1841–1895) was a patron of the arts, collector, and author
of many writings on aesthetics.

[7] In her book *Der Meister von San Francesco* (Tübingen: Rainer, Wunderlich
Verlag, n.d.), p. 26, Isolde Kurz refers to San Francesco as "das Haus des
Glückes" (the house of happiness).

theory at least, from morality and current views on the conduct of life."[8] But this 'amoral' trait did not prevent him from being extremely kindhearted, generous, and willing to go out of his way to help others.[9]

Dietrich von Hildebrand's mother, Irene Schäuffelen, was born in Heilbronn, April 7, 1846. She was the child of a second marriage, for her mother, Augusta Schäuffelen, had married a rich widower to whom she bore three children—two girls, Hedwig and Irene, and then a boy, Alfred. When Hedwig died at the age of sixteen, Irene's mother was inconsolable. She was a widow at the time, and her eldest child had been a special source of joy to her. Augusta went daily to the cemetery and was quite brokenhearted. Even though Irene was only twelve, she recognized that a radical change of scene was necessary in order for her mother to recover. She persuaded her to move to Dresden, where Irene made the acquaintance of several intellectuals and artists of talent and began to lead a lively social life. Mother and daughter attended plays, operas, and concerts, and Irene, an intelligent, spirited, and charming child, soon acquired a great deal of culture. She read much and had an outstanding talent for languages and a spontaneous attraction to whatever was beautiful. She had a strong personality and induced her mother to cater to her *Wanderlust*. Her younger brother, Alfred, much to his displeasure, was put into a boarding school, and Irene,

[8] Ethel Smythe, *Impressions That Remained* (New York: Alfred A. Knopf, 1946), p. 310.

[9] This is shown by his care for Karl Stauffer, a Swiss artist who had been unjustly incarcerated, first in a Roman prison and then in an insane asylum in Florence, because of his affair with the married daughter of a high-ranking Swiss official. When the scandal broke out, Adolf Hildebrand was the only one who came to the man's rescue; he managed to get him freed and sent him to Switzerland, to his sister, Emmi Vogt, who took care of this broken man in a most touching way. Unfortunately, Stauffer later committed suicide.

chaperoned by her mother, decided to visit Italy. They traveled over the then formidable Gotthard Pass (just south of the Swiss city of Lucerne) and arrived on the other side of the Alps.

The impression that Italy made on Irene, who had now become a lovely young woman, was overwhelming. It was love at first sight, a love to which she remained faithful her whole life. Her rich artistic sensibility was aroused by the world of beauty and poetry she discovered. Her vitality, which her son would inherit, was boundless. She could not drink in enough of the world of culture and beauty. She traveled widely, always accompanied by her mother—to Spain, Ireland, and Norway.[10]

Young Irene benefited from whatever she saw. The world of culture formed her mind and soul, her entire outlook on life; and this young woman, whose formal education had been limited, grew up to be one of the better-educated, cultivated *grandes dames* one could meet. Her knowledge of fine arts, of architecture, painting, and sculpture, was outstanding, as was her acquaintance with the great works of music. Her command of Italian, French, and English was remarkable. She read Greek and Latin literature, Dante, Shakespeare, Cervantes, Goethe, and Schiller. Great writers and poets were her spiritual friends, and they helped form and enrich her personality. She possessed to perfection the lovable and forgotten art of conversation. She knew how to deal with the great of this world and also how to put at ease the artisans, workers, and servants, who respected and loved

[10] Extensive travels in the nineteenth century were not common for young ladies in their teens; most of them did not have a longing to discover the world. Trains were slow, and traveling was often a strenuous affair. Only those taken by *Wanderlust* would abandon the comforts and security of a well-run home for the adventures that were often the fate of travelers.

her. She had no diploma but was "educated" in the best sense of the word.

Irene grew up to be a most attractive young woman, combining beauty with a charming personality. Her charms did not remain unnoticed. She was hardly eighteen when, passing over a narrow bridge in Germany, she was seized and kissed by a fashionable-looking young man. Taken by surprise and baffled by this unexpected token of affection, she nevertheless felt morally bound to accept his abrupt proposal of marriage. Franz Koppel by name, he was a writer and had been a *Korpsstudent*. He was also burdened with debts, whereas Irene was rich.

Irene soon recognized that she was heading for unhappiness. Her fiancé lived in another world. He preferred light music to Beethoven, popular and amusing comedies to Shakespeare. Moreover, he emanated a certain *Trivialität* (vulgarity) that was abhorrent to her. She wanted to liberate herself from this groundless engagement, so one day she summoned the courage to tell Franz that she wanted to break a bond that was choking her, spiritually, artistically, and intellectually. Hoping to obtain her release, she offered to pay all his debts. Franz objected, claiming that it was against his honor to accept a large sum of money from a young woman who was not to become his wife. In an unchivalrous manner he told her that, if she persisted in her refusal to marry him, he would shoot himself, a trick that has victimized many a young girl.

Under this threat, Irene yielded. She had a noble idea of love and marriage, and yet she was about to enter into an intimate union with someone whom she did not love. To her the prospect was sheer torture. In her despair, she set one condition to her consent: that if the marriage proved to be deeply unhappy for her, Franz would release her and grant her a divorce. She wanted this clearly stated in writing, and she asked him to sign a paper stipulating the conditions under which she had agreed to the marriage.

This is how Irene became Mrs. Franz Koppel. The strain on her was such that she fainted during the marriage ceremony.

As expected, the marriage turned out to be a complete failure; there was no communion of souls between Irene and her husband, and, in spite of the joy she felt upon becoming the mother of a little boy, Alfred,[11] she soon decided to make use of the privilege she had requested before her marriage. Franz was slow in granting her request. Several times he convinced her to give the marriage another try. Irene yielded to his wishes, but each time she became more convinced that no *modus vivendi* could ever be found between them. The marriage was purely conventional and conditional, that is, no marriage at all.

To forget her sorrow, Irene started traveling again and headed for Italy. Here she made the acquaintance of Adolf Hildebrand. The impression she made on him was like the impression Juliet made on Romeo—overwhelming love at first sight. After facing innumerable obstacles and difficulties, Irene obtained a divorce from Franz Koppel. She relinquished half of her fortune to him but was given custody of little Alfred, who was formally adopted by Adolf Hildebrand in 1877 when she became his wife. That is how Irene came to San Francesco.

She was an ideal partner for her husband,[12] beautiful, talented, and cultivated, with a warm and lovable personality, which her son Dietrich inherited. In the course of the next thirteen years, she was pregnant eleven times. She had five miscarriages but gave her husband six healthy children, five

[11] Alfred Hildebrand-Koppel (1870–1896).
[12] Kurz, *Der Meister von San Francesco*, p. 19.

girls and a boy—Eva (Nini), Elizabeth (Lisl), Irene (Zusi), Sylvie (Vivi), Bertel (Bertele), and Dietrich.[13]

The joy of the family at Dietrich's birth was great: finally, after so many daughters, a male heir had been given to Adolf and Irene. From the moment of his birth, this child was surrounded by the special love of his mother and of his five sisters, who vied with one another in showering their little brother with affection and sharing with him whatever talent they possessed. His sisters were to have a profound influence on Dietrich's personal and artistic development.

Adolf and Irene were blessed with children who possessed remarkable talents. Again, Ethel Smythe writes of the Hildebrands: "The family consisted of several children, mostly girls—all of them budding sculptors, painters, or poetesses."[14]

Nini, the eldest, the *grande dame*, was a strong, radiant personality, graceful, with unfailing taste and elegance. She played the piano with great talent and danced superbly. Lisl was beautiful. Her face was so admirably sculpted by nature that one could not take one's eyes off her. Her bearing was regal. Impulsive, warm, and generous, she lived on and from beauty. Her artistic talents were outstanding.[15] While still a teenager, Lisl painted frescoes on the walls of San Francesco, and she developed into an artist whose talent should one day be fully recognized. Her paintings emanate originality and delicacy of touch and reflect her reverent and tender love for nature. Totally unworldly, she never tried to become famous, to advertise her work, or to stoop to the demands that the

[13] Eva, born on January 1, 1877; Elizabeth, born on November 24, 1878; Irene, born on January 22, 1880; Sylvie, born on January 29, 1884; Bertel, born on May 16, 1886, and lastly, Dietrich, born on October 12, 1889.

[14] *Impressions That Remained*, p. 309.

[15] In a letter from H. Thoma to Adolf Hildebrand, he refers to the paintings of young Lisl, aged fourteen, as *"ein Wunder"* (a miracle); in *Adolf von Hildebrand und seine Welt*, p. 399.

modern "artistic" world (often commanded by financial or fashionable considerations) makes upon those who wish to gain recognition in their lifetime.

Zusi, too, was a full-fledged artist, a gifted sculptor. She married Fedja Georgii, a student of Adolf von Hildebrand's. Talented as she was, her works never reached the greatness of her older sister's. But she also had a fascinating personality, warm, unconventional, in love with life and beauty. She radiated a *joie de vivre*, a zest that made her the center wherever she was. Her husband adored her. All her children were devoted to her.

The fourth Hildebrand daughter, Vivi (the only one I was not privileged to meet—even though she had married a Belgian painter and lived in Brussels, where I was born), was very different from her older sisters. Reserved, shy, and reflective, she was less dynamic, less effervescent than the other Hildebrand children. Intelligent, inquisitive, and reverent, she radiated a gentle goodness and meekness that fascinated those who knew her. By nature, Vivi (the last of the six Hildebrand children to enter the Church, in 1921) was *naturaliter Christiana*, kind and friendly. She refrained from rash judgments, desiring to be fair toward everyone. Mysterious and introverted, she had a particularly strong influence on her brother through her enchanting imagination (her short stories were delightful) and her talent for enlivening every experience. She was especially creative in making connections—a landscape with a piece of music or a song with an everyday event. For example, she connected passing through the Brenner Pass on the way to Florence with the Quartet in D Minor of Mozart and the death of a pet cat with a popular melody.

The youngest of the five Hildebrand daughters, Bertele (at first named Quintilla,[16] to express her parents' disappoint-

---

[16] In Latin, "the fifth female".

ment at having another daughter), was a "world" all to herself. Already as a very young child her passion for music was extraordinary. It was clear that her life would be dedicated to what she herself called "my love-adventure with music". She was a most original and unconventional person. She never allowed stale opinions to filter through her experiences or to influence her view of life. She had received the rare gift of allowing things to speak for themselves and was not influenced by what "they said" about them. Every word coming from her lips was stamped by primeval freshness and genuineness. She could speak the deepest thoughts with so little pretension that only one whose soul was attuned to authentic greatness could perceive her peculiar enchantment and depth. Naïve in the extreme, helpless, not a great linguist (unlike her sisters), she was nevertheless highly intelligent, but her intellectual sharpness was hidden under the cover of a certain helplessness and even clumsiness. Incapable of learning in the conventional way, she read very slowly, contemplatively, but so deeply that she became an expert on Dante, Shakespeare, Goethe, and Stendhal. The commentaries she wrote testify to the depth of her interpretation. She was a great conversationalist, particularly *tête à tête*. The charm of her personality was such that she belonged to the small group of extraordinary women who impress to such an extent that one does not even raise the question as to whether they are beautiful.

But if ever there was a Doña Musica (the name of a character in Paul Claudel's masterful play *The Satin Slipper*), it was Bertele Hildebrand. She lived in the world of music. She lived on music, from music, for music. Her brother said that she was constitutionally incapable of falling in love with anyone except an outstanding musician. Her greatest love was Beethoven, but, as he was long dead and buried, she gave her heart when she was a very little girl to the great conductor

Hermann Levi,[17] by then an elderly man and a close family friend of the Hildebrands. Noticing her passionate love for music, he enjoyed entertaining the child with his piano playing. At the age of fourteen, Bertele became engaged to Wilhelm Furtwängler,[18] who said that Bertele was the most musical person he had encountered in his life. This engagement was broken after a few years, but the unpublished letters between Bertele and Willi Furtwängler (which are still extant) testify to the fact that music was the bond that linked them. It is hard to believe that they were written by teenagers; they have a level of depth and maturity inconceivable today. Later, Bertele married the outstanding composer and pianist Walter Braunfels.

This relationship to music was the very substance of Bertele's being. Shortly before her death in August 1963, she fell into a coma. Her family was ready for the worst, when all of a sudden she regained consciousness. "I just heard the third movement of Beethoven's Archduke Trio," she whispered, "and it brought me back to life." She then asked her grandchildren to play it for her.

What has been said is enough to sketch the sort of world into which Dietrich von Hildebrand was born—a world in which art reigned supreme, a world of culture, a world of beauty. Nothing tasteless, let alone vulgar or ugly, was permitted to enter San Francesco. Fashion magazines were forbidden. Only classical music resounded through its halls. Adolf Hildebrand was a passionate player of chamber music; his wife and daughters sang and played the piano or the

---

[17] Hermann Levi (1839–1900) conducted the first performance of Wagner's opera *Parsifal* at Bayreuth.

[18] Wilhelm Furtwängler (1886–1954), a contemporary of Dietrich von Hildebrand, later in life became a celebrated conductor.

violin. From his cradle on, young Dietrich heard Bach, Haydn, Mozart, and Beethoven. In addition, as Adolf's reputation grew, the great artists and thinkers of the day began flocking to San Francesco.

It would be fascinating to draw up a list of all the famous men and women who rang the old-fashioned bell of San Francesco and, later, visited the house on the Maria Theresia Strasse in Munich. Hermann Levi, Conrad Fiedler, Felix Mottl, William Gladstone,[19] Henry James, Franz Liszt, Isolde Kurz,[20] Rudolf Otto,[21] Hugo von Hofmannstahl,[22] Rainer Maria Rilke,[23] Hippolyte Jean Giraudoux,[24] all were guests in the Hildebrand home. Richard Wagner and his wife, Cosima,[25] were frequent visitors; when she became a widow in 1883, Cosima continued her acquaintance with the Hildebrands. In the spring of 1893, Adolf wrote to his wife that Queen Victoria might visit them in San Francesco.[26]

What was striking about Adolf von Hildebrand and his family was their natural, unpretentious relationship with the great or famous of this world: neither withholding respect and deference nor in any way subservient toward those of superior rank or position, Adolf and his wife moved among them with grace and warmth.

[19] William Gladstone was prime minister of Great Britain from 1868 to 1874.

[20] Isolde Kurz (1853–1944) was a poet and author of stories of Italy and the Renaissance.

[21] Rudolf Otto (1869–1937) was a German theologian, philosopher, and historian of religion. His best-known book is *The Idea of the Holy* (1917; New York: Oxford University Press, 1958).

[22] Hugo von Hofmannstahl (1874-1929), Austrian poet, dramatist, and essayist, wrote several librettos for Richard Strauss' operas.

[23] Rainer Maria Rilke (1875–1926) was an Austro-German poet.

[24] Hippolyte Jean Giraudoux (1882–1944) was a French novelist, essayist, and playwright.

[25] Cosima Wagner (1837–1931) was the daughter of composer Franz Liszt.

[26] Letter of Adolf von Hildebrand to Irene, Spring 1883, in *Adolf von Hildebrand und Seine Welt*, p. 399. This visit never took place.

The von Hildebrands were able to relate just as graciously to those of less exalted social status. Irene von Hildebrand was the mistress of two very large houses. Apart from San Francesco, her husband had a mansion built in Munich, where he had received the assignment of designing a fountain—the Wittelsbacher Brunnen. From 1898 on, Irene and her children spent six months of the year in Florence and six months in Munich. Adolf was compelled by his work to stay mostly in the Bavarian capital, but he returned to San Francesco whenever he had a moment of respite. Having six children living at home (Alfred was studying at a university in Germany) and innumerable guests, Irene needed a large number of servants. She had a talent (which her children inherited) for dealing with her household staff, whose members both respected and loved her. For the generations raised after World War II, it is difficult to picture how positive the relationship between masters and servants could be. Servants partook of the family's joys and sorrows, and their masters took a lively interest in their personal lives.[27]

---

[27] At the turn of the century, Irene von Hildebrand engaged a peasant family headed by the young Giulio Ceri. He lived with his wife and three children in the peasant house on the campo. Through the years, he became more and more an integral part of San Francesco. He died in the von Hildebrand villa in the early 1950s, but by then his beautiful daughter, Giulietta, was playing a prominent role in the household as cook and friend. (Giulietta was such a special person that she is mentioned in R. W. B. Lewis' book *The City of Florence* [New York: Farrar, Straus, Giroux, 1995], p. 239.) She lived in the house most of her life, and when she died (1985), the whole family mourned, for everyone loved her deeply. She was very pious, a daily communicant, and fully deserved the affection that she received. She had a passion for cats (as had all the von Hildebrands) and fed a large number of those ever-hungry animals living in the campo. However, only those "born in San Francesco" itself were allowed to enter the house. Her brother Piero and his lovely wife, Elvira, moved to the Tealdi House (one of the houses that belonged to Adolf von Hildebrand and was located on the campo). After the First World War, the Tealdi House belonged to Georges and Vivi Baltus. Piero remained superintendent there for

In Munich, during World War I, Irene von Hildebrand engaged as cook a young woman named Martha Hummert, who remained part of the family until her death after the Second World War. When Adolf and Irene died and their son moved into the Maria Theresia Strasse house, she worked for him and his wife until they left Germany in 1933.

The contrast between the graciousness of the von Hildebrands and the irascibility of some of her previous employers is illustrated by a story Martha Hummert related about the wife of the composer Richard Strauss.[28] Frau Strauss was a petulant and somewhat hysterical woman.[29] Martha related how impossible Frau Strauss was to live with and how badly she treated her servants. One day, Martha decided that she could no longer tolerate such behavior, and she gave her notice. Richard Strauss, who liked her and appreciated her great talent as a cook, met her on the staircase as she was preparing her departure and begged her to reconsider her decision. Martha replied that she was sorry to have to tell him that Frau Strauss was impossible to live with, to which Richard retorted, "But I, too, have to put up with it." Martha answered, "Yes, Herr Doktor, but I have not chosen to marry her!"

The moment baby Dietrich opened his eyes, all he saw were loving faces and works of art—paintings, sculptures, and Bolognese furniture. He heard lovely old songs and classical music. Dietrich took his first steps in a Florentine campo that comprised a hill commanding one of the finest views of

---

many years until his death. One of his sons, Stefano, now lives on the campo with his wife and children. Any descendant of Adolf and Irene von Hildebrand arriving in San Francesco always makes a point of immediately paying a visit to Elvira or to her son Stefano.

[28] Richard Strauss (1864–1949) was an outstanding German composer.

[29] See Barbara Tuchman, *The Proud Tower* (New York: Macmillan, 1966), p. 309.

Florence, framed by trees. It is no wonder that the first public lecture Dietrich gave, at the age of seventeen, was on aesthetics and that he was still writing about the subject in his eighties, when he composed two large volumes on this topic.[30] In this work, von Hildebrand distinguishes sharply between luxury and beauty—a confusion so widespread in our society. In San Francesco there was neither luxury nor effeminate comfort; beauty and authentic culture reigned supreme.[31]

Humanly speaking, one can hardly imagine a more felicitous family background. Young Dietrich—the last visible fruit of a great love—was received into this world with enthusiasm, for at last Adolf and Irene had an heir. In a letter to his friend Conrad Fiedler, Adolf gives expression to his joy, which was fully shared by his wife and five daughters.[32] But when Bertele, aged three years and five months, was allowed to see the long-expected little brother, she exclaimed, "Ma non é mica un fratellino; é una scimmia" (But this is not at all a little brother; it is a monkey), a remark that was typical of her and that greatly amused her whole family.

According to the custom of the time, little Dietrich was given a wet nurse, and he thrived on rich Italian milk. He was so lively that his nurse once exclaimed, "Questo bambino é un vero terremoto!" (This child is a real earthquake!). He was to remain one his whole life long. Until late in life, when he developed severe heart trouble, Dietrich's vitality was such that he would exhaust most of his friends and acquaintances. He had inherited this vitality from both his parents, a vitality evident in a story he relates about an Englishman who visited San Francesco. While lunching with his guest, Adolf Hilde-

---

[30] Dietrich von Hildebrand, *Ästhetik*, vol. 1 (Stuttgart: Kohlhammer and Habbel, 1977); *Ästhetik*, vol. 2 (Kohlhammer and Habbel, 1984).

[31] Kurz, *Der Meister von San Francesco*, p. 23.

[32] *Adolf von Hildebrand und Seine Welt*, p. 334.

brand embarked on a discussion about various art theories with a dynamism and fire that was overwhelming. The Englishman listened and, from time to time, he would say quietly, "I see." When the meal was over, he turned to the artist's wife and said, with typical British humor, "Madam, your husband is disgustingly healthy." Those words became famous in the von Hildebrand family.

As a child, little Dietrich was quite unruly and went into tantrums when his wishes were not respected. Once he threw a sardine can at his mother's head because she had not yielded to his will. Another time, he refused to see her for a while because she had used a trick to get him into bed. She had told him she wanted him to go down the corridor, whereupon his nurse leaped out and grabbed him! Only four at the time, he nonetheless considered this stratagem immoral, a breach of trust, and his older sister Nini had to be sent to placate his wounded feelings. Another time, he hit his governess with a toy whip because she refused to let herself be locked up in the cellar! He hit her nose, and she cried plaintively, "I fear my nose is broken." Fortunately, it was not, but from then on, whenever little Dietrich went into a tantrum, his beautiful sister Lisl, who had a very fine nose, would cover her face with her hands from fear that it would suffer damage. It is interesting that this mischievous child became later in life an unusually friendly, cheerful, and even-tempered man, never given to moods or erratic behavior.

When Dietrich reached school age, his parents chose to entrust his education to a French governess, Mademoiselle Böhrer (of French Swiss extraction). For three full years, the little boy's instruction in all subjects was given exclusively in French. Mademoiselle Böhrer also taught her pupil an impressive number of French stories and old French songs, which he loved and never forgot. Mademoiselle was a typical

Francophile and inculcated in her pupil a deep love for France that he retained his whole life. By the time Dietrich was nine years old, he was as fluent in French as he was in Italian and German. When he was a teenager, Dietrich learned English. The life at San Francesco and in the house on the Maria Theresia Strasse in Munich was so international and cosmopolitan that it was easy for the young boy to pick up foreign languages.

After the tenure of Mademoiselle Böhrer, Dietrich had private tutors and was therefore spared the depressing ambiance of many schools, the dullness and pedantry of some teachers, and the cheerless and sweaty atmosphere of the classroom. Moreover, private tutoring guaranteed that no time was wasted in horseplay, disciplinary problems, and the slowness or unwillingness of some students to learn. His teachers were carefully selected by his parents, and they accompanied the family to Munich or Florence, as the case might be. Several of them achieved recognition later in life in their own field of expertise; for example, Ludwig Curtius in archaeology and Alois Fischer in philosophy.

Comparing his first three tutors—Walter Rietzler, Dr. Wühl, and Ludwig Curtius—Dietrich wrote that, whereas the first both instructed and challenged his pupil, the second only instructed him (and did it well), and the third, Ludwig Curtius, both instructed and educated him. For, if the young boy did his homework carelessly, Curtius punished him by forbidding him to play with his friends. Once the punishment was particularly painful, because Dietrich had developed a friendship with an American boy. The very day this boy was to come to San Francesco to say goodbye because his parents were going back to the United States, Curtius forbade his pupil to see him. All he was allowed to do was to tell him that he was being punished and to say goodbye.

As for his tutor Walter Rietzler, it was his misfortune to fall in love with the beautiful Lisl. She was not indifferent to his attentions. Both shared the same love for great music and literature. They read together and took walks together. Irene von Hildebrand did not look on this association with a kindly eye; unconventional as she was, she nevertheless could not picture her beautiful, aristocratic-looking daughter married to a man whose earthly prospects were not brilliant. One day, Mrs. von Hildebrand found her daughter, who had let her hair down her back, listening with rapture to Rietzler, who was reading poetry to her. She strongly expressed her disapproval of this "pastoral" scene, and Rietzler's fate was sealed. His contract was not renewed. His student was upset by this decision. Not only did he like his teacher, but he sided with the lovers. Young as he was, he told his mother that her attitude struck him as harsh and unloving. But Irene was not only adamant; she sharply reproved her son for his interference in matters he was not equipped to judge.

Is it surprising that the next candidate Irene von Hildebrand chose as tutor for her son was cast from a very different mold? Dr. Wühl was definitely not the type of man who would appeal to any of her lovely daughters. He was hand-picked because his appearance did not favor romance. He typified pedantic and unpoetic German teachers, but he was efficient, and his student learned well under his tutelage. The boy found him unattractive, however. The contrast between the world he was living in and the cut-and-dried person who was tutoring him was not likely to awaken his sympathy. One day Dr. Wühl slapped Dietrich in the face, accusing him (probably rightly so) of impertinence. The teenager was so outraged at this treatment (for his parents never used physical punishment on him) that he started to whistle, to show his radical disapprobation. (In Europe, whistling is a sign of contempt.) It is surprising that he did not get another smack. But he immediately reported the matter to his mother, who called Dr. Wühl to task and censured his educational methods. His contract was not renewed.

The young boy had not always made things easy for this teacher. One day, he convinced his mother to let him take his tutor for a drive in the dog-cart (an open, horse-drawn, two wheeled vehicle), which his sister Lisl drove so expertly. Irene von Hildebrand, knowing that her son had had very little practice, was reluctant to yield to his wishes. But it was not easy to say no to her youngest, who had a very strong will and who saw no reason to give up the beautiful plans he had made. He pressured her to assent to his wishes, and she finally yielded, on condition that he drive only on the main road, up to the Carthusian monastery, and then turn right back. The boy promised, saying to himself that, if things went well, there was no reason whatsoever for not making a tempting detour and returning to San Francesco by the back road, through the lovely Florentine hills.

Everything went well up to the monastery. Encouraged by his flawless performance, the young boy, imagining himself an expert coachman, decided to ride roughshod over his mother's orders, and, instead of turning back, he turned right. It was exhilarating to travel through this enchanting landscape, which commanded a lovely view over Florence. When he arrived at the top of the hill, he pictured in his mind how exciting it would be to go downhill at full speed and, letting down the brake, whipped his horse to go into a gallop. But at that point, things went awry. The carriage began swaying madly from one side of the serpentine road to the other. At a sharp turn, it hit a rock and crashed to pieces; the young driver managed to jump out, but his teacher disappeared under the ruined vehicle, muttering, "Jetzt ist der Dreck fertig" (Now we are in a fine mess). Dr. Wühl, who had mistrusted his pupil's expertise from the very beginning, was not in the best of moods. The disobedient young driver, though unhurt, saw that he was in serious trouble. By now, he should have been back in San Francesco, and he found himself far away, the dog-cart totally ruined. He decided to look for help at a nearby Italian farm. A friendly peasant volunteered to take teacher and student back to Florence in his *baroccino* (a small cart Italian peasants use to transport hay or wheat). The dog-cart had to be left behind.

It took a while before the trio were on their way. The peasant drove his donkey, and Dr. Wühl and his crestfallen pupil sat at the rear of the *baroccino*, legs dangling, leading the horse by its reins. But a donkey is a donkey, and this lovable but stubborn animal, not understanding the urgency of the situation, decided to walk as leisurely as possible, grazing at its convenience. The young boy was becoming increasingly worried, calculating how long it would take them to get back to San Francesco at such a snail's pace. The sun was setting, and every moment the situation became more precarious. He urged the peasant to hasten the pace, but he answered that the only way to do so would be to put the horse in the shafts and to have the donkey take the place of the horse. They had to stop at another farmhouse to make the change. By now it was dark and ominously late. But, although the horse trotted cheerfully, the donkey refused to collaborate, maintaining that grazing was more pleasant than running. At one point, as Dr. Wühl and his pupil were holding the donkey's reins, the donkey stopped altogether, yanking teacher and pupil off the *baroccino*. It was the second fall for Dr. Wühl; this time, he was pressing his ribs and moaning pitifully. His pupil, more fortunate, was unhurt. Finally, they arrived back on the main road and met a carriage that the distracted mother had rented, sending Lisl and Zusi to find the remains of their little brother. The joy of the culprit's mother was great when she saw him safe and sound, but Dietrich knew from experience that Irene, like most mothers who have worried themselves almost to death, could suddenly become irate if she were to find out that the agony she had gone through was in fact caused by the carelessness of her offspring. He therefore had to maneuver cleverly, and when Irene asked him to explain the long delay, the half-penitent boy had to use all his cunning to blur the facts and create as confused a picture as possible. Dr. Wühl did not know the area surrounding Florence, and his explanations were necessarily vague. Dietrich's attempt to hide the fact that he had disobeyed his mother's orders succeeded pretty well, and he was much relieved when the interrogation was over.

Dietrich proved to be a talented and precocious student, although he made sure that his studies did not absorb him to such an extent that he had to sacrifice listening to music, reading beautiful books, making excursions, or seeing his friends. He remained faithful to this principle throughout his life. Work was important, and he could work with incredible intensity, but not so as to make it the most important thing in life. He always gave priority to his personal and religious life.[33]

Thanks to the intellectual and artistic world into which he was born, the conversations of his parents at mealtime, and the exchanges he had with his sisters, Dietrich's intellectual and artistic maturity far exceeded his years. His parents praised Cervantes' *Don Quixote* as the greatest novel ever written, but they told their son, aged eleven at the time, that he was still

[33] See "Efficiency and Holiness", in *The New Tower of Babel: Modern Man's Flight from God* (Manchester, N.H.: Sophia Institute Press, 1994).

too young to appreciate this masterpiece fully. They said he should postpone reading it until he was more mature and capable of giving the book the admiration it deserved. That was the wrong thing to say to the young boy. It piqued both his curiosity and his vanity. He decided that he would take *Don Quixote* from the library and read it in bed at night. From the first page, he was so captivated that he could hardly put the book down. In a brief space of time, he read the two-volume edition from cover to cover. Incapable of keeping his enthusiasm to himself, he told his mother how riveted he was by this masterwork. Delighted by her son's response, Irene forgave him his disobedience.

Together with Shakespeare's works, *Don Quixote* remained one of the great literary passions of Dietrich's life. He read this book some fifty times. After he had had a heart attack in Mexico in January 1964, being bedridden for several weeks, he asked his dear Mexican friend Robert Ibañez Parkman to lend him a copy of *Don Quixote*. The latter replied that he possessed it only in Spanish, a tongue Dietrich did not know at all. "It does not matter in the least", he answered. "My wife can read it to me, and, because of my knowledge of Italian, I can easily guess the meaning of a few words in every sentence, and this will guarantee my enjoyment, for I know the work so well that a couple of clues will suffice." This proved to be true. While I was reading it to him, he kept laughing again and again, telling me what the next episode was going to be.[34]

In addition to encouraging his budding passion for great literature, Dietrich's family life cultivated in him a deep,

[34] Dietrich lived a thought crucial in his book *What Is Philosophy?* (Milwaukee: Bruce Publishing Co., 1960; repr. London: Routledge)—namely, the contemplative theme, as distinct from the purely noetic theme. Simply to know the content of a book is not to "possess" it; one must go beyond the mere curiosity of being "informed" about its content and truly contemplate its artistic structure.

lifelong love of music. With such musical parents and sisters, his love for the most sublime of all arts started early. He was captivated by the beloved sonatas of Beethoven and Mozart, played by his sisters, and by the chamber music his father played with his friends. Dietrich had a phenomenal musical memory, and his knowledge of this field was such that, in later life, professional musicians asked several times whether music was his field of expertise. The moment that beautiful music was played, he who was ordinarily so buoyant and dynamic became contemplative and receptive. He could listen for hours without moving, except to point out to those close to him the most sublime passages of a work.

This love of music was further deepened when the family moved to Munich in 1898. The six months spent in the Bavarian capital had the advantage of exposing the von Hildebrand children to the rich musical life of the city, renowned for its dedication to art. Young Dietrich had numerous opportunities to attend operas and concerts. He heard *The Marriage of Figaro, Così fan Tutte, La Serva Padrona,* and *The Magic Flute,* the score of which his sisters had played for him beforehand. Soon he knew the last by heart, and he responded to it with all his youthful enthusiasm.

One of the great artistic experiences of Dietrich's youth was the discovery of Wagner's music. As mentioned earlier, Wagner, who died in 1883, had visited the von Hildebrands in Florence, and Wagner's widow, Cosima, remained in contact with the family. Musical as he was, however, Adolf von Hildebrand never cared for Wagner's music. It was not his "cup of tea". He did not like to show his emotions, and the intensity of Wagner's passion went against his grain. However, he liked Bruckner, and he used to say, "That is my

---

[35] Josef Anton Bruckner (1824–1896), Austrian composer of symphonies and religious music.

Wagner." [35] But his son's appreciation of Wagner was very different. There is no doubt that not only did Dietrich understand Wagner's message in a unique way, but he had a special affinity with this genius. He saw Wagner as the challenger of the right of love over pure convention and brutal force. Senta's fidelity saves the Flying Dutchman from damnation, in the opera of the same name. Elizabeth in *Tannhäuser* stands for purity, and through her loving prayers brings back to contrition her sinful admirer, Tannhäuser. Alberich in the *Ring* cycle typifies greed and raw sensuality stripped of any love.

As a youth, Dietrich had several enriching male friendships, all with young men older than he who shared his love of music—among them, Hermann Solbrig and a young man identified only as Raff. Both Solbrig and Raff were accomplished pianists, and young Dietrich often urged them to play for him the scores of Wagner's operas, while he listened for hours on end. Raff also read the libretti with him and opened up to him Wagner's philosophy as it was expressed in his works.

When the *Ring* was on the program at the Munich opera house, the teenager arrived to stand in front of the box office by 6 A.M., wait for a couple of hours until it opened, and buy a ticket either for a seat in the *Galerie* or for standing room. At 4 P.M., he was back at the opera house, waiting for an hour and a half until the doors opened at 5:30. Then, in a mad rush, he would climb five flights of stairs to make sure of getting a good place. The performance started at 6 and lasted until 10:30 for *Rheingold*, longer for the *Walkyrie*, *Siegfried*, and *Götterdämmerung*. All in all, Dietrich stood for nine full hours, but had it been announced that the whole performance would start all over again, he would gladly have stood for another five hours.

His endurance shows that young Dietrich had inherited his father's "disgusting health" and his mother's vitality. Love is such an incentive that it conquers fatigue.[36] This willingness to put up with inconvenience for the sake of a noble enjoyment was deeply characteristic of Dietrich's personality.[37] His whole life long, he would think nothing of discomfort and unpleasantness if that was the price he had to pay for the enjoyment of a noble good. One day, as he suffered from a severe toothache, he claimed that the pain vanished while he was listening to Wagner.[38]

Given his passion for Wagner, it is no surprise that a high point of Dietrich's youth was his trip to Bayreuth, which he undertook in the summer of 1906, after he had received his *Abitur*[39] and was about to enter the University of Munich. He, to whom Wagner's music meant so much, knew that seeing and hearing Wagner's operas in the setting designed by the master himself would provide the perfect opportunity to savor the artistic riches of his genius.

Soon after his arrival at the "Wagnerian capital", young Dietrich went to the *Wahnfried*, the "sacred" place of Wagnerians, where the master had lived and reigned. As Adolf von Hildebrand's son, he was received most graciously. But, to his deep regret, he felt that no member of the Wagner family

---

[36] On the supernatural plane, one finds an analogy in the lives of saints who endure suffering, pain, and fatigue with a smile because their hearts are burning with love of God.

[37] In this he differs radically from C. S. Lewis, who writes in *Surprised by Joy* (171) that to escape pain was for him more important than to achieve happiness or enjoy some positive good.

[38] Later in life, von Hildebrand became indignant when people claimed that Nazism incorporated the spirit of Wagner. For him, it was Alberich (the evil character of the *Ring of the Niebelungen*), not Wagner himself, who was a Nazi hero; the Wagnerian ethos constantly brought forth the fearful conflict between good and evil, and the horror of brutal force. The whole tragedy of the *Ring* is based on the craving for gold, which becomes a curse.

[39] The qualification for university entrance in Germany; equivalent to the French *Baccalauréat*.

truly reflected the greatness of the world he had discovered in Wagner's music.

Cosima Wagner was an impressive personality. She was the "duchess" of the realm and was treated as such by her children, friends, and acquaintances. When her daughters came into the room, they would curtsy in front of their mother and then kiss her hand, a ritual that none of them would have dreamed of omitting. She was a strong, talented woman, but young Dietrich felt keenly that, somehow, she neither embodied nor was rooted in the world of depth and seriousness that typified Wagner's operas. Cosima's philosophy of life, which the young man had heard expounded several times in the course of her visits to Florence and Munich, was tainted by a slight scepticism and a touch of frivolity that were antithetical to the Wagnerian ethos. Cosima did not show these traits in her public role as queen of *Wahnfried*, but they became apparent as soon as one spoke *tête à tête* with her. Once, in Florence, Cosima's disparaging remarks about *Fidelio*, which young Dietrich had just heard and which had moved him deeply, disappointed him keenly. He was to discover that *Tristan and Isolde*, probably because it was inspired by Wagner's love for Frau Wesendonck, was underrated in the *Wahnfried* and called "excessive" by Cosima's son, Siegfried. This was heresy to Dietrich and deeply upsetting. To him *Tristan and Isolde* was the culmination of Wagner's genius, incorporating as it did the moral ethos of all his works, the longing for redemption, and the ardor and metaphysical fervor of his music.[40]

Cosima's eldest daughter, Daniela (whose father was Hans von Bülow and who was now Frau Thode), was attractive and had an elusive charm that was very appealing. She was lively and intelligent. The second daughter (also a child of

[40] It is worth mentioning that Pope Pius XII and C. S. Lewis were both great admirers of Wagner's music.

Cosima's first marriage) was Countess Gravina. She was less attractive than her sister and did not seem very intelligent. Cosima's third daughter, Isolde, Wagner's child, strongly resembled her mother, even though she also had traits of her father; she had something mysterious about her and an alluring intensity. She was married to a mediocre conductor named Beidler, who, as Cosima's son-in-law, was allowed to conduct several of Wagner's operas. The fourth daughter, Eva, was the one whom the young Dietrich saw most during his visit. She bore a marked resemblance to her father. Eva was very friendly to the young man. They took long walks together and discussed the merits of Wagner's music. She was bright and had a pleasing appearance. Siegfried, the youngest child and the only boy, was the family member Dietrich knew best, for he had frequently visited the Hildebrands in Italy and in Munich. Dietrich's relationship with him, however, was not as deep as the one he shared with Eva. Although he treated Siegfried with great friendliness, Dietrich had scant sympathy for him.

Wahnfried had the charm of a highly cultivated but very formal world. In spite of the fact that the Wagner family did not meet his expectations, Dietrich's love for Wagner's music deepened. From a musical and artistic point of view, the days spent in Bayreuth completely met his expectations. Not only was he allowed to be present at dress rehearsals, but he attended the performances in the Wagners' box. All in all, he heard the complete *Ring*, *Tristan and Isolde*, and *Parsifal* three times each. Conductor Felix Mottl's rendering of *Tristan and Isolde* was uniquely satisfying; the singers were outstanding. The whole presentation was majestic, introduced by trumpets announcing that an opera was about to begin. In addition, thanks to the Wagners, the young man met most of the luminaries who came to Bayreuth.

Apart from the enchantment of Wagner's music, Dietrich's visit to Bayreuth marked the first time in his life that he was "on his own" and treated as an adult. When he was a child, he was always unhappy to hear his mother tell him that early youth is the happiest time in life. He wanted to reach maturity, to be fully awakened, and he saw this as a prerequisite for true happiness.

Although the Wagner family was very gracious to him, Dietrich felt obligated after a while to leave Bayreuth so as not to abuse their kindness. With a heavy heart he returned to Munich. But, after ten days, his longing was so great that he took the train back to Bayreuth. Because of their touching eagerness to share the young man's interest in Wagner's music, both his mother and his eldest sister, Nini, joined him for a few days, but to his deep regret neither of them was deeply moved by the magic of Wagner's music. Somehow, they remained outsiders, but their lukewarm response, while it saddened him, in no way influenced him negatively. What he experienced in listening to Wagner's music was so convincing that no one could have shaken his conviction that Wagner was one of the very great musicians of the world. But, as he loved his mother and Nini deeply, it was a source of grief that they could not share his enthusiasm, a grief that was certainly shared by Irene, who was especially close to her youngest and who loved him so tenderly. Indeed, Irene's desire to share everything with her son was so deep that she started studying Latin and Greek when she was over fifty, to keep up with young Dietrich's studies. She enjoyed reading the great classics of literature to him and with him, discussing the works, and exchanging impressions. They read together Homer and Plato, Goethe and Schiller, among others. She was often present during his lessons, and she loved to deepen her own knowledge.

Humor played a great role in the von Hildebrand household and was in rich supply among parents and children. They loved to engage in playful merrymaking. Dietrich relates that when he was fifteen, his former tutor Ludwig Curtius gave a lecture in Munich for a women's organization. Men were not invited. Two of his sisters were planning to go to Curtius' talk, and young Dietrich had to find a way of contravening what he considered to be a stupid prohibition: the exclusion of men. Possibly inspired by Viola in *Twelfth Night*, he decided to disguise himself as a girl; his sisters lent him their clothing, and to hide his identity better he wore a large hat with a veil. Although he took long steps, he was not recognized, and he managed without difficulty to enter the hall where the talk was given. He sat next to his sister Zusi, for whom Curtius had a marked affection. But throughout his lecture, Zusi could not refrain from giggling. The lecturer noticed it and was clearly offended: what could be so funny about his talk? He was disgruntled until, when the lecture was over, his ex-pupil rushed to the podium and embraced him warmly. Curtius recognized the young boy and understood the source of Zusi's behavior. He joined in the fun, for indeed the boy really looked comical in his new attire.

The von Hildebrands enjoyed *Unsinn* (nonsense, banter, jokes). Isolde Kurz relates in her book[41] that one day an English clergyman came to San Francesco. He was a missionary going to China and was trying to raise money for his work. Adolf von Hildebrand told the servant to tell him that he himself was Chinese and was preaching his own religion in Florence. The clergyman showed great interest, asking where and when this preaching was taking place. He said that he had

[41] *Der Meister von San Francesco*, p. 101.

heard about this and was desirous to hear the Chinese preacher. The next Sunday, following the instructions he had received, he came to San Francesco in the burning August heat, to be told by the servant that that very day the Chinese preacher was delivering his homily in Sofiano!

Young Dietrich hated to be left out; as a child, he envied his sisters, who retired to their bedrooms at night and happily chatted together until they fell asleep. Being the only boy, he had no companion. But he hated being alone, and soon he formed the habit of inviting friends to his home so that he would have company. This sense of communion was to mark his whole life. There never was anybody who was less of a "loner" (or more gregarious) than Dietrich von Hildebrand; love and friendship occupied a central role in his life.

In his youth Dietrich had a passion for horseback riding; he loved to ride full speed through the Florentine fields. Once, enjoying such a gallop with Wilhelm Furtwängler (with whom he shared the services of his tutor Ludwig Curtius) and his parents' coachman, Ireneo, they inadvertently rode through a cornfield, creating havoc in the harvest. The peasants were understandably furious and got ready to greet the culprits with pitchforks. But the wily Florentine coachman, who was responsible for bringing his charges safely home, told the irate peasants that the two boys were the sons of the Count of Turin (a very popular cousin of King Victor Emmanuel).[42] All of a sudden, much to the pleasant surprise of the two youths, the pitchforks disappeared, and they were greeted with reverent bows! As soon as they had reached the main road, Ireneo informed his young charges of the trick he had used to guarantee their safety.

[42] Victor Emmanuel III was king of Italy from 1900 to 1946.

Because of his close relationship with his mother and sisters, Dietrich showed a deep affinity for the "feminine" from a young age. This sensitivity was given its first expression when the boy, aged ten, wrote a play (to the great satisfaction of his father, who would have welcomed his son's becoming a writer) in which the hero delivered a passionate encomium on the virtues of the fair sex. He eloquently sang the praises of the heroine: "Women are definitely superior to men. They are more poetic, more attractive, more lovable; they have softer voices", and so forth. Obviously, the young author was trying to put into words his loving admiration for his mother and his five sisters. "But", the monologue ended, "men have one outspoken advantage over women, namely, that whereas the latter love men, who deserve it less, men love women, who deserve it more." [43]

Young Dietrich often fell in love, but mostly with girls who were older than he and with whom he could share his intellectual and artistic interests. He always made a point of entertaining them with beautiful, leather-bound editions of his favorite books. Living as he did, with people who had a high degree of culture, his intellectual and artistic maturity far exceeded his years, but, as could be expected, the various young women who touched his heart did not take the expressions of devotion of a teenager seriously. More than once he tasted the sorrow of unrequited affection.

Again, his closeness to his mother deserves to be emphasized. There was not only a deep love between them, but also a profound affinity—a trait that is very important in human relationships and an essential presupposition for the most beautiful ones. There was between them what Leibniz calls

[43] That was already the seed of his now-famous *Wertantwort* (the response-to-value) in his *Ethics*: Dietrich von Hildebrand, *Christian Ethics* (New York: David McKay, 1953).

"a preestablished harmony"; they synchronized humanly, intellectually, and artistically.

His father, on the contrary, intimidated him. Adolf von Hildebrand had such a powerful personality that his son did not feel quite at ease with him. In fact, father and son, both with strong personalities, had very different structures and were bound to have conflicts. Dietrich's early youth was totally centered on the feminine element. Quite early in life, the boy became aware of how profoundly his father's *Weltanschauung* differed from his own. Apart from their disagreement about Wagner's genius and about the role and importance of philosophy in life, Adolf von Hildebrand's ethical relativism, his pantheistic bent, and his moral unconsciousness were upsetting to his son. In some way, one can say that for years there was a tacit "tug-of-war" between father and son. The father was idolized by his five daughters, whose basic principle was that such a lovable and talented individual could do no wrong. But the young boy wanted to pull his sisters away from their father's influence, particularly concerning ethical and religious questions. His mother, on the other hand, was a great admirer of Kant's ethics, but, like her husband and her daughters, she had no serious religious concern. The young boy regretted this deeply, but he knew that he was right, and he set his mind upon "conquering" his sisters by opposing their father's dominance of them.

It must be added, however, that the more mature Dietrich became, the more he learned to appreciate his father's remarkable talent, and he gained a more complete image of his father's personality, seeing his weaknesses against the background of his innate nobility, his great generosity, and his human goodness.

But it never occurred to anyone to call Dietrich soft and

effeminate.[44] Deep as the influence of his mother and his sisters was, he was masculine in the best sense of the term, displaying a manliness that was coupled with a warm, loving heart and a deep affectivity.[45] As a man, he was best capable of understanding the charm and mystery of femininity, for it is one of the sad aberrations of certain feminists (and I am thinking here of Simone de Beauvoir) to accept as dogma that a man, being male, cannot understand a woman.[46]

What his mother and sisters gave Dietrich was a rare sensitivity for the mystery of femininity; a high regard for the female personality; an intuitive understanding of her spiritual, psychological, and intellectual structure; and a deep reverence for the female being. Thanks to his youthful experiences with noble women, Dietrich never became a victim of the macho complex or of the almost childish belief that women—being less "theoretical" than men—are less intelligent and unworthy to be a man's intellectual partner. On the contrary, he was convinced that the female touch, the female approach, the

[44] Alphonse de Lamartine (1790–1869) was a French Romantic poet and statesman, whose poetry is marked by a certain delicacy and softness, a style that may stem from the fact that he, like von Hildebrand, was surrounded by five sisters. But sociological and psychological explanations can have severe weaknesses; often the opposite conclusion could just as well be drawn from a sociological assertion.

[45] These qualities are the roots of von Hildebrand's book The Heart (Chicago: Franciscan Herald Press, 1977; originally published as The Sacred Heart: An Analysis of Human and Divine Affectivity (Baltimore: Helicon Press, 1965). He makes a crucial distinction between dynamic affectivity (buoyancy, vitality, anger, and so forth) and tender affectivity (tenderness, sweetness, warmth—the latter qualities are particularly incarnated in women), an insight that might be traced back to his own personal experiences.

[46] See de Beauvoir's remarks on poet and playwright Paul Claudel in The Second Sex, trans. H. M. Parshley (New York: Alfred A. Knopf, 1971), pp. 224–31. The author of this famous book speaks much about "transcendence" but misses the most important meaning that this word can have: to go beyond and above oneself. To de Beauvoir, transcendence essentially means to go into the world, to enter the workforce and help form (or deform) it.

female view of things were of great importance to the male intellect. He often said that in the course of his life he had met more remarkable women than remarkable men. Usually he preferred to talk to women rather than to men, who, while often having a remarkable expertise in one field, tend to believe that they are competent in all fields. He highly appreciated the receptivity of women and enjoyed reading his manuscripts to those who had a genuine interest in them. But this spiritual affinity with the feminine did not prevent him from having enriching and deep male friendships.

His own manliness was tempered by "female" virtues: the precedence he gave to the human over the nonhuman, to the concrete over the abstract, to living over nonliving things, to persons over things, to friendship and love over his career. He hated violence, brutality, and any form of cruelty. A boy with whom he played as a child had a passion for catching butterflies, which he would kill and then pin in his scrapbook. Little Dietrich much preferred living butterflies to dead ones, and he made a point of shaking the trees and bushes when his companion was out hunting these poetic insects, much to his friend's displeasure. When Dietrich was a teenager, briefly attending an English school in Florence, he made the acquaintance of a group of English and American boys whose parents were living in Italy. He invited the boys to the campo, but soon they started fighting viciously, kicking and striking one another. Horrified by this behavior, he begged them to desist. When they paid no attention to his plea, he started crying. His companions made fun of him and called him a sissy. Little did he care. To him, meaningless violence was not only hateful but a caricature of true masculinity.

Later, von Hildebrand opposed the idolization of brutal force incarnated first in Prussian militarism and then in Nazism. He remarked that usually the less spiritualized by culture a people are, the more they are likely to overestimate physical strength and place it at the pinnacle of their subjective hierarchy of values. Sparta conquered Athens, Macedonia conquered Greece, Alaric conquered Rome, Prussia dominated Germany, the Turks defeated the Arabs, and in all these cases the conquerors were less cultured than the nations they conquered.

As further evidence of his affinity for the feminine, Dietrich, unlike most men, never knew the temptation of giving the precedence to his career over family and affective ties that is the tragedy of many marriages. It was incomprehensible to him that a man would sacrifice those dear to him for the sake of worldly success. He considered this a "sin" against the hierarchy of values. How often did he tell me that this hierarchy had been a guiding thread of his life, and these were not mere words, because he lived according to it.

He was convinced that happiness on this earth and beatitude in heaven are essentially related to persons and to love. Much as he appreciated beauty in impersonal beings, and the Platonic heaven of "Ideas", he knew intuitively that they can only hint at Someone beyond them, who alone can fulfill the deep longing that God has put into the human heart. We shall see again and again how deeply rooted in St. Augustine's philosophy his thought was. He often quoted the words "Fecisti nos ad te, Domine, et inquietum est cor nostrum, donec requiescat in te" (For Thou hast made us for Thyself, O Lord, and our hearts are restless until they rest in Thee).[47] Convinced that God was personal in the most profound sense of the word, he, like Kierkegaard, nurtured a strong dislike for any form of pantheism. He rightly saw that an impersonal divinity was a contradiction in terms and that pantheism is

---

[47] St. Augustine, *The Confessions*, bk. 1, chap. 1.

often an expression of metaphysical pride, of a sense of self–importance that one can have for being part of a huge whole.[48]

Another trait of Dietrich's personality evident early in his life and again related to his affinity for the feminine was his eagerness to learn from those who were more knowledgeable than he. He was keenly aware of the fields that were his forte and of those in which others were more competent. He never had to labor against the tendency to assert himself by taking himself as a norm. He never fell into the weakness decried by Socrates in *The Apology* of assuming that, because a person is proficient in one field, he must be accomplished in other fields as well.[49] There was no trace in him of the pride that claims, "I discovered it all by myself." On the contrary, he loved to relate that his full appreciation of a great painting (for example, Tintoretto's *Susanna in the Bath*, in the Vienna Museum) was due to his sister Lisl or that it was thanks to Bertele that he came to appreciate fully a particular piece of music. He wanted to learn, to open himself to enriching experiences, but he never said that a work of art was beautiful simply because one was supposed to say so. He was profoundly receptive, and this receptivity enlivened him to such an extent that he was then rewarded by "seeing" what had been explained to him, and it fully became his. Many times I heard him say, "This is a thought that I owe to my beloved teacher Reinach; this was inspired by Scheler; this is a jewel that my *alter ego* Siegfried Hamburger [his greatest friend] gave me."

Love, truth, and beauty: these factors were to remain prominent throughout Dietrich's life. But there was one thing

---

[48] Hence von Hildebrand's early rejection of the philosophy of Spinoza, a philosopher whom his father admired.

[49] Plato, *The Apology*, 21c–23c.

that was sadly lacking in San Francesco, and that was religion. Both Adolf von Hildebrand and his wife were noble pagans. They were lovable, warm, noble-hearted personalities, but neither had any religious interest. Officially they were Protestants, but they never attended religious services or discussed religious matters. They were, however, reverent, and they were far from endorsing the cynical liberalism fashionable in the nineteenth century. Their children were baptized by a Protestant minister, but the supernatural significance of this great event escaped them completely. To baptize one's children was a Western tradition, and this tradition was the limit of their religious horizon.

Even though little Dietrich dearly loved his mother and her influence over him was great, her lack of religiosity, of which the child soon became aware, in no way influenced him. None of Dietrich's beloved sisters was religiously inclined, even though the two younger ones had each a soul that could have been called *naturaliter Christiana*. Indeed, Lisl, the most beautiful and the most talented, once told her little brother that it was ridiculous to compare Christ to geniuses like Michelangelo, Beethoven, or Napoleon. She viewed the Savior of the world as a noble and good man, but how could these qualities be compared to genius?

But God's grace is more powerful than sociological conditions, and the young boy, totally deprived of religious food, was nevertheless powerfully attracted to religion.[50] A couple of episodes will shed light on the workings of grace in his soul. His youngest sister, Bertele, told me that when she was eight and a half and her brother was just five years old, she shared a bedroom with him. Before going to sleep, the children were chatting, and Bertele told her brother that their

---

[50] The same was true of Gabriel Marcel.

mother had said at table that Christ was the Son of God just as all men can be considered to be God's children but that there was nothing special about Him. To her amazement, her young brother jumped up in his bed, stretched out his hand, and said solemnly, "And I swear to you that Christ is God." An astonishing response, surely—but a harbinger of the confession of faith that he would make in 1914 upon his entrance into the Catholic Church.

The boy soon learned to read, and the first book that he read from cover to cover was a biblical story that his mother had bought because it contained pictures that children could color. Little Dietrich read the book three times with a degree of fascination: somehow he felt that this book was not at all like the fairy tales that had been read to him. He perceived the solemnity of God's voice addressing Himself to Abraham. He enjoyed reading and rereading this book while his sisters were taking dancing lessons in the living room of the von Hildebrand's villa. The contrast between the mundane world of the dance and the sacred world of the Bible kept him spellbound. From this early age on, he could never endure people who flouted religion or were irreverent toward it. His own deep reverence remained a part of his character throughout his life. Many of his writings illumine this crucial virtue, so neglected nowadays. Early he sensed that irreverence has a blinding effect on the mind, that it dulls the heart and nips in the bud any response to value.[51]

At age six, little Dietrich was baptized by a Protestant minister, Mr. André. The boy took the ceremony very seriously, and he resented the semi-humorous, semi-ironical comments of his sister Nini, who considered the whole affair to

[51] See *The Art of Living*, rev. ed. (Manchester, N.H.: Sophia Institute Press, 1994), pp. 1–11.; also *Liturgy and Personality* (Manchester, N.H.: Sophia Institute Press, 1986, 1993).

be purely conventional and devoid of meaning. Dietrich was chubby as a child, and, when he donned his white apron, his sisters teasingly called him "the little priest". But this epithet did not offend him in the least.

When the boy was eight, Lisl took him to Milan and showed him the cathedral, drawing her brother's attention to its architectural beauty. But she became annoyed when he insisted on genuflecting in front of every single altar—and there were many of them. "If you proceed with this silly performance and continue to make all this fuss, I won't show you the cathedral", she declared. This remark made no impression whatsoever upon her brother. Much as he loved his sister, he felt that, in this case, he was right and she was wrong, and that he was therefore under no obligation to yield to her demand.

This story is typical of Dietrich von Hildebrand's life. I have never met anyone who was less swayed by peer pressure, public opinion, the general consensus, "the spirit of the time", and the like. He knew all too well that "what they say" is mostly empty prattle and that what is fashionable today will be outmoded tomorrow. His norm was this: Is it right or is it wrong? Is it true or is it false? Is it or is it not pleasing to God? And he conformed his conduct to those criteria.

When he was a child, he used to prostrate himself in front of a reproduction of Donatello's *Head of Christ* that his parents had placed in their living room above the door because of its artistic beauty. Once his mother opened the door and caught sight of her son in this adoring posture. Deeply moved, she gently closed the door. She was much too reverent to try to change or suppress spontaneous inclinations in her son's soul.

This sense for the sacred was reinforced when, at fourteen, Dietrich heard for the first time Bach's *Passion according to*

Saint Matthew, which overwhelmed him. (He was to hear it performed some fifty times in his life.) Once again, he tasted the flavor of the supernatural, for this unique work puts in music what St. Matthew expressed in words. His heart was touched to its core by the "Erbarme Dich" (Lord, Have Mercy). He sensed the quality of "another world", one that infinitely transcends the beauty our senses reveal to us. In a gentle, secret way, grace was deepening its hold on the boy's soul.

When he was fifteen, his mother asked him whether he would like to be confirmed. Without hesitation, Dietrich turned down this suggestion, on the ground that he took religion much too seriously to perform a religious act as a mere formality. He definitely wanted to be a Christian, he told his mother. But having no idea whether Protestantism was the true form of Christianity or not, he could not possibly commit himself yet.

His independence of his beloved family was further evidenced by his passionate interest in ethics. Much as he loved beauty, he could not endorse his family's view that aesthetic values were supreme. At age fourteen, while he was taking a walk with Nini, she tried to convince him that moral values were purely relative, depending upon the time, place, and circumstances in which men found themselves. To her surprise, her brother vigorously challenged her views and offered a whole barrage of arguments to prove her wrong. A bit ruffled by this attack, Nini tried to regain her ascendency over him when, upon returning home, she called her father to the rescue: "Imagine, Father, Dietrich refuses to acknowledge that all moral values are relative."

"Nini," the father answered, "do not forget that he is only fourteen."

The boy was piqued, and answered, "Father, if you have

no better argument than my age to offer against my position, then your own position must rest on very shaky grounds."

Soon afterward, Dietrich paid this sister a visit. Having married Carlo Sattler, a painter and architect, in 1902, Nini had just given birth to her first child, Bernhard, in August 1903. In the course of this visit, the young boy once again gave evidence of his serious metaphysical concerns. Venturing on an intellectual discussion, Nini explained to her brother that she could not fathom why people were concerned about inane questions such as the immortality of the soul. Her brother was indignant and replied, "Nini, how can you uphold this nonsensical view? Don't you understand that the question of whether or not we have an immortal soul is of crucial importance?" Unbeknownst to the teenager, he was repeating what Pascal had written in his famous *Pensées* (section 3, no. 194).

A key feature of Dietrich's philosophy was already emerging in his mind: the hierarchy of values, the conviction that there are things that rank higher and are more important than other things, that this order is fully objective and is to be respected. To know whether or not we have an immortal soul is infinitely more important than to know that the earth is or is not in the center of the universe. It is typical of a great personality that he has a clear perception of this hierarchy and lives accordingly. It was an idea that he developed later in *Liturgy and Personality* (1932).

Another trait of Dietrich's character that deserves attention is his reverence toward the sexual sphere—a logical consequence of his deep reverence for femininity. Dietrich could never sever this mysterious sphere from a loving self-donation to another person, a commitment for life, in the framework of marriage. Even though his own father's life had not been flawless, even though later in life Dietrich had friends (such as

Max Scheler and Hermann Solbrig) whose lives were reprehensible, he could never tolerate or be close to those whose sins originated, not in passion or weakness, but in cynicism and irreverence. In his last ethical work, *Moralia* (Regensburg: Josef Habbel, 1980), he distinguishes between sins of weakness and sins of wickedness. There were two operas whose libretti were deeply disturbing to him: *Carmen*, because the heroine plays with José as a cat plays with a mouse; and *Madame Butterfly*, because Pinkerton was to him plainly detestable. And as much as he loved Verdi's *Othello*, whenever he listened to this great opera on recordings, he would stop after the "Ave Maria". The scene of the murder was too upsetting to him.

A holy wrath would take hold of Dietrich when men spoke contemptibly or disparagingly of women. He hated the attitude of such men and could not stand their company. It appears that grace had favored him at a time when he had no idea that such a mysterious reality as grace existed.

One episode sheds light on how deeply the boy understood the depth and seriousness of the sexual sphere. As noted earlier, the Hildebrands had a whole array of servants, many of whom were very attached to the family. Dietrich was often found in the servants' quarters and in the kitchen. He loved to talk to them, hear about their love stories, their families, their lives, and their problems, and he always treated them with great affection. He, in turn, was loved by them, something I was given to witness when, much later in life, in Florence I met some of them, for whom the arrival of *"Il Signor Gogo"* (his nickname) was a feast.

Once Dietrich found out that one of these servants had had several amorous adventures. The young boy expressed his disapproval. "Ernesto, how can you possibly do that?" he exclaimed. To which the servant answered, "Signorino, you misunderstand me; non lo facciamo per cattiveria; lo facciamo perché ci fa sentire bene" (We don't do it out of wickedness; we do it because it is pleasant). Later on, in his *Ethics*, Dietrich called this attitude "motivation by the purely subjectively satisfying". Dietrich had received a special grace, and it is to this grace (which came to full bloom when he entered the Church) that we owe the sublime works that he later wrote on the virtue of purity.[52] This attitude was not only theoretical; it was conscientiously practiced, even at a young age. Once his father had a female model of flawless beauty, a real Venus. When Dietrich was asked whether he would like to look at this masterpiece of nature, the boy, who was then a teenager, answered without a moment's hesitation that he wanted to reserve the discovery of the beauty of the female body for the moment when he would find the partner with whom he would share his life in marriage.

The unique features of the background and youthful character of Dietrich von Hildebrand bear witness to the truth of the dictum of Catholic theology that *Gratia supponit naturam* (Grace presupposes nature). Thanks to their privileged background, all the von Hildebrand children were spared the psychological disorders so prevalent today—inferiority complexes (a subtle form of pride), repression, lack of objectivity, unhealthy self-centeredness, odd psychological twists, and also what Adolf von Hildebrand called "unnecessary feelings". None of Dietrich's sisters was "crushed" by the gifts of the

---

[52] These include *Reinheit und Jungfräulichkeit* (*Purity and Virginity*) (Cologne, Munich, Vienna: Oratoriums Verlag, 1927), later published in English under the title of *Purity* (Steubenville, Ohio: Franciscan University Press, 1989); and the article "The Role of Reverence in Education" in *The New Tower of Babel* (repr. Manchester, N.H.: Sophia Institute Press, 1994), pp. 145–56. The papal nuncio to Germany, Bishop Eugenio Pacelli (later Pope Pius XII), wrote him a letter of congratulation when *Reinheit* was first published.

others. There was no rivalry among them. They were like a quintet, each playing her own instrument and rejoicing in the beauty of the whole. They were classical in the sense given to this term in one of his books.[53] His love for beauty, his passionate devotion to truth, his reverence toward the religious and sexual spheres: all these were unmerited graces evident in his youth that "predestined" him to embrace Roman Catholicism in his twenties. The seeds of this fruitful conversion would be sown at the University of Munich.

[53] See Dietrich von Hildebrand's chapter on this subject in his *Liturgy and Personality*.

CHAPTER 2

University Years and Conversion
1906–1914

Dietrich von Hildebrand became *civis academicus* in the autumn of 1906. He had just turned seventeen years of age. From that moment on, he spent most of the year in Germany, but he never missed a chance of crossing the Brenner to enjoy holidays at his beloved San Francesco.

Dietrich arrived at the university intent on studying philosophy. He had made this decision two years earlier, at the age of fifteen, upon discovering Plato's dialogues, some of which he read in Greek. He had noticed that he had an innate talent for detecting errors and equivocations in arguments and for unraveling a confused line of reasoning, and he set his mind upon developing this gift. Despite his father's contention that philosophy was not a "serious" intellectual pursuit,[1] Dietrich had an inner conviction that it was clearly and definitely his calling. This conviction never wavered, and he remained faithful to his commitment to philosophy until the very last day of his life. He once told me, "When you

---

[1] See Adolf Hildebrand's letter to his daughter Nini, May 1895, in *Adolf von Hildebrand und seine Welt* (Munich: Verlag Georg Callwey, 1962), p. 428.

notice that I can no longer philosophize, call the priest urgently; the end is near."

At the university, Dietrich commenced his philosophy studies under Theodor Lipps, whose lectures made a great impression upon him. Lipps' noble personality emanated spirituality and expressed his dedication to what he was convinced was true. This trait appealed to his new student. Lipps attracted him particularly because of his defense of an objective, valid ethics and, therefore, because of his rejection of ethical relativism. Moreover, he was impressed by the distinction Lipps made between *sensation* and *feeling*—a distinction that later blossomed in Dietrich's own life and in his works. But, as the pupil observed, Lipps' epistemology did not harmonize with his ethics, showing that he had not fully succeeded in liberating himself from "psychologism", prevalent at the time, which regarded human knowledge as merely a "content of consciousness", accessible only to the knower. In fact, psychologism made man a prisoner of his own mind.

On the other hand, neither Alexander Pfänder's courses nor those of Alois Fischer (who had been Dietrich's private tutor from 1903 to 1906), impressed him. The first repeated himself constantly and delivered very dry lectures, while the second was neither challenging nor inspiring. Lipps alone appealed to the young philosopher.

He soon joined the Akademischer Verein für Psychologie (Academic Association for Psychology), an organization that met weekly at Café Heck in Munich.[2]

The level of conversation was very high. After one of the members delivered a lecture, it was discussed at length. The

---

[2] The group had been founded in 1894 by Lipps. These evening meetings were attended by various faculty members and students majoring in philosophy, including Alexander Pfänder, Moritz Geiger, Alois Fischer, Herr Gallinger, and Herr von Aster; Professors Lipps and Cornelius also came from time to time.

young man learned more there than at the university itself. He was both intellectually challenged and fascinated, and every new meeting was sheer joy to him. He appreciated the gift of being in close contact with talented and outstanding minds, exchanging ideas with them, and discovering that they likewise defended the objectivity of truth and the possibility of attaining certainty in knowledge! There he met Heinrich Reinach, the younger brother of Adolf Reinach. The latter was soon to play a key role in Dietrich's philosophical development, and Heinrich was to become a great friend.

It was at the Akademischer Verein für Psychologie that the young man gave his first public talk, in January 1907. The topic he had chosen to address was "Stoff und Form in der Kunst" (Matter and form in art). His main concern was to distinguish between the artistic content of a painting and the non-artistic elements linked to it, such as its title, the fame enjoyed by the person depicted, historical or literary references (e.g., the battle of Waterloo, or Ulysses visiting Circe), which might awaken a person's interest. But these elements, he said, should play no role in a true appreciation of a work of art.[3] His talk was well received, although it triggered a lively discussion. The older men were impressed by this young talent and congratulated him on his inaugural performance. This praise was both encouraging and gratifying. A week later, the discussion continued, and Adolf von Hildebrand accompanied his son to offer support for his position.

At Easter time 1907, young Dietrich made the acquaintance of Adolf Reinach, a man six years his senior. Dietrich had already heard a great deal about him, both from the

---

[3] This thought received its full development in D. von Hildebrand's work *Ästhetik*, published posthumously by Kohlhammer in two volumes.

latter's brother, Heinrich, and also from his friend Raff, who had introduced him to Wagner's music.

From the first moment of their acquaintance, Reinach made a deep impression upon Dietrich, who immediately sensed Reinach's superior philosophical talent and his intellectual stature, coupled with a noble and attractive personality. Even though Dietrich entertained great hopes from this first meeting, the reality went far beyond his anticipation. He sensed Reinach's unconditional thirst for truth, his intellectual discipline and thoroughness, his moral stamp. Reinach struck him as a person totally free of prejudice and receptive to the "voice" of being. He had an outstanding precision and clarity of mind, and he immediately awakened one's trust because one could sense his integrity. He radiated an atmosphere of moral strength, of absolute purity, and of an outspoken moral greatness. The two men spoke about Lipps. They shared the same admiration for his personality and his moral stance. But Adolf Reinach made the young man keenly aware of the limitations of Lipps' ethics and, above all, of the unsoundness of his epistemology, caught in the tangles of psychologism.

At the time that young Dietrich met Adolf Reinach, the latter already had his doctorate in philosophy and was then working toward a degree in law at the University of Tübingen; he remained in Munich for a brief time only. Nevertheless, he was to reenter Dietrich's life shortly. In the course of the summer semester of 1907, the young philosopher gave his second talk at the Akademischer Verein, once again on an aesthetic theme: "Tiefe und Vollendung" (Depth and perfection).[4] The gist of his thought was that a work of art can be "perfect" within its own framework and yet not

[4] Once again, this was a distinction that reached its full development later in his two-volume work on aesthetics.

possess the "depth" that another work, less perfect in form, can possess. For example, Shakespeare's *Cymbeline* does not possess the formal perfection of *Les Précieuses Ridicules* of Molière, but the first work is deeper.

The talk was, once again, a success, and the speaker was elected president of the Verein. It was an honor but a very infelicitous choice. A more unfortunate idea could not have entered the heads of this distinguished assembly. Dietrich von Hildebrand was then and ever remained the worst possible organizer. He was unpractical and disorderly; he often forgot to make the necessary preparations; and he completely over-looked details that should have been attended to. In this he strikingly resembled C. S. Lewis (e.g., as related in *Surprised by Joy*), but Lewis was wise enough to refuse such an "honor" when it was offered to him.

Another important experience was in store for the young philosopher. Moritz Geiger, who was lecturing at the University of Munich at the time, had a rich uncle in the United States who had invited his nephew to visit him. Moritz decided to take a semester off, and in July 1907 his friends at the Verein organized a farewell party for him in a restaurant. That evening turned out to be a memorable one for Dietrich, for it was then that he made the acquaintance of Max Scheler.[5] Scheler had managed to transfer from the University of Jena (where he had received his *Habilitation*) to Munich. He was now *Privat Dozent* at the university. He was lavishly gifted, endowed with an extraordinary philosophical talent, and he was to play a decisive role in Dietrich's young life.

At Geiger's farewell party, Dietrich happened to sit next

---

[5] Dietrich had previously heard a lecture given by Scheler at the Psychological Association. But at that time Scheler was still strongly marked by Kantian thought, and his talk did not meet Dietrich's approval; and no personal contact took place.

to Max Scheler, and they began to talk. He wrote in his *Memoirs*:

> Scheler unfolded before my eyes the whole magic of his friendliness, for Scheler could be enchanting when he chose to; he dedicated himself completely to me, and opened up for me the breadth and depth of his remarkable mind. Whatever he said was deep, rich in content, interesting. He represented quite another "world" from that of the other professors. He was much more cultivated, and had a much richer contact with being. The "world" that his personality emanated reflected a rich field of experiences, and Scheler had, moreover, a warm, personal touch.

From the first moment of their acquaintance, Dietrich was captivated both by Scheler's mind and by his personality. What he felt for this man, fifteen years his senior, was neither the esteem that he had for a real philosophical power, such as that possessed by Pfänder, nor the sympathy he felt for Geiger. In Scheler, Dietrich recognized a real genius. He was being drawn into a dazzling, enriching, spiritual world. Scheler had a brilliant way of formulating ideas. Moreover, there was nothing "professorial", nothing pedantic, pompous, or self-important about him. Ideas flew from his mind as fresh spring water gushes forth from a mountain, joyfully, without effort. It was for the young von Hildebrand a new experience. Never before had he encountered a mind whose genius "overflowed", as it were, the way a river overflows its banks and fecundates the thirsty earth. The impression Scheler made on him also differed from the one Reinach had made on him a short time before. After they met, in the spring of 1907, Reinach became a philosophical authority for Dietrich.

Through his moral nobility, his uncompromising truthfulness, and his deep moral seriousness, Reinach awakened in Dietrich an esteem so deep that it bordered on veneration. Yet Reinach did not have the riveting charm of Scheler. The latter fascinated the young man with his brilliance and the charm that emanated from his whole being, his way of expressing himself, his very laughter.

In his enchantment and fascination, Dietrich seemed to forget that he was attending a farewell party in honor of Geiger. Judged in hindsight, Dietrich could be accused of unfriendliness, for he practically ignored the presence of the other guests, absorbed as he was in conversation with Scheler. This was one of Dietrich's weaknesses. When he was focused on something, he seemed congenitally incapable of taking account of other elements or obligations. He, who was ordinarily so polite, did not for a moment suspect that his concentration on Scheler could have been interpreted as rude and resented by the other guests.

That evening in July 1907 was of decisive importance for the philosophical and spiritual development of Dietrich von Hildebrand. His meeting with Scheler was, no doubt, one of the great intellectual events of his life. He went home in a state of intellectual inebriation. He decided to take Scheler's lectures, in addition to those of Lipps, and also to attend a seminar conducted by Pfänder.

Dietrich's friendship with Scheler, which lasted for some fourteen years, deserves close examination. Wrong as it is to interpret Dietrich von Hildebrand's ethical views as modeled on Scheler's—in fact, as he himself repeatedly said, he owed his philosophical formation to Adolf Reinach, whom he called "my true teacher"[6]—his acquaintance with Scheler

[6] See his article in *Philosophie in Selbstdarstellungen*, vol. 2 (Hamburg: Felix Meiner Verlag, 1975), pp. 77–127.

was to him a boundless source of delight and inspiration. From the very first moment, Dietrich knew that he had met an extraordinarily gifted philosopher. Tragic and undisciplined though Scheler was as a person, he radiated genius. Everything he touched turned to gold. He had an uncanny gift for shedding light on whatever subject he addressed, from the most profound to the most insignificant. Whatever he said was interesting, challenging, original.[7]

The young Dietrich was fascinated by this mind. For months he and his new friend spent hours in Munich cafés, until late into the night, discussing any topic that happened to strike their fancy. Scheler was, without doubt, pleased by this friendship. It granted him an ideal interlocutor, someone who was receptive and yet who challenged some of his positions. Dietrich soon saw how tragic it was that a man so lavishly gifted was inwardly torn apart and unhappy, and he wished with all his heart to help Scheler come back to what he firmly believed was his true self.

Dietrich loved Scheler with all his heart, and love, he knew, implies both a readiness to sacrifice for one's friend and to interpret his failings and mistakes lovingly, for these are

---

[7] An example is an incident that occurred to Scheler in the fall of 1910. One evening, Scheler was walking along the river Isar in Munich at a place where the river runs between rocky cliffs that rise high above its bed. All of a sudden, he lost his footing and slipped rapidly downhill toward the water. It was a long fall, and as he was falling he saw, in a flash, his whole life pass in front of him. Fortunately, the mishap occurred in autumn, and the ground was cushioned with an abundance of leaves and foliage that eased his fall. He was severely bruised, but he did not break any bones. Nevertheless, he was shaken, and Dietrich, to whom Scheler went for help, took him to his doctor. The patient had a fascinating way of describing his experience and made it so vivid and lively that one seemed to be witnessing it or even living it oneself. He had an amazing talent for observing his own feelings and then describing them to others in the liveliest colors. What he related was never stamped by the commonplace typical of many people's narrations of their experiences.

seen against the background of his "true" self—a thought that he developed later in his *opus magnum* on love.[8] But, with time, Dietrich saw more and more clearly the tragic discrepancy between Scheler's genius and his childish, petulant, and capricious personality. There was a gap between Scheler's amazing gifts and his total lack of self-control. He gave in to every whim and craving, was a chain smoker, was addicted to coffee and aspirin, and was unable or unwilling to restrain himself.

Despite Scheler's failings, Dietrich never lost sight of the greatness of his personality and intellect, which continually enriched the young man's mind. But his greatest debt to Scheler was that the latter's thought, still steeped in Catholicism, opened up for him the way to the Church by convincing him that she had both received and retained the fullness of revealed Truth.

This was to young Dietrich a revelation. Although born and raised in a Catholic country, he had never met a Catholic, let alone a convinced and practicing one. He was totally ignorant of the Church's doctrines. Two of his tutors (Ludwig Curtius and Alois Fischer) were fallen-away Catholics. He had been trained to enter churches as places rich in artistic beauty, but his parents were blind to their sacred character. Reverent as Dietrich was toward religion, he was nevertheless baffled by Scheler's assertion that the Roman Church was the one true Church of Christ, and he asked him to explain why he claimed this supremacy for the Catholic Church. With ease, Scheler brushed aside the dormant prejudices against the Church that the young man had picked up from both his tutors and his milieu. Then Dietrich's remarkable readiness to learn, his receptivity toward those

[8] *Das Wesen der Liebe* (The essence of love) (Stuttgart: Kohlhammer; Regensburg: Habbel, 1971).

who knew better than he, came to the fore. Scheler told him
that the Church produced saints. "What is a saint?" the
young man inquired. Once again, Scheler deployed the full
scope of his genius. He applied all his gifts to sketching the
essence of sanctity, and he illustrated his teaching by mentioning Francis of Assisi, describing his life in the most vivid
terms. Scheler's arguments about holiness were so powerful
that they convinced his young friend that the life of a Saint
Francis of Assisi could not be explained by purely natural
ethical categories; his holiness had to come from another
source.[9] Unwittingly, Scheler had opened for his young
friend the path to conversion. Slowly but surely, the face of
the Holy Catholic Church began to shine more and more
clearly. It was a slow process. It took several more years for
Dietrich von Hildebrand to enter the Church, but, thanks to
Max Scheler, he was on his way.

The seed of friendship, planted so auspiciously in the summer of 1907, continued to take root the following winter,
during which Dietrich attended Scheler's course on Greek
philosophy at the university. Whereas Alois Fischer's course
on the same topic, which he had taken previously, had not
impressed him, Scheler's lectures delighted him. He found his
presentation of hedonism, cynicism, and Stoicism masterly.

Their café meetings continued, and in addition to exerting
his influence in philosophical and religious matters Scheler
succeeded in modifying Dietrich's political views. Previously,
under the influence of his tutor Alois Fischer, who came
from a modest background and had even, for a while, lived in
dire poverty, the young man was sympathetic to socialism. It

---

[9] Later von Hildebrand wrote a book about St. Francis of Assisi, entitled *Not
as the World Gives: St. Francis' Message to Laymen Today* (Chicago: Franciscan
Herald Press, 1963; repr. Steubenville, Ohio: Franciscan University Press under
the title *The Image of Christ.*

rightly struck him as unfair that accidental circumstances of birth or background should prevent a person from developing his talents.[10] Through his discussions with Scheler, he now perceived clearly the danger of an earthly messianism and of the shallow (but tempting) belief that state laws can bring about a transformation of this earth and solve all its problems. It became clear to him that this transformation can be accomplished only through the purification of every single individual, a purification that, as he saw more and more clearly as time went by, can be achieved only by grace, which is dispensed through the Church. Socialism claimed to be a human solution to social and economic problems. Scheler opened up to the young man the treasures contained in the social teaching of the Church, rooted in the supernatural. While keeping his loving concern for the underprivileged, Dietrich came to see the problem in a totally different light. Thanks to Scheler, a great inner clarification took place in the young man's thought. To the last day of his life, he remained grateful to Max Scheler. From the time of his conversion until his death, Dietrich von Hildebrand was a daily communicant. His prayer life was so intense that, unwittingly, he often prayed aloud, even though only in a whisper. Every single day that I attended Mass with him, when the priest prayed for the living and the dead, I heard him mention Max Scheler's name.

At the same time as he was pursuing his studies in philosophy and enjoying his friendship with Scheler, the young Dietrich was avidly drinking the cup of life. There were delightful parties at the Hildebrands' home, 23 Maria Theresia Strasse; with his friends he went to plays, concerts, balls, operas, and operettas, as well as taking hiking excursions in

[10] It is often said: "He who is not a socialist at twenty has no heart; he who is a socialist at forty has no brain."

the beautiful surroundings of Munich.[11] During one of these hikes, the family's shepherd dog, Rhino, started chasing a hare. Young Dietrich ran wildly after him to prevent him from catching his prey. Walter Braunfels, who had become Dietrich's friend and later became his brother-in-law, shouted, "For goodness' sake, don't strain yourself. There are plenty of hares." To which Dietrich answered, "I care about the individual." This funny remark is typical of him. From his youth, he had a keen understanding of the uniqueness of every individual and a strong dislike for every form of pantheism, in which the individual vanishes into its species or into the immensity of the whole.

One more significant event marked Dietrich's life in 1907: he became engaged to Märit Furtwängler. The families von Hildebrand and Furtwängler had known each other for years. As noted earlier, Wilhelm, Märit's older brother, and Dietrich had shared a private tutor, Ludwig Curtius. Wilhelm was engaged for several years to Dietrich's youngest sister, Bertele—something that surprised no one, because of her passionate love for music. But, to her great sorrow and disappointment, one day, out of a blue sky, Willi told Bertele that their relationship was too spiritual and intellectual to lead

[11] As his friendship with Scheler deepened, Dietrich always included him in these excursions. It was on one such outing that Scheler exhibited one of his many eccentricities—singing. The young people had arrived at an inn. There was a piano with a music sheet for an old *Schlager*, or popular song. Scheler asked Hermann Solbrig, who used to play Wagner's music for Dietrich, to accompany him, and he started singing. His performance was hilarious, because he sang without ever pausing, even when a pause was called for. Scheler had the habit, while singing, of shaking his head in a very peculiar way; and finally, he was producing all sorts of tones that did not belong to the music. Later, Dietrich thought these performances bordered on the ridiculous; but at that time, his enchantment with Scheler was such that he saw them against the glorious background of Scheler's personality and talent and would have resented anyone's making fun of Scheler's performance.

to marriage. Bitterly disillusioned, the young girl allowed herself to become attracted by a brilliant young musician, Walter Braunfels, a friend of Dietrich's. Noticing that Walter had feelings for Wilhelm's sister Märit (nicknamed Märchen: German for fairy tale), Bertele told her brother that Märit was in fact attracted to him and had told her that she recalled with longing a very brief "falling in love" that she and Dietrich had experienced when they were mere children.

Bertele's communication overwhelmed her brother; for the first time in his life, he was loved first. Convinced that love was the most beautiful and most important thing in human life, he—who had fallen in love so many times and had suffered much because his love was never requited—in his youthfulness and immaturity, let himself be overcome by the thought that finally there was a lovable young girl who had fallen in love with him. Understandably, earlier he had suffered from a series of disappointments when, time and again, his respectful and loving advances had been turned down. Once, after a particularly painful rejection, he sought solace with his sister Nini, who told him that, as he was much too young to get married anyway, he should not take it so much to heart. "I know that I am much too young to get married," he responded, "but I am not too young to love." That was typical of him. It was love that was all important, but, simultaneously, he realized that an unrequited love cannot lead to happiness—it is like snatching air.

Despite the fact that Bertele's claim had no solid foundation, the young man actually talked himself into believing that he returned the love of the sweet-looking Märchen. Yet, he had to admit to himself—and this troubled him—that he was not feeling for Märchen the type of enchantment he had experienced so many times before. But he had a very strong will, and he, who had so often fallen in love, now had to "will" himself into loving, until he actually convinced himself that he truly loved Märchen. But he was baffled by the fact that the young girl, who was definitely not in love with him, responded so little to his advances. He could not reconcile her passivity with Bertele's assurance that she loved him. Nevertheless, after various ups and downs, the two young people did get engaged; Märit was fifteen, her fiancé two years older. The engagement lasted for a couple of years.

Because Dietrich always wanted to share whatever he experienced with those he loved, he soon introduced Märit to Scheler and persuaded her to attend the latter's lectures. He little suspected that this meeting was going to have consequences for all three of them, as Scheler eventually fell in love with Märit and married her.

Having spent two and a half enriching years at the University of Munich, during which his mind matured, Dietrich decided to transfer to the University of Göttingen for the summer semester of 1909 to study under Edmund Husserl, author of the ground-breaking work *Logical Investigations*. He had been introduced to this great work through an excellent lecture given by Moritz Geiger at the Akademischer Verein. The young man had then read the first volume of this book in the spring of 1907 and was enthusiastic. "It was for me like experiencing a sunrise", he wrote in his *Memoirs*. "Skepticism and psychologism were refuted once and for all, and Husserl's book opened up the blissful promise that the human mind could attain absolute certainty." He then felt that the time was ripe to leave Munich and study under the master himself.

It was a hard decision for him to make. He loved Munich passionately—its culture, its musical life, its charm. He believed himself to be in love with Märit; his friendship with Scheler was a constant source of inspiration; his beloved family and numerous friends and acquaintances lived in the Bavarian capital. But Scheler encouraged him to go and convinced him that attending Husserl's lectures would benefit him greatly. Ever devoted to his friend, Dietrich decided to follow his advice. Moreover, he had the feeling that to be separated from Märit for a while would be good for both of them—their engagement was not giving him the joy he had anticipated. Being far away for a while would give both him and Märit a chance to reexamine the nature of their relationship and to determine whether it was likely to lead to a happy marriage.

Even so, he did not rush to leave his beloved city. His brother-in-law, the Belgian painter Georges Baltus, who in 1904 had married the fourth Hildebrand daughter, Vivi, was in Munich at the time. Although a dilettante, he was a talented theater director, and he was working on an amateur performance of Shakespeare's *As You Like It*. The actors had rented a small theater in Munich, and the opening night was to be early in May 1909. Märit played the role of Phebe, and later Scheler told his young friend that when he saw her perform, with her lovely blond hair and radiant blue eyes, he fell in love with her.

Young Dietrich always considered that personal concerns were more important than professional ones, so even though by attending the performance he would inevitably miss one whole week of lectures at Göttingen, he did not hesitate; he stayed in Munich. On the other hand, not wishing to arrive at the university shockingly late, he sacrificed attending the marriage of his dear sister Bertele to Walter Braunfels on May 9, 1909.

Dietrich's description of his arrival in Göttingen is priceless. One cannot imagine a more brutal contrast than that between the enchantment of *As You Like It* in poetic Munich and the drabness that greeted him upon arriving in Göttingen. He took a room in a hotel and from the first moment felt that he had landed on another planet. He came from a world of beauty, nobility, poetry, and charm, and suddenly he found himself having lunch with a group of traveling salesmen whose only topic of conversation was comparing the merits of the various hotels and inns in which they had stayed. It was like a bad dream; the town struck him as petty, small, and philistine. He must have fully recognized, at that moment, how blessed his life had been up to then.

But the young man's first impressions of this famous university town were unfair. His experience with the traveling salesmen could have been duplicated anywhere. On his way to a friend's house, he traversed street after street lined with tasteless small villas inhabited by professors; once again, the impression was depressing. But soon he discovered the old Göttingen, which had charm and which he learned to appreciate.

That very afternoon, Dietrich paid a visit to Husserl. He was excited at the thought of finally making the acquaintance of someone whose book had made such an impression upon him and the whole circle of his friends at Munich, including Alexander Pfänder, Moritz Geiger, and especially Adolf Reinach. He had, however, been warned that Husserl's personality was no match for his mind. Even so, he looked forward to meeting this now-famous thinker.

Husserl received his new student with great friendliness. He had a winning simplicity about him and was kind and natural. But he did not impress Dietrich as a great personality. The difference between him and Scheler was striking. Husserl had nothing of the latter's brilliance and intellectual "glow". Meeting Scheler was bound to make one realize immediately that he was of extraordinary intellectual stature. Reinach too, although in a different way, made the same impression. Both men were "personalities" in a sense Dietrich later defined in his *Liturgy and Personality* (1932). Husserl was no "personality" in that sense.

Even so, Husserl was appealing by virtue of his simplicity and unpretentiousness. He in no way acted the part of the "famous man" and was not typically professorial. But it was clear that he was touchy, and he could not conceal the fact that he was offended because his new student had missed the first week of his courses, as well as his seminar.[12] Naturally, this pedantry struck Dietrich as ridiculous. How could someone take university life that seriously! After all, there were more important things in life than taking courses! In short, the young man never regretted having skipped one week of courses for the sake of enjoying a performance of *As You Like It*. All of a sudden, he felt that he had landed in a narrow world, totally centered on the university, professors, courses, diplomas—all viewed with an awe that to the young man's mind was totally out of proportion. The pseudo-sacrality of the professorial world was disconcerting and disheartening to him.

Fortunately, the situation was redeemed as soon as Husserl and his new student engaged in a philosophical discussion. That was where Husserl revealed his true self. However, he managed to irritate young Dietrich once more by making allusions to various sculptures, assuming that the son of a famous sculptor would understand his point better if brought to bear on the world of marble! Dietrich found this assumption naïve. Nevertheless, Husserl made several remarks that were both deep and enriching.

---

[12] That Husserl was extremely touchy and easily offended is confirmed by Edith Stein in *Aus dem Leben einer jüdischen Familie* (Freiburg im Breisgau: Herder, 1965), p. 230.

Upon leaving Husserl, Dietrich had mixed feelings. On the one hand, Husserl's *Logical Investigations* had opened a new world to him. It was like a dawning light against the dark sky of the prevalent philosophy. Husserl was clearly a much greater thinker than Lipps, but Lipps was a more impressive personality. Spoiled by his background, the young man had probably assumed that a great mind or great artistic gifts go hand in hand with a great personality. He was thinking of his own father, of Scheler, of Reinach. He now knew that it need not be the case.

He rented a room in a house situated on a pretty street called "the Jewish street" and soon made the acquaintance of other students, several of whom became friends—especially an outstandingly talented Latinist, Günther Jachmann. But, typically, one new acquaintance, although not devoid of charm, displeased him from the start, for Dietrich felt that he had an irreverent attitude toward women. This new acquaintance struck him as frivolous, and that sufficed to choke in Dietrich's soul any deep sympathy for him.

He also made the acquaintance of a whole series of young girls—but found one more unattractive than another. What a contrast between the beauty and grace of his mother and his five sisters, who for many years had long, flowing hair, while the various professors' daughters all had the unfortunate habit of tying their hair in a knot on top of the head—a fashion that struck him as unpoetic and pedestrian. There was no Rosalind, no Portia, no Viola among them! He described them as charmless and dull.[13]

As noted previously, humor constantly peppered the lives and conversations of the von Hildebrand family. To find himself in a dull, conventional world of *petits bourgeois* was to

---

[13] Following St. Paul, Dietrich von Hildebrand had a special love for long hair in women. To him, it belonged to the charm and aura of femininity.

young Dietrich a challenge. He decided that he would not adapt himself to this drabness but would try by every means, as long as he remained in Göttingen, to shake these northern Germans out of their straitjackets. His role was *épater le bourgeois*, to astonish or baffle the stolid citizens of Göttingen, whose code of behavior irritated him. He absolutely refused to conform to its stodgy protocol. He started a "cultural revolution", introducing dances that were not fashionable in the small university town. In no time, Göttingen knew that an *enfant terrible* had joined the student body.

Dietrich faithfully attended all of Husserl's lectures, but he systematically cut the other courses for which he had registered. Under Scheler's influence, he had chosen to minor in zoology and botany, two branches of knowledge in which he had no interest. Scheler had talked him into it, because, impressed by his young friend's knowledge of literature, history, music, and languages, he thought that a scientific formation would benefit him greatly. It was a most unfortunate piece of advice, for soon Dietrich saw the magnitude of his mistake. The lectures bored him; dissecting frogs disgusted him. After sitting in the course several times, he played truant for the rest of his time at Göttingen. In European universities attendance at class is not obligatory, but students are responsible for knowing course material. As most professors endlessly repeat themselves, the students buy lecture notes, cram them into their heads before exams, and then pass or fail as the case may be.

Whenever he could, Dietrich escaped from Göttingen on the night train to Munich. He was so robust that a sleepless night did not bother him at all, and any excuse was good enough for him to return to Bavaria. Late one night, after one of the numerous parties he attended, Dietrich and a couple of friends took refuge in the only café still open in the wee hours of the morning, at the railway station. They were conversing cheerfully when, all of a sudden, it was announced that the express train to Munich was about to enter the station. One of Dietrich's companions, Theodor Conrad, said jokingly, "How tempting it is to jump on the train and go south." Dietrich needed no encouragement—no sooner said than done. A few minutes afterward the three young men, all in dinner jackets, found themselves in a compartment, going south. The idea of this adventure was exhilarating, but once they found themselves moving fast away from Göttingen, their enthusiasm abated somewhat. Neither young Dietrich nor Conrad had enough money to pay his fare. Moreover, Conrad was very poor, and he suddenly weighed the consequences of his rash decision. Fortunately, the third young man had money and offered to advance the fare for the three tickets. Once in Munich, Dietrich took Conrad to the Maria Theresia Strasse, where his mother, assuming that they had been a bit tipsy to have made such a wild decision, said to her son, "Praised be your tipsiness, thanks to which I have the joy of seeing you!"

Her son had not been tipsy at all, but he had simply been in one of his humorous moods and was not able to resist the temptation of doing something a bit wild. Not only did Irene von Hildebrand pay for her son's trip, but, upon being told that Conrad was poor, she offered to pay for his trip as well. That was typical of her nobility and generosity. Having breathed Munich's poetry to their hearts' content, the three young men, quite proud of their adventure, took the night train back to Göttingen in time for their courses on Monday morning.

Back at the university, the young philosopher found Husserl's teaching a great disappointment. The professor was giving a course on the history of philosophy, and there was an abysmal difference between Scheler's dazzling presentation in

Munich and what Husserl had to offer. Scheler's lectures were fascinating, brilliant, always incisive and inspiring. Husserl, totally absorbed by his own writings, prepared his courses superficially. He was the type of professor who is so absorbed in his own research that teaching has no attraction for him. His course was badly organized, and he allowed himself to be carried away by his personal thoughts, in no way concerned that they were unrelated to the subject he was supposed to discuss. Much of what he said was incomprehensible. From a historical point of view, this course was valueless. It was the case of a powerful mind and a deplorable teacher, for writing and teaching are two very different things, and rare are those who possess both talents to an equal degree. Husserl's seminar, however, was much more interesting, that is, when the students succeeded in forcing their professor to remain centered on the topic under discussion, a role that young Dietrich immediately assumed with great success.

In the late spring of 1909, after a Pentecost vacation spent with his family in Munich, Dietrich returned to Göttingen and heard, to his great joy, that Adolf Reinach had decided to get his *Habilitation* under Husserl and had become the latter's assistant. Thanks to this happy turn of events, Dietrich was going to start the most important and serious part of his philosophical formation. Reinach taught a course on ethics, and the young man was fascinated by the distinction his teacher made between the values of a state of affairs, which he termed the "right", and the moral value of the person, which he termed the "good". This distinction was to bear rich fruits later in Dietrich's numerous ethical works. It was the seed of his all-important distinction between "morally relevant goods", such as the life or property of a person, and "moral values", such as justice, purity, generosity, and truthfulness, as qualities of the person. After delivering his lectures, Reinach left Göttingen for a while.

In the meantime, Dietrich's relationship with Husserl was developing positively. The latter was particularly affable to him, and the young man discovered many attractive and lovable traits in his professor, who, apart from his outstanding talent, was a kind and lovable man. But his wife, Malwine, did not win Dietrich's sympathy. She was very talkative, and much of what she said had little or no content. Moreover, she had a special talent for making tactless remarks.[14] Malwine did not share Husserl's timidity. She was much more assertive than he and had more vitality. But her husband clearly had great admiration for her. They had three children—one girl and two boys—one of whom, Wolfgang, was to lose his life during the First World War.

The Husserls had concealed from their children the fact that they were of Jewish descent. They were both formally Protestants, and they were very anxious to hide their origins. Their daughter, Elli, however, soon found out, thanks to Husserl's new student. Dietrich made a point of informing a young woman named Putti Klein, the daughter of a professor at the university, that Husserl and his family were Jewish. She, being Elli's friend, hastened to share this piece of information with her. Whether Husserl was upset upon finding out that his well-kept secret had been violated is not known. Having had since his youth many Jewish friends and acquaintances (Hermann Levi was Jewish; so were Raff, Scheler, and Reinach), Dietrich found the Husserls' dread of having their origin disclosed not only absurd but totally incomprehensible. He was so free of any sort of prejudice, so far removed from bigotry in any of its forms, that he could

---

[14] Edith Stein makes the same point: *Aus dem Leben*, pp. 175, 268–69.

not respect a position that, to his mind, was both unwarranted and irrational. He radically rejected anti-Semitism, and it was inconceivable to him that Jews should be ashamed of their blood.

The summer semester of 1909 came to an end, and Dietrich joyfully returned home. Upon arriving, he heard that Max Scheler was vacationing in Zell am See, in Austria, and he decided to spend a few days with him. No doubt, he was anxious once again to enjoy Scheler's personality and be stimulated by his mind. The days Max and Dietrich spent together in the Austrian resort must be numbered among the finer moments of their friendship.

The young man (who was not yet twenty at the time) arrived via the towns of Kufstein and Wörgel and was warmly received by Scheler. It was the year of Emperor Franz Josef's jubilee; he had been reigning for sixty years, one of the longer reigns recorded in history.[15]

Dietrich immediately fell under the spell of Austria and its courteous people. He felt a deep spiritual affinity with this country, which continued throughout his life, though Italy was and remained his first love. He loved Austria's tradition and culture, its majestic landscape and architecture, and its Catholic spirit.

The days the two friends spent together were marked by increasing intimacy and trust. As a token of friendship, Scheler related to his young friend the story of his life. He spoke at length about his youth and his tragic marriage to Amélie von Dewitz. Scheler's wishful thinking often colored his interpretation of the facts. He spoke of his life the way he imagined it to be, which was not in every detail the way it was. Only

[15] He died seven years later.

after many years of friendship did Dietrich learn to distinguish between the fact and fiction of Scheler's account of himself. Even then he never discovered the truth regarding some of the episodes Scheler described on this trip.[16]

Scheler's father was Protestant, but he had converted to Judaism in order to marry Scheler's mother, who came from an Orthodox Jewish family and whose father requested this "conversion" as a condition for allowing the marriage. Little Max was outrageously spoiled by his domineering mother, who treated her other child, a daughter, with great coldness. Scheler's sister met with a terrible end. She was murdered by her fiancé in 1904, and Scheler had the sad task of accompanying the police in the search for her body, which was found in a wood.[17] The fact that he was both dominated and indulged by his mother had sad consequences. Never taught restraint, Scheler never learned to discipline himself, to control his impulses and whims. That weakness was to be the undoing and the downfall of a great mind and a presage of the many tragic situations in which he later found himself.

Young Scheler was brought up as a Jew, but he received no religious formation.[18] As a young boy, however, he was impressed by the simple but deep faith of the Catholic maids who worked in his home in Munich, and he was attracted by the beauty of baroque architecture. While in gymnasium,[19] he came under the influence of a Catholic priest, through whom he discovered the Absolute and somehow divined the world

[16] I am reporting what Max Scheler told Dietrich von Hildebrand while calling attention to discrepancies I have uncovered, in subsequent footnotes.

[17] According to Wilhelm Mader, Scheler's sister committed suicide. He notes that this incident is never referred to in Scheler's extant letters and that to the end of his life Scheler avoided talking about it. See Wilhelm Mader, *Scheler* (Reinbek: Rowohlt, 1980), p. 31.

[18] Mader's book contests this statement.

[19] The German equivalent of college-preparatory high school.

of grace incarnated in the Catholic Church. He told Dietrich that this discovery led to his conversion and baptism.[20]

In 1893, when Scheler, at the age of nineteen, received his secondary school degree, he decided to celebrate by taking a trip to Italy with a friend. The two young men arrived in Brüneck, where, upon entering the restaurant of the hotel where they were staying, Scheler noticed a woman several years his senior looking ominously at him. He said to his friend, "You know, there are some women who should wear on their breast the skull and crossbones label, like those put on bottles of poison." Though he had instantly intuited the dangerousness of this woman, by the very next day he had become her lover. This accidental affair with Amélie von Dewitz was to mark Scheler for the rest of his life.

Amélie was a refined but hysterical woman with a demonic streak.[21] She was the wife of a Prussian aristocrat, who truly had had enough of her. Upon finding out that she had a young lover, he gladly granted her a divorce. Scheler soon married Amélie,[22] and they then moved to Jena, where Scheler studied under Professor Eucken and received his doctorate.

Scheler's life soon became a living hell. He now apprehended that he had married a "witch", whose perverse desire to hurt was the mainspring of her actions. When he had

---

[20] After Dietrich's death, I learned that Scheler's conversion story is not corroborated by the facts, as shall be seen later.

[21] Mader confirms that Amélie von Dewitz was mentally unbalanced. She suffered from psychosomatic illnesses and had to be hospitalized several times (*Scheler*, p. 20).

[22] According to Mader, Amélie's mother was Catholic and insisted that Scheler be baptized in order to marry her daughter. Not one to take such "formalities" very seriously, Scheler agreed. The date on his baptismal certificate shows he was baptized two weeks before contracting his invalid marriage with Amélie. My husband died ignorant of this fact. Despite his later understanding of Scheler's character, he would have been aggrieved to learn the actual circumstances of his friend's baptism.

finished writing his doctoral dissertation, Amélie, perhaps motivated by jealousy, burned the whole manuscript while he was out of the house. In another jealous rage, she slapped the face of Professor Eucken's wife in public.[23] More than once Amélie threw open the window facing the street of their home and screamed that her husband was in bed with the wife of a well-known publisher. She particularly enjoyed feigning suicide. She would make a small cut on her breast and play a death scene, expecting Scheler to perform the role of the despairing husband. If he "failed" in his part, her hysterical cries resounded through the neighborhood.

Scheler remained in Jena with Amélie until 1905. He was by then in a state of psychological and moral bankruptcy and could no longer endure his wife. In spite of her protests, they separated. First he went to Berlin, where he led a completely dissolute life. Then he went back to Munich and started teaching as a *Privat Dozent*. Amélie would not let him be, and in 1907 they tried to live together once again. The experiment failed, and in 1908 the break between them became final. Still determined to make life miserable for Scheler, Amélie began a whole series of intrigues against him.

Dietrich's response to this long, sorry tale was one of deepened affection and profound pity. He felt touched by Scheler's confiding in him and compelled to help his friend out of the morass of misery and sin into which he had fallen. That such a genius should find himself in these foul circumstances broke his heart. How could someone who had been granted such sublime religious and philosophical insights lead a life that was so radically opposed to his intellectual vision?[24]

The surprising thing about Scheler was that, while relating

---

[23] Mader writes that she menaced Frau Eucken with a gun (*Scheler*, p. 30).

[24] Max Scheler exemplified the mystery that is man: on the one hand, his thought and writings helped many people find their way to God; on the other

these unsavory details to his young friend, he was animated neither by bitterness nor by hatred. He narrated them with a cool detachment, very much as if he had been only a spectator of these dramas instead of one of the principal actors. He repeatedly said that he knew himself to be a great sinner, and he never tried to exonerate himself by putting all the blame on Amélie. This evenhandedness made a deep impression upon his young friend, who considered it incredibly noble. But later he was to discover that this trait in Scheler arose from a certain moral indifference. Was Scheler intellectually fascinated by the entanglements of his own "drama"? God alone can pass judgment upon this tragic character.

Scheler nurtured a passionate interest in observing people —their foibles, their mannerisms, their idiosyncrasies, their personalities. This interest was triggered by a mixture of psychological curiosity and the enjoyment of a rich gamut of experiences. He never passed judgment on people's behavior, but he was clearly amused by their foibles and follies. He once said to his young friend, "To me, men are like animals in a zoo. I love to watch their antics. You are an exception." (Whether he truly meant that or simply said so as a sort of *captatio benevolentiae* is a question that I leave open.)

Scheler's attitude is illustrated by his treatment of Günther Jachmann, the outstanding Latinist whom Dietrich had met in Göttingen. He had visited Dietrich's parents in Munich and proved to have a special understanding for Adolf von Hildebrand's artistic gifts.[25] Dietrich introduced Jachmann to

---

hand, he himself tragically opted for a sort of religious schizophrenia. It was not the first time in the history of the Church that a man whose life is sinful has been an instrument of grace. God can raise children to Abraham out of stone.

[25] See his superb article dedicated to this great artist on the occasion of his death, published in a volume containing reproductions of some of Adolf von Hildebrand's outstanding artworks.

Scheler, who immediately took to him. The three men continued talking until the early hours of the morning, Scheler displaying his scintillating mind and intellectual treasures. After Christmas 1909, however, Scheler suddenly turned all his attention to Heinrich Reinach and dropped Jachmann in a rather rude fashion. Scheler was dominated by his arbitrary moods. A person might catch his interest for a while, but when he thought that he knew that person, the interest dissipated. He had little or no continuity, and therefore, too, he soon lost interest in the women whom he conquered. Enjoying the human zoo, he wanted change and variety, and he had had enough of Jachmann.

Nevertheless, in the course of those few days in Zell am See, Scheler had once again revealed the depth and nobility of his mind, which at that time had not yet been affected by his sexual aberrations. Dietrich was intellectually inebriated by the wealth of insights being poured upon him; and, beyond the insights that Scheler generously showered on him, there shone the light of the Roman Catholic Church. Dietrich's deep attachment to Scheler was in large part a consequence of the fact that the latter was for him a mediator pointing the way to the Church. Moreover, Dietrich sensed that his deep affection for his older friend was reciprocated, and that Scheler truly rejoiced in his personality, his idealism, and his passionate commitment to truth. Indeed, the hotel proprietress had told the young man that when Herr Doktor Scheler received the letter announcing that his friend would visit him, he had said to her, "This letter changes my whole life."

The beautiful days in Zell am See had to come to an end, and Scheler suggested that they return to Munich via Salzburg. Thus it was that Dietrich saw for the first time this uniquely beautiful city, a city that was to play an important role in his later life. The days in Zell am See and in Salzburg cemented the friendship between Max and Dietrich. One needs a great deal of confidence in someone fifteen years younger to open oneself as Scheler had to his young friend, and Dietrich was deeply touched by this sign of trust. He had a loving heart, and Scheler's happiness and welfare became matters of the greatest importance to him. The devotion of the younger man to the older was, indeed, boundless.

Later in life, Dietrich von Hildebrand characterized friendship as a type of affection in which the *intentio benevolentiae* (the desire to do good to the loved one) takes precedence over the *intentio unionis* (the desire for union), in contrast to spousal love, in which both are very much in the foreground.[26] Dietrich's devotion to Scheler in the ensuing years was his way of living this *intentio benevolentiae*. He never missed a chance to help him, to cater to his needs, to foster his legitimate interests. Moreover, toward Scheler, this *intentio benevolentiae* was characterized by a total selflessness. The young man truly burned for the good of his friend, and he was ready to make any sacrifice for his sake. Scheler certainly liked his younger friend a great deal, but his capacity to serve or to give selflessly was no match for that of his admirer. Moreover, Max Scheler enjoyed being admired, understood, loved by a friend. His attachment to Dietrich had a very different note, for he was definitely not inclined to make sacrifices for others.

I have mentioned that, since his youth, Dietrich could not tolerate a cynical attitude toward sexuality. It might strike others as strange that he had such devotion to a man who proved to be a profligate. But the reason is easy to find. Scheler was not a cynic. He was a man overwhelmed by his sexual passions, for he had never learned to control his desires, even the most insignificant. He was a tragic character,

---

[26] See *Das Wesen der Liebe.*

clearly his own worst enemy, torn between what he knew to be right and his uncontrolled impulses. His young friend had one deep wish for him, and that was that he might find a Senta (the heroine in Wagner's opera *The Flying Dutchman*) who would pull him out of the muddy swamp in which he lived. Far from rejecting Scheler the sinner—for Pharisaism was totally foreign to him—Dietrich ardently wished that his friendship, which so strongly appealed to what was best in Scheler, could be instrumental in helping him find his moral and religious moorings.

Nevertheless, while deeply concerned about Scheler's personal troubles, Dietrich continued to find his genius a source of delight. In December 1909, while both were in Munich, they attended together a performance of Shakespeare's *Coriolanus*. Dietrich was already acquainted with several of Shakespeare's comedies, and he had a special understanding for their enchanting poetry. Through Scheler, he now fully discovered the power of Shakespeare the historical dramatist. Scheler opened another door, and from that moment on Dietrich began a lifelong study of Shakespeare's works. He read all his plays, rereading some of them many times. And when he was a dying man, Shakespeare's works were on his table. He was so enthused about his new discovery that he wrote his mother, who was in Rome at the time, in order to share it with her. She immediately wrote back, telling him how happy she was about this development.

A few months earlier, Scheler had given a talk on the difference between the Christian love of neighbor and humanitarian love. It was a superb lecture and contained the nucleus of the ideas later fully developed in his book *Ressentiment im Aufbau der Moralen* (The role of *Ressentiment* in the building up of morality). Scheler's criticism of Nietzsche and of the latter's arguments against Christian love was a source of joy to Dietrich, for whom it was a breakthrough to a deeper understanding of the Christian ethos, an uplifting clarification that gave him a deeper insight into the Church. Once again, God was using Scheler, the sinner, to open for Dietrich the world of the supernatural.

Meanwhile, as his friendship with Scheler prospered, the young man's engagement to Märit Furtwängler proved more and more of a disappointment. Their affection had no deep roots. It was unsubstantial and based more on wishful thinking than on a real "value response". They both became increasingly conscious that it could not lead to marriage. While remaining good friends, they decided toward the close of 1909 to end their engagement, and they mutually agreed that they were free to form other attachments.

This step was all the more desirable because, while in Göttingen, the twenty-year-old Dietrich had met a young woman who made a deep impression upon him. Her name was Margarete Denck. He had met her at a dinner party when he first arrived in Göttingen in the spring of 1909 but had not taken special notice of her. A bit later, he encountered her again at a dance and discovered to his amazement how different she seemed from the other Göttingen girls he had met. She did not look dull or ordinary; she had a charm and poetry about her and an enchanting way of laughing. She was four years older than he, had lost her father when she was about six, and had been raised by her maternal grandmother, who lived in Göttingen. Like Dietrich, she was nominally Protestant but did not practice her religion. She was extremely musical, played the piano with talent, and shared not only many of Dietrich's cultural interests but his religious longing as well.

They talked at length. She told him that she had been engaged to a man whom she had loved but who had abandoned her for another. This explained the sadness and reserve expressed on her lovely face. He felt a deep pity for someone who had been so unfairly treated and had clearly suffered deeply. With a loving heart, he could feel a deep sympathy for others. Throughout his life, he wished ardently to be instrumental in making others happy, to heal their wounds by introducing them to another "world", to the intellectual and artistic world in which he had been raised and, later on, to the glorious world of faith. Pity was ever one of his leading motivations. It was a key to many of his actions. But if pity played a role at the beginning of his interest in Margarete (Gretchen), it was only a starting point. Soon, he truly and deeply fell in love with her. The more the twenty-year-old student came to know Margarete Denck, the deeper became his attachment. The relationship became serious on his side, and he decided to introduce her to his parents in Munich.

While finding Margarete attractive and lovable, neither Adolf nor Irene von Hildebrand was at all enthusiastic about the thought that their son might marry her. Not only was she older than he—a secondary concern—but she came from northern Germany and from a very different family background. She was shy and reserved and did not fit the image they had envisioned of their future daughter-in-law. They knew that their son loved and revered his five sisters, and both had wished that his future wife would come from a similar mold. This was definitely not the case with Margarete. Moreover, they thought that Dietrich was much too young to commit himself seriously.

To the young man, however, all these considerations were totally groundless: he loved Gretchen, and he loved her more and more as time went on. He believed that love should conquer all petty obstacles, and it never occurred to him for one moment that he should yield to his parents' wishes and give up Gretchen, as they clearly wished him to do. On the other hand, he had not completed his studies and was financially dependent upon them. He was the last person in the world, however, to be swayed by financial considerations, and he had firmly decided to look for a teaching position in a high school or, in the worst of cases, to take any position rather than give up what he considered the most important thing in life—love.

Like a golden thread in a seamless garment, this trait ran throughout Dietrich's life: he never even knew the temptation to sacrifice what was objectively important in itself (in his terminology, a *value*) for the sake of money or financial security. He lived up to this principle so consistently that for many years, as will be seen, he often found himself in severe financial straits. These financial consequences reached their climax when he gave up all earthly security because of his refusal to live in Nazi Germany.

The young student had told Gretchen about his still-existing engagement to Märit; and, when his new friend came to Munich for the first time, Dietrich introduced them to each other. Interestingly enough, Gretchen, who at the time was definitely not in love with Dietrich, said to him with great earnestness, shortly after meeting his fiancée, "I urge you not to marry this young woman. She is not the right wife for you." This remark made a deep impression upon Dietrich, and it was soon afterward that the engagement was terminated.

Young Dietrich apprised Max Scheler of his situation. Scheler, who in the meantime had acknowledged to himself that *he* loved Märit, was overjoyed, all the more because he had reason to assume that she reciprocated his feelings. As his first marriage had been a purely civil one, from a Christian point of view Märit could become his true, legitimate wife. Dietrich was convinced that Scheler was on the way to a *vita nuova*.

As Dietrich's attachment to Gretchen continued to grow, he invited her to come to Munich for longer periods of time. She stayed with one of his sisters, usually Nini. He introduced her to Scheler, and for several months, the four of them—Dietrich and Gretchen, Max and Märit—led a joyous life. They went to plays, parties, balls, operas, concerts, and even operettas, which Max Scheler loved and which Dietrich enjoyed tremendously in spite of the strong disapproval of his sister Bertele, who chided him for his "infatuation" with music that her artistic sense could not endorse. Her brother was quite conscious of the chasm separating Bach, Mozart, and Beethoven on the one hand and Lehar, Suppé, and Strauss on the other, but he was young, and operettas were fun and amusing; moreover, Scheler always managed to throw an enchanting glow on whatever was experienced in his company.

Even though Dietrich had decided not to take courses for a semester, his mind continued to be stimulated by his frequent contacts with Scheler, who often came to the Maria Theresia Strasse, where he gave talks, read books to his friends, and fascinated everyone who met him with his brilliance.

Dietrich now hoped that Scheler's love for Märit, and their marriage, would conclude the sad episode of the preceding sixteen years of Max's life. He was convinced that a deep and true love can operate miraculous changes in a person's soul, changes that no counseling could achieve. In his youthful idealism, the young man was convinced that love would transform Scheler—and, for a while, it seemed that that was the case. He was therefore overjoyed when Scheler confided to him that he loved Märit with his whole soul and that this profound emotion was making a new man out of him. One wish of young Dietrich was that his friend would marry Märit and embark on a new life. He was convinced that Scheler would now return to the Church and live a life in full harmony with his philosophical insights. Alas, many obstacles had yet to be overcome before this wish could be realized.

A huge stumbling block to Scheler's hope of marrying Märit rose up before him in 1910. His ex-wife, Amélie, had reported to a socialist newspaper, the *Münchener Post*—a sort of tabloid always eager to publish sensational and scandalous stories—that the "professor of ethics" at the University of Munich was allowing his ex-wife, Amélie, to starve, while he was enjoying the luxury of traveling with his girlfriend, whom he had registered as his wife in a hotel. The scandal broke out with the violence of a tornado and made headlines all over Germany. Sensationalism took over, and the professor's adulterous relationships were the topic of every wagging tongue. To her dismay, Märit's mother found out in this manner that her daughter was no longer engaged to Adolf von Hildebrand's son (an engagement that she had fully welcomed), and that she had now fallen in love with a scandalous character. Poor Märit had to endure many scenes. But her ex-fiancé came to the rescue. He tried to convince Mrs. Furtwängler that Scheler was an exceptional man of extraordinary talent and that she should be flattered that such a genius wished to marry her daughter. He had had a tragic life, yes. But a deep love, the love he now had for Märit, would heal the old wounds and enable him to start anew.

Dietrich's appeal helped somewhat, but Mrs. Furtwängler made it clear to Märit that she would not give her consent to a marriage with Scheler unless he was publicly exonerated of the charges leveled against him in the *Münchener Post*. Very much against his will, therefore, Scheler was forced to sue the newspaper for libel. In the meantime, Mrs. Furtwängler sent her daughter to Berlin and exacted from her the solemn promise that she would not correspond with Max. What was to follow was a sad story.

Reluctant as he was to sue, Scheler was at that time so deeply in love with Märit that he was ready to go to any length to win the consent of her mother. But it was a risky situation. First of all, Scheler's life had been far from blameless, and it was easy enough to level accusations against him. Second, it was clear from the start that the socialists in Munich wanted to cast aspersions on a Catholic professor. Even though Scheler had been excommunicated as a result of his first marriage and was not practicing his faith, he was still considered a Catholic, and his teaching was strongly marked by a Catholic ethos. Finally, at the trial, both the judge and the jury were clearly biased against him. (The judge was the same one who had conducted the famous Eulenburg process a few years earlier.)

The *Münchener Post* had leveled three charges against Scheler. First, he was accused of letting his wife, Amélie, starve while he enjoyed trips with other women, and during the course of one of the trips, in Lusin Piccolo, he had allegedly registered his paramour as his legitimate wife.[27] Second, Scheler was accused of borrowing money (stated with the vulgar expression *anpumpen*, roughly the equivalent of the English expression "to hit up" or "touch" someone for cash) from one of his students, a violation of the code of honor of any university. Third, Scheler was accused of having "hooked" the fiancée of one of his students (namely, Märit)—the charge again was leveled in crude German slang.

Dietrich was outraged. The few encounters he had had

[27] In his book on Scheler, Wilhelm Mader claims that this accusation rested on a misunderstanding (*Scheler*, pp. 37–38).

with Amélie had convinced him that that poor woman, animated by a vitriolic hatred, had only one aim in life, to ruin Scheler's career. It was in no way true that she was starving. She had money of her own, while Scheler had great difficulties making ends meet with his modest salary as *Privat Dozent*. The third charge was so ridiculously false that Dietrich offered to testify in Scheler's defense. He was willing to put his own reputation on the line for the sake of his friend. Obviously, it was not to his advantage, because the whole affair was bound to be unsavory, but the young man, who was definitely a bit of a Don Quixote, never allowed his personal interest to play a role when it was a question of truth or falsity, right or wrong.

The details of this depressing incident are outside the theme of this book. As to the first charge, it is enough to note that during the trial it became clear that Scheler's ex-wife was not without financial means. Moreover, she had been allowed to testify before having taken an oath, and that was clearly illegal. She gave shameful details about her husband's private life, presenting him as totally perverted. Even though that testimony was irrelevant to the matter of the trial, it made a strong impression on the jury. Amélie's daughter from her first marriage also was called to testify on her mother's behalf, and her testimony was peppered with offensive details. It was obvious that she had been well coached by her mother—another of the many illegalities during the trial.

Regarding the second charge, it was true that Scheler, who was chronically in need of money, had borrowed six hundred Marks from one of his students. However, the "student" in question, Archibald Fuchs, was not a matriculated student of the university but, captivated by Scheler's genius, had merely audited Scheler's courses. But the facts of the case were badly misrepresented. Influenced by Scheler's mind and personality,

Archibald Fuchs had converted to Roman Catholicism. He had become attached to his mentor and nurtured the thought of entering a religious order. Fuchs was rich, and he had said to Scheler that he was planning to give him his whole estate upon leaving the world. Scheler then asked whether he could advance him 10,000 Marks—a huge sum of money at the time, but Scheler was crippled with debts. Fuchs declined to give him this sum but lent him 600 Marks, which, although welcome, did not fully alleviate Scheler's financial woes. Scheler had agreed to repay Fuchs within a year, which, as could be foreseen, he did not do. Fuchs then turned against Scheler. Dietrich had met Fuchs previously, for Scheler had introduced him as a friend to the von Hildebrand household, and found he had scant sympathy for a man who looked like Mephistopheles, who was a morphine addict, and whose face was scarred by the various *Korpsstudent* duels he had fought.

The third accusation against Scheler was blatantly false. The engagement between Märit and Dietrich had been severed by their mutual consent. Interestingly enough, Dietrich's deep affection for Scheler had made him aware that the latter was more important to him than Märit. This fact opened his eyes to the tenuousnous of his attachment to the young woman, for it was evident that a fiancée should have affective priority over a friend.

True to his word, Dietrich came down from Göttingen to testify and made a point of being present for the duration of the trial. He became deeply upset at the illegal way in which the lawsuit was conducted and alarmed at the thought that his friend's name was being dragged through the mud.

When called upon to testify, he stated, with a strong, clear voice, that he had indeed been engaged for a while to Fraulein Märit Furtwängler, but that both parties had concluded that they were not compatible and had parted amicably. He added that it was his joy now that his dear friend Max Scheler loved his ex-fiancée and that she, in turn, fully reciprocated this love. Condescendingly, and with a voice loaded with irony, the judge said to him, "You are a very idealistic young man."

As was to be expected, given the handpicked jurors, the illegality of the procedures, and the whole tenor of the trial, Scheler lost his case. When Dietrich heard the verdict, he broke into sobs. In a way, he took the outcome much more to heart than did Scheler himself. The latter was, of course, shaken at the thought that marriage with Märit seemed now out of the question. He was not only publicly disgraced, but he also lost his *venia legendi*, that is, for the rest of his life he would be barred from teaching at any German university. His name *had* been dragged through the mud; he had become a social leper.

Upon leaving the courthouse, Dietrich met Archibald Fuchs and gave him back a paltry sum of money that he had previously borrowed from him, saying that, from now on, he would have nothing to do with him. Sharp words ensued. Günther Jachmann at that moment proved to be a true friend to the disconsolate young man and tried his best to intervene. Dietrich then invited Günther to his parents' house. The next morning, a *Korpsstudent* rang the bell at 23 Maria Theresia Strasse and told the servant that he wanted to give a message to Dietrich von Hildebrand. Dietrich was taking a bath, so he asked Günther to go in his stead. The *Korpsstudent* told him that he had been sent by Archibald Fuchs, who, offended by the sharp words Dietrich had addressed to him the previous day, challenged him to a duel unless he agreed to take back his words and formally apologize. Günther relayed this information, whereupon Dietrich asked his friend to inform the *Korpsstudent* that he could not take back anything he had said because it was all true. Moreover, he considered duels to be immoral, and he absolutely refused to accept the challenge to fight one.

When Dietrich returned to Göttingen, he was greeted at the railway station by Gretchen. She was in full solidarity with the stand he had taken and was outraged at the way the trial had been conducted. To Dietrich's joy, Adolf Reinach also expressed his deep sympathy for Scheler, whose future was now in jeopardy. Soon afterward, Dietrich received a letter from a student organization in Munich, informing him that because he had dared to refuse a duel he was from now on considered *Satisfaktionsunfähig*—the worst penalty that could be imposed on a *Korpsstudent*—that is to say, anybody could insult him, for he was officially deprived of the right to avenge himself. Even though Dietrich was usually terribly slow to answer letters, he immediately took up pen and ink and wrote back that their declaration impressed him as much as if he had been excommunicated from some Chinese Buddhist sect. He never heard from them again, probably because, given the prevalent mentality, this student organization must have concluded that anyone who remained unaffected by the severity of their censure was clearly insane.

Despite the disgrace that the trial had brought upon Scheler, his devoted friend was determined to help him rebuild his life as much as possible, by inviting him to come to Göttingen, sharing both his room and his monthly allowance. After a few days, Dietrich took a train to Berlin, to relate to the anxious Märit what had happened during the trial's proceedings. He also wanted to be able to assure the dejected Scheler that his fiancée remained totally faithful to him. Märit was delighted to see her ex-fiancé, and he soon came back to Göttingen and was able to calm Scheler's fears. Märit's love had in no way abated.

Soon afterward, Scheler did go to Göttingen. He had lost

not only his reputation but also all his means of support. Dietrich tried unsuccessfully to collect a series of signatures from well-known professors urging Scheler's reinstatement. He traveled with Scheler to Jena with this intention. Interestingly enough, a professor he knew well told him that his own life was similar to Scheler's but that he did not want this fact to make the headlines!

As was to be expected, in view of the trial's outcome, Märit's mother was now adamantly opposed to the marriage of her daughter to Max Scheler. She also exacted a promise from her daughter not to write to this man, who was now a pariah. According to German law, Märit could not get married without her mother's consent (her father had died a few years before). But once again Dietrich took the side of the lovers and offered to be the go-between. Märit addressed her letters for Max to Dietrich, and he played the postman. Usually so careless and forgetful about practical things, he performed this task with great care, until Märchen, reasoning that she was not bound to keep a promise that had been forced on her, relieved her ex-fiancé of this task.

Dietrich concocted a plan for Scheler in Göttingen, organizing a seminar in a café and convincing students and friends to attend Scheler's lectures; Scheler was thus able to earn a modest sum of money, enough to cover some of his everyday expenses.

Dietrich had by this time definitely decided to pursue his doctoral studies in Göttingen. What prompted this decision was primarily his growing interest in Margarete Denck. Moreover, Theodor Lipps, his first teacher at the University of Munich, had recently died, and he could easily convince his parents that it was best for him to continue his studies under Husserl. When the latter heard of this decision, he was not overly pleased. He sensed, correctly, that his student's main motivation for staying at the University of Göttingen was Fraulein Denck and not his courses. However, in the meantime, Adolf Reinach had become *Privat Dozent*, or lecturer, in Göttingen, and for Dietrich this was a tremendous boon, for Reinach was the ideal teacher. Here he was going to have a chance to be formed by this remarkable man who combined love for truth with depth, discipline, and clarity. Again and again, Dietrich von Hildebrand said and wrote that his true teacher and mentor was Adolf Reinach. Scheler had inspired and stimulated him, but the young philosopher never considered himself to be his "disciple". Soon after their first acquaintance, he had noticed flaws in Scheler's thought, and later, in his doctoral dissertation, he clearly distanced himself from Scheler's ethics.

Husserl, who was both shy and conventional, not at all pleased to hear that Dietrich had invited Scheler to come to Göttingen, told the young man that, given the scandal that had just taken place, he ought to understand why Scheler could not possibly be received in the Husserl home. Once again, Dietrich did not hesitate to put his head on the block for a friend. Since he had decided to study for his doctorate under Husserl, the latter's goodwill was all-important for his future. Worldly prudence should have taught him that it was unwise to challenge the person on whom his professional fortunes depended. But Dietrich never practiced prudence, this "doubtful virtue", as Saint Francis of Sales calls it.[28] Without a moment's hesitation, the new Don Quixote said to his professor, who was thirty years his senior, "Dear Professor, you ought to know that every unkind word addressed to Scheler is something that I take personally. I am in complete solidarity with him, and I respect him." Husserl must have

[28] See, for example, J. P. Camus, *The Spirit of St. Francis of Sales* (Tournai: Casterman, 1946), pp. 246–47.

been impressed by the young man's courage, for soon afterward he did receive Scheler into his home, and the sad episode was forgotten. Much as Dietrich deplored Scheler's promiscuous life—and Scheler knew this full well—he saw him as a tragic figure, perverted by a sick woman, a man who suffered from his sinfulness but was incapable of breaking the bond that controlled him.

Thus Max Scheler settled down in Dietrich's rooms in Göttingen, and the friends commenced housekeeping together. The constant contact with Scheler's mind was exhilarating, but to live with a genius who was totally undisciplined was no sinecure. Scheler had one basic principle, which he applied rigorously: "I do not want to treat myself pedagogically", which meant, in essence: I want to follow my wishes and my whims, and I absolutely refuse to keep my nature and temperament in check.

To save money, Max and Dietrich decided to dine in their room at night on cold cuts and bread. Although Dietrich's allowance was very generous, when it was divided in two the situation became precarious. Scheler nevertheless always insisted on buying such a quantity of meat that, in spite of two healthy appetites, much of it was left over and had to be given to the dogs, for they had no refrigerator. One day, Dietrich remarked that it would be wiser to buy just the amount of cold cuts needed. This was enough to trigger Scheler's anger. In order to assert himself and teach his young friend that he was not to be "educated", the very next day he purposely bought an enormous amount of meat that could not possibly be eaten, and most had to be thrown away. Dietrich wisely decided that it was better to yield to his friend's bizarre behavior than to begin a feud that could endanger their friendship. That Scheler might yield to reason was entirely out of the question, and the young man loved him too deeply to argue with him on so minor an issue. The cold cuts continued to "go to the dogs"!

Wasting food was not their only difficulty. Every morning, Scheler would call their landlady and shout, "Frau Schmidt, please bring me my mail." When the answer was "*Herr Doktor*, there is no mail for you today", Scheler would go into a rage: "How dare you say that I have not received a letter? Of course my fiancée has written, and you are keeping it from me. Please, bring it to me immediately." "But, *Herr Doktor*," the unfortunate Frau Schmidt would answer, "why in the world would I keep your letters to myself?" Scheler's wrath would then turn to the mailman when he came for the second delivery around noontime. "Give me my letter", he would command. Once again, the response was, "*Herr Doktor*, there is no letter for you today." Then Scheler would truly lose control over his temper: "I shall go to the postmaster and complain about you. You have no right to withhold my correspondence!" Luckily for the hapless mailman, Märit wrote frequently, but not as often as she should have, according to Scheler's impetuous wishes, and every single time she failed to do so, the same tragi-comedy was repeated.

From time to time, Max and Dietrich had breakfast in a restaurant. Max always ordered two boiled eggs. He insisted that they be so soft that they were practically liquid. After a few minutes, he would call the waiter and demand, "Bring me my eggs." "They are not yet ready, *Herr Doktor*", was the answer. Scheler would storm back: "How stupid of you to say that! Of course they are ready! I told you that I wanted them to be almost liquid. Therefore it is clear that they are ready. Bring them immediately!" The waiter would begin to lose his patience, and an unpleasant exchange of words would erupt. One day, this silly quarrel threatened to develop into a real fight, and the other guests were eagerly watching the show. Dietrich decided to end the brawl by making use of a trick that he had once used successfully with his lovable but irascible brother-in-law, Walter Braunfels. The latter had started a row with musicians performing in the von Hildebrands' house, because it was late and he wanted them to stop playing. But young Dietrich, who was enjoying himself immensely and did not want the party to come to an end so soon, had signaled to the musicians by touching his forehead in such a way that they would understand: pay no attention to Walter's request, for he has a bat in his belfry. The musicians, delighted to prolong their work, had winked to the young man in reply—that they had gotten the message—and played with renewed fervor.

Dietrich now decided to play out the same scenario in the restaurant. Unbeknownst to Scheler, he touched his forehead to inform the waiter that his friend enjoyed less than perfect sanity. The waiter, thus convinced that his customer was truly deranged, became so ostentatiously courteous that Scheler turned to Dietrich and said, "What is the matter with the fellow? He was so rude a moment ago, and all of a sudden he has become so polite!"

Shortly after Scheler joined Dietrich in Göttingen, in 1910, the two friends planned to pay a visit to the great Russian novelist Tolstoy, whom they admired deeply. Dietrich's parents had offered him a trip around the world, but, as was typical of him, he turned down this generous offer, not wanting to travel alone. His parents would, of course, have been willing to finance the two on a trip to Russia instead, but, just as their plans were maturing, they learned that Tolstoy had died.

During the school year 1910–1911, Dietrich attended Reinach's lectures in Göttingen with passionate interest. This academic year marked the most important time in his intellectual formation, for he was approaching philosophical maturity. Reinach's lectures were masterpieces. His presentation was unique, incorporating a sound historical foundation, precision, clarity, and depth. One could not imagine a finer teacher. For his devoted student, it was a continuous intellectual banquet. The lectures Reinach gave on both Plato (whom Reinach revered) and Descartes made an impression on him that lasted for life. At the same time, the Philosophical Association[29] that Dietrich had founded with Theodor Conrad, like the Verein he had belonged to in Munich, continued to be enriching and challenging. Many outstanding new students had joined it: Jean Hering from Alsace, Siegfried Hamburger from Kattowitz (he was to become von Hildebrand's close friend), Hedwig Martius (a remarkably talented young woman who later was Edith Stein's godmother), Alexander Koyré, and Roman Ingarden, a Pole. All were outstandingly gifted young people who did honor to both Husserl and Reinach.

In the course of this year in Göttingen, Dietrich spent much time with Hedwig Martius (who later married Theodor Conrad). He appreciated more and more how remarkable she was, and her contributions to the Philosophical Association were superb. There was a striking contrast between her extraordinary intelligence and her childlike, lovable personality. She was kind, innocent, simple, ready to help others, and very modest in appearance. When she stepped into a room, no one could have suspected what a powerful mind God had given her.[30]

During the summer of 1911, an important meeting took

[29] The Göttinger philosophische Gesellschaft.

[30] Although a prolific scholar, Hedwig never obtained a professorship in Germany. Being a woman was no trump at the time, as it is now! Some of her better-known works are: *Der Raum, Bios und Psyche* and *Abstammungslehre.*

place at Husserl's home, with Max Scheler, Adolf Reinach, and Dietrich von Hildebrand in attendance. Its purpose was the founding of the *Jahrbuch für Philosophie und phänomenologische Forschung* (Journal of philosophy and phenomenological research). Alexander Pfänder had been informed of the plan and had agreed to become a member of the committee. It was an important hour for philosophy, as this review was to preserve outstanding contributions to human thought. Scheler offered to write a work on ethics for the *Jahrbuch*; Reinach, a work on the philosophy of law; Husserl intended to publish his work *Ideen* (Ideas).[31]

During the meeting, Scheler, who had a touch of sadism in him, enjoyed making Husserl nervous. While discussing the birth of the new journal, he kept turning the pages of a book by Theodor Lessing in which the latter related how, during a visit he had paid to Husserl some years before, Husserl had tried to deny his Jewish origins. Scheler knew about the passage and relished Husserl's embarrassment at the thought that he might find it. It was typical of Scheler, but certainly not kind, however regrettable Husserl's attitude had been.

Having met Reinach, Adolf and Irene von Hildebrand, deeply impressed by his personality, had invited him to accompany their son to Florence during the Easter vacation of 1911. They both shared Dietrich's loving admiration for this man of integrity and moral rectitude. It was a joy for young Dietrich to open to his revered teacher the treasures of Florentine art and architecture. But besides these cultural discoveries, Reinach and Dietrich made the acquaintance of two young men, Giorgio Papini, who later became an ardent Roman Catholic, and Giuseppe Prezzolini, who later taught

---

[31] The plans were drawn up in early 1911; Reinach oversaw the production of the first number.

Italian at Columbia University in New York. At that time, they were both philosophical relativists, subjectivists, and idealists. The four men entered into a fierce discussion that had a dispiriting effect on both Adolf Reinach and Dietrich. There was an intellectual chasm between them that no argument could bridge. To be treated unjustly or not to be given the money promised for a lecture never upset Dietrich. He brushed these aside as of little importance. But when he heard fallacious arguments, he became upset, so much so that he actually lost sleep. He responded to philosophical errors the way a musician reacts when he hears someone sing off-tune while thinking he is giving a fine performance.

During this visit to Florence, Adolf Reinach and Dietrich von Hildebrand also made the acquaintance of the famous philosopher Franz Brentano, Husserl's own teacher, who, for this reason, was highly respected by the Göttingen circle. Brentano was an ex-priest who had left the Church because he refused to accept the dogma of papal infallibility. He was at that time an elderly man, but when Dietrich was a young boy he had often met him in the streets of Florence, for Brentano lived close to the Porta Romana and therefore a stone's throw from San Francesco. He was an impressive personality, with the appearance of an Old Testament patriarch. Now, he received his guests very kindly but started expounding his views on sensation as if he were on a podium. Dietrich observed that he had a powerful mind; and while Husserl was superior to his teacher as a philosopher, Brentano was definitely the greater personality.

The picture I have drawn so far of Dietrich von Hildebrand's life shows how happy his youth had been. But life was going to teach the young man that suffering is an inevitable ingredient of our earthly existence. His brief engagement to Märit

had been a disillusionment, and he had no doubt been affected by it. But his optimism resurfaced. When he broke this
youthful bond, it left no scar or bitterness in either him or
Märit. By then, he had already met Margarete (Gretchen)
Denck, the woman he would eventually marry.

When Dietrich introduced Gretchen to his parents, he
sensed intuitively that, although they found her attractive and
lovable, they would not welcome a deeper commitment on
his part, for reasons I have mentioned. Moreover, Dietrich
had not completed his studies and was still too young to bear
the responsibilities of marriage. His parents had looked differently on their son's engagement to Märit. First, the two
families were friends, and second, the question of marriage
was never raised because the couple were so young. With
Gretchen, who was twenty-six, the situation was quite the
reverse. The question of marriage was clearly and inevitably
in the foreground. Adolf and Irene von Hildebrand refused to
give Dietrich their permission to marry Gretchen, and this
had the effect of a legal prohibition because the law required
a young man of Dietrich's age to have the written permission
of his parents in order to marry.

Though anguished that his father and, particularly, his
mother would not permit him to marry Gretchen, Dietrich
embarked on a path contrary to their wishes, feeling justified
by his love for Gretchen. He dismissed his parents' arguments
against the union as superficial and invalid and consummated
his relationship with her without the benefit of lawful marriage. In the minds of the young lovers, taking this step meant
making a commitment for life.

Their decision led to an extremely painful episode. One
day, in the late spring of 1911, Gretchen informed Dietrich
that she was pregnant. This news meant that marriage was
now not only his deepest wish but also his urgent moral

obligation. Both Adolf Reinach and Max Scheler were consulted, and it was decided that Reinach, for whom Adolf and Irene von Hildebrand had high regard, would go to them as an "ambassador" on their son's behalf. Eloquent as Reinach tried to be, both Adolf and his wife remained adamant against the marriage. Nevertheless, they offered to continue to support their son financially while he was writing his dissertation. They suggested that he and Gretchen move to either Berlin or Vienna and live "in hiding" until the child was born, that is, until February 1912. There is no doubt that both Adolf and Irene still wanted to give their son a way of "escape" in case he were to discover that Gretchen was not the right wife for him. Dietrich sensed this attitude and was outraged by it. Did his parents understand him so little that they could think for a moment that he would abandon Gretchen, especially now that she was a mother? Unhappy as he was with their decision, Dietrich still had no choice but to submit to his parents' will. Reinach, who behaved admirably in this whole episode, tried to convince him that time would bring a solution, that as soon as the baby was born, Adolf and Irene would relent and grant him permission to marry.

The year between the spring of 1911 and the spring of 1912 entailed intense suffering for Dietrich. He had remained faithful to his firm decision never to separate love and sex. And yet he had placed himself in a position in which he was giving the impression that he was not seriously committed to Gretchen, a thought that drove him toward despair. He was not a practicing Protestant. He knew nothing about sacramental marriage, yet he wanted to avoid giving the impression that his love for Gretchen was anything less than a lifelong and sacred bond.

In the document he left me, Dietrich von Hildebrand relates the psychological torture he suffered when, upon arriving in Vienna, he had to see a lawyer to advise him of his situation, for he needed his help to register with the police, a requirement for foreigners settling down in Vienna. Obviously, he had to register Gretchen as Miss Denck and not as his wife. When he went to see the lawyer to explain his situation, he was so ill at ease and stammered so much that, at first, the lawyer thought he was dealing with a criminal affair. Finding out that it was "only" a question of pregnancy out of wedlock and that the young man was going to marry his fiancée as soon as he received parental permission, the jovial Viennese made it clear that that sort of thing was not the stuff of tragedy.

After settling down in the Austrian capital, the young philosopher started working intensely and systematically on his doctoral dissertation. Originally, he had wanted to write his thesis on an epistemological theme, and he had suggested to Husserl the topic "Error and Illusion". But Husserl strongly advised him against what was too ambitious a project for a doctoral thesis, requiring him to come to grips with the most crucial questions of human knowledge. Dietrich accepted Husserl's advice and decided to turn to an ethical theme, "The Nature of Moral Action", a topic to which Husserl gave his approval.

Moral questions had always been at the very center of Dietrich's interest, so his new subject fascinated him, and he started working on his thesis with his usual intensity. The work was nearing completion when, one day, standing in front of a food store where Gretchen was shopping and contemplating the attractiveness of the wares displayed in the window, it suddenly occurred to him that their appeal differed radically from the appeal of values. In a flash, he discerned that whereas the appetizing wares derived their importance from the viewer's response to their appeal, the importance of *values* was intrinsic to their very being. Their importance was rooted in their essence, independently of any response given to them.

Values called for a proper response of appreciation. They *deserved* this response, while the response given to tempting foods was up to the individual. In other words, Dietrich discovered that there are two radically different categories of importance, two very different forms of motivation. The first he called *value* (that is, the important in itself), and the other, the *merely subjectively satisfying* (that is, something whose importance is derived exclusively from the appeal it has for an individual person).[32] To clarify this difference, we might say that gratitude is the response due to the *value* of a generous action, something intrinsically good in itself, whereas the importance that beer has for a person depends exclusively on whether or not he happens to like it.

This discovery constituted a clear break with Scheler's ethics, based on the thesis that pleasure also was a value, although low on the scale of importance. But Dietrich saw clearly that if this were the case, choosing pleasure over a value could be explained only as an intellectual error, and this obviously did not correspond to observation. He saw with overwhelming clarity that pleasure appealed to a totally different "center" in the human soul. It was therefore not a question of "higher" and "lower", but a question of two different sources of motivation that were radically different from one another. This discovery, made in front of a food store in Vienna, became the backbone of his numerous works on ethics.

At first, this revolutionary insight upset him. He was putting the finishing touches on his doctoral dissertation, and he recognized that, on the basis of what he had just perceived, he would have to rewrite the whole work. But his love for

---

[32] See Dietrich von Hildebrand, *Christian Ethics* (Chicago: Franciscan Herald Press, 1972), chapter titled "The Categories of Importance".

truth and his delight in the magnitude of his discovery was such that, with renewed vigor, he harnessed himself to the task. The more he worked, the more he recognized the depth and fruitfulness of the insight that had been granted him. He never knew the temptation of making compromises with truth for the sake of convenience or personal advantage. He rewrote his whole thesis, and in a very short span of time it was completed. In December 1911, he went to Göttingen and submitted it to Husserl for approval. A month later, Husserl wrote him that the dissertation was accepted. He suggested some minor stylistic changes, but it was clear that the work pleased him greatly.

Overjoyed that his mentor had accepted his thesis, Dietrich's one great concern was now the imminent birth of his child in early February, a birth that turned out to be dramatic. The baby was very large, and Gretchen, exhausted after hours of labor, no longer had the strength to give birth. Finally, the doctor had to take the baby with forceps, and in the process he almost pierced one of the baby's eyes. The young father was present during those agonizing hours, encouraging Gretchen, who was suffering excruciating pains, and holding her while the physician was trying to grasp the child's head. The moment the child—a son—was born, Gretchen seemed to recover from her torment in the most amazing way, whereas the young father's legs were shaking under him, and he nearly fainted from exhaustion.

The parents named the boy Franz because of their devotion to Saint Francis of Assisi, whose personality Scheler had sketched so powerfully for them. The name Franz was an unfortunate choice, however, because it was also the name of Irene von Hildebrand's first husband. No doubt, too, Adolf von Hildebrand was disappointed that this grandchild carrying the von Hildebrand name was not named after him.

His son's birth was to Dietrich von Hildebrand a profoundly religious experience. It moved him to the depth of his being and made him aware of the mysterious collaboration between God and man that takes place in procreation. It threw a new light for him on the mystery of the sexual sphere and deepened further his sense of reverence for this sphere, which can either elevate man or degrade him deeply.

The child was a handsome little boy, with big, radiant, blue eyes, the joy and delight of his parents. Soon he proved to be precocious, manifesting unusual musical talents. When he was two years old, he could spontaneously sing the second voice of any song that he heard. The proud father and mother discovered the beauty of paternity and maternity in the love and responsibility they had for this little creature, who partly owed his existence to them. Dietrich never expected that one could love a baby as much as he loved little Franzi. The child became the apple of his parents' eyes.

As Adolf Reinach had predicted, soon after the birth of their grandchild, Adolf and Irene von Hildebrand relented and allowed their son to marry Gretchen. They chose not to attend the wedding, however, which took place in Vienna in May 1912. Only Zusi and Vivi came to the ceremony, celebrated in a Protestant church.

His dissertation completed, Dietrich had to go back to Göttingen to take his oral examination and defend his thesis. He was told that, whereas Husserl considered his dissertation to be the most outstanding he had ever directed, Scheler considered Hedwig Martius' work still better. Reinach's judgment was that both works were equally remarkable.

Unfortunately, Scheler had given his young friend very bad advice in urging him to minor in zoology and botany. Bored by scientific courses, Dietrich had systematically absented himself from them. The professors of the science faculty hardly knew his face. In order to pass his comprehensive, however, he had to have a good command of the material covered. So he decided to cram in as much factual knowledge as possible. Thanks to his powerful memory, he felt that he was satisfactorily prepared.

The two professors who examined him were known to have a strong dislike for Husserl and his philosophy, and they extended this dislike to his favorite disciple.[33] They decided to teach the young man a lesson. They questioned him on the most arcane aspects of their disciplines and told him that he lacked a scientific bent of mind. They literally interrogated him as if he were in the dock, and Dietrich was well aware that he was not performing well. He left the examination room crestfallen.

In spite of Husserl's efforts to grant him a *summa cum laude*, which would have been important for his career, the two scientists were adamant. All they could grant him was *cum laude*. Husserl tried to make up for this by giving him a *summa cum laude* grade for his dissertation, writing on its cover *opus eximium*, "superb work", but the final grade, the one that counted, was *cum laude*. The new Doctor himself was not overly surprised by the outcome of his examination. Nevertheless, he was disappointed. He knew what Husserl thought of him. He knew now that he had been unwise to follow Scheler's advice. Had he chosen history and music, he would have come through with flying colors—and without much work. It was too late now to cry over spilled milk, however, and he never allowed himself to be depressed by things that he considered to be of secondary importance.[34]

---

[33] That Edmund Husserl was not popular among his colleagues at Göttingen and that they looked unfavorably on "phenomenology" is affirmed by Edith Stein in *Aus dem Leben*, pp. 175–76, also 187.

[34] See Karl Schuhmann, "Husserl und Hildebrand", *Aletheia* 5 (1992): 6–33.

Coincidently, 1912 proved to be the wedding year for two of Dietrich's closest friends. In August, Adolf Reinach married Anna Stettenheimer, a young woman he had met in 1906–1907 in Tübingen, where she was studying natural sciences at the university. And in Munich, Mrs. Furtwängler finally relented in her fierce opposition to her daughter's marriage, and Max Scheler and Märit Furtwängler were married in the Ludwig Kirche in December.[35]

Scheler, still ostracized from German universities, had to find another means of support. Fortunately, he found a position at a publishing house in Berlin, but, understandably, he wished to go back to teaching. Since all university doors were closed to him in Germany, he turned his attention elsewhere. In 1913, having heard that there was an opening at the University of Cairo, he managed, with Adolf von Hildebrand's help, to be recommended to Pasha Fuad, an Egyptian prince (and the great protector of the university), by the king of Bavaria. Scheler wrote him a letter in French that had been penned by a woman named Annette Kolb (later a well-known writer), who had a perfect command of that tongue because her mother was French. By means of this letter, Scheler was able to present himself as someone who was fluent in the tongue of Corneille and Racine, but this was far from the case.

When Scheler heard that Prince Fuad had just arrived in

[35] Apart from the difficulties created by Märit's mother, Max had to deal with Amélie, who refused to grant her husband a divorce. She relented only when she obtained, as a compensation, the sum of 60,000 gold Marks, which Märit (Märchen) had inherited from her father. Because of her age, however, the young girl could not avail herself of her money. She had to find someone willing to advance this impressive sum, with written guarantee of complete reimbursement when she came of age. She found an "anonymous" person willing to do so. Märit then became Mrs. Max Scheler. See Wilhelm Mader, *Scheler*, p. 42.

Munich and was staying at the Hotel Regina, he became very excited. Petulant as he was, he immediately sought to see the prince's secretary, but he had to hide the fact that his French was inadequate. He needed Dietrich's help and came to him in a state of great agitation, asking him to accompany him in an attempt to convince the secretary, who was Italian, that he, Scheler, would be the ideal candidate to fill the vacant post in Cairo. He knew that the courses were normally given in Arabic but that French could be used as a substitute.

Dietrich—always willing to help his friend—acceded to his request. Scheler had the rather fantastic idea that his courses could be translated into Arabic, and that he could then read the text. With his usual lack of realism, he had convinced himself that going to Egypt was the ideal solution to his problems. Well aware how dim the prospects of success were, Dietrich would never have dreamed of turning down a request from Scheler. His friend's welfare was of the utmost importance to him. So they went to the Hotel Regina and asked to see Fuad's secretary, who was apprised, of course, of Scheler's letter to the prince.

The secretary turned out to be an extremely elegant man, Italian by birth, who immediately addressed Scheler in Arabic. Poor Scheler became flustered and could mumble only "Not yet, not yet." To ease the situation, Dietrich decided to speak Italian for fear that, if he spoke French, Scheler's ignorance of the language in which he was supposed to teach would immediately become apparent. Surprised to be addressed in his mother tongue, the secretary asked the young man, "Does Professor Scheler also speak Italian?" Dietrich had no choice but to admit that Professor Scheler had no knowledge of Dante's tongue. "But then," the secretary asked, "why speak a language that Professor Scheler does not understand?" That decision was, of course, fatal, because Scheler's

French was hardly better than his Italian, a fact he desperately wanted to hide. "I shall take you to see the prince", the secretary announced.

Neither Max nor Dietrich wanted this honor, and they pleaded as excuse that they were not properly dressed for such a meeting. But the secretary assured them that the prince did not stand upon ceremony and that their dress did not matter in the least. Before they had time to object, they were standing in front of the great man in whose hands lay Scheler's fate. The situation became more hilarious when the prince, whom Dietrich addressed in French, said excitedly, "Deitsch spreken, Deitsch spreken" (*Deutsch sprechen*), with such an accent that it was clear he knew only a few words of German. He too wanted to hide the fact that he did not know French. At this point, Dietrich looked upon the interview as a farce, a Shakespearean comedy in which he merely was playing a ridiculous role for friendship's sake.

The secretary took over and started to explain the importance of being fluent in Arabic. The students in Egypt were rather primitive, he said, and unless a teacher had perfect command of their tongue, they would never be able to understand the subject. He asked Dietrich if he knew the famous Orientalist Littmann. Even though he had never heard his name before, he said that, of course, this great man's name was not unknown to him. Scheler, however, declared that he had never heard anything about him. Dietrich stepped on his foot, to warn him that such an admission was not furthering his cause. To his frustration, Scheler exclaimed, "Why did you step on my foot?" The secretary continued: "Surely, you both know the famous Professor Turini, who taught in Cairo. He could best explain to you the situation prevalent in the east." Dietrich started singing the praises of Professor Turini, whose name also was not known to him.

But Scheler ruined the game: "Turini? I never heard the name before." Once again, his friend stepped on his foot, and Scheler irritably said, "Why do you keep stepping on my foot?" He added with a note of bitterness, "I feel that you are not truly furthering my interests. You are not doing your best to convince him of my qualifications for the post." This was unjust, but Scheler could easily be unjust when irritated. Needless to say, nothing came of this madcap interview. The adventure had been doomed from the start, but, once again, Dietrich had proved to Max that he could unconditionally rely on his help.

With his marriage and the completion of his doctorate, Dietrich now embarked upon an extremely happy period of his life. He was married to the woman he loved. He had completed his studies, and his academic career was beginning in earnest. Shortly after he received his doctorate, his former tutor, Alois Fischer, recommended that he be invited to give a series of lectures on ethics to the Teachers Academy in Munich. He was accepted, and the fee he received for these talks was the first money he ever earned. It was the beginning of a speaking career that would eventually take him to seventeen countries.

Dietrich had inherited his mother's *Wanderlust* and was always looking for occasions to satisfy this passion for travel. In 1913, Adolf von Hildebrand bought a car, cars being at that time a rarity. Having traveled much by train, Dietrich viewed this new mode of locomotion as ideal: not only could one enjoy the landscape, but one could stop at any time to enjoy it contemplatively. Adolf and Irene decided to go to Florence by train early in March 1913 and had appointed a chauffeur, Philip, who, along with the head of the Ford company in Munich, Mr. Jacques, was to drive the car down to

Florence for this maiden journey (meant to test the function-
ing of the car). No one else was to ride with them.

This restriction was a blow to Dietrich's dream of taking a
long drive in a car; it struck him as irrational to deprive him
of this joy. Typically enough, instead of discussing the matter
with his father, he decided to say nothing but to make arrangements with the chauffeur to take him and Gretchen as
additional passengers. He was not ready to pass up the chance
at a beautiful experience for his father's arbitrary decision.
Little Franzi was to remain in Munich with his nurse, and
then his father would go back north to fetch him and bring
him to San Francesco for the Easter vacation.

The trip was to begin on March 13, 1913. Dietrich was in
a high state of excitement during the days preceding. For a
great experience is not limited to its actual enjoyment; there
is something called *Vorfreude*, anticipated joy, and afterward,
there is a resounding of this joy in the soul, and the gratitude
one feels at having experienced it. It is like the three musical
movements of the same symphony, which enrich and complete each other.

But the trip turned out to be a drama indeed. March can
be bitterly cold on the north side of the Alps; the roads were
icy, slippery, and in primitive condition. The moment the
chauffeur (who was a tyro, having received his driving license
only a few days before) started driving the car uphill, he
showed his inexperience and took the curves much too fast,
risking his passengers' lives, as well as his own. Yet Dietrich
insisted that the collapsible roof of the car be kept open so
that the sky could be enjoyed, as well as the landscape, and
the cold was so bitter that they were freezing. It is amazing
that none of the four caught pneumonia. At one point, the
car stopped suddenly: it had hit a block of ice, which had
pierced the gas tank! After all sorts of complications, the car

was put on a train to Innsbruck for repairs, which took a couple of days. As the Brenner pass was still very icy, the travelers wisely decided that, once repaired, the car would be sent by freight to Bressanone, on the south side of the Brenner, and that they would proceed from there to Florence. After briefly enjoying the beauty of the Tyrolian capital, Dietrich and Gretchen decided to go on ahead to Bressanone and wait for Philip and Mr. Jacques there. Both of them enjoyed this lovely town, so full of charm, tradition, and poetry. Finally, the car arrived in good condition, and the quartet were on their way to Florence. They stopped first in Verona, proceeded to Mantua and Modena, which they admired briefly, and continued on to Bologna, where they spent the night. They were now ready for the last leg of their trip: driving over the Apennines. How dramatic an experience this was is difficult to imagine for today's travelers, who benefit from the beautiful Autostrada del Sole. But, in 1913, it was another matter. Not only did the car run out of gas (the travelers had to wait until the Bologna–Florence bus passed by and helped them out), but also the road was narrow, bad, and twisting. Like a horse smelling the stable, Philip again drove much too fast, endangering himself and his passengers. More than once, Dietrich and Gretchen thought that their last hour had come, but they all arrived safely in San Francesco. Dietrich was a little apprehensive at having circumvented his father's wishes. But Adolf, upon hearing how much his son had enjoyed the trip, decided that it was wiser to drop the whole matter.

This episode throws a clear light on Dietrich's lifelong and passionate love for beautiful experiences. It was difficult for him to renounce a noble enjoyment for reasons considered irrational. Like the little boy of twelve who wanted to drive a dogcart, he wanted to enjoy a beautiful trip in a mode of conveyance that to his mind was ideal, and he "rode roughshod" over the obstacles. Typical also was the contrast in his soul between his innate fear of danger and his blindness to peril if the "theme" was beauty and the enjoyment of a great experience. When the latter was the case, the hazards of a situation receded in his thinking. I have already mentioned that he usually concentrated all his attention on one theme and had difficulty registering other themes that should also have drawn his attention. No doubt, he and Gretchen could have lost their lives through Philip's daredevil driving. But just as he never regretted having cut a whole week of courses at Göttingen four years earlier, so he never regretted contravening his father's wish.

After a day spent in Florence, he prepared to return to Munich by train to fetch little Franzi. Returning also was Mr. Jacques, whose presence with the automobile was no longer necessary. They decided to take the night train. When they arrived at the border, all passengers had to leave the train with their luggage to pass customs before entering Austria. Dietrich had taken only a very small piece of luggage, which he had put in the net above his seat. When the train stopped at the border, a sleepy Dietrich took a bag and proceeded to the station, where the inspection was taking place. Everything seemed to go well, until a commotion arose, and a very upset woman informed the customs officers that a small bag containing all her jewelry had been stolen; the passengers were prohibited from leaving the station. All of a sudden, the woman saw the luggage that Dietrich was carrying and exclaimed: "There it is; this man has taken my jewels." Her bag and Dietrich's were of the same size, and the sleepy, absentminded traveler had mixed them up; the bag she had picked up contained only pajamas and toilet articles. Even though the situation was very painful for Dietrich, he and his companion could not help but break into such hearty laughter that they easily convinced the hysterical woman of their innocence. They reboarded the train and slept peacefully until Munich, where little Franzi was happy to see his father.

The moment had come when Dietrich had to give his whole attention to a pressing concern that had been his for months. Even though a desire to enter the Church had been growing in his soul, the pressure of his personal and academic life, the tensions and difficulties that he had gone through, had prevented him from concentrating on what he now knew to be the most important thing in life—one's relationship with God. The seeds that Scheler's philosophy had planted in Dietrich's soul were now close to bursting forth in full bloom. Gretchen had followed the same itinerary, and she too was anxious to prepare for her reception into the Roman Catholic Church. Amazingly enough, however, it was Lisl Brewster-Hildebrand who gave them the final "push". To his astonishment, Dietrich heard that his beautiful sister—married to an American, Christopher Brewster, who had become an Italian citizen—had entered the Roman Catholic Church. She invited Dietrich and Gretchen to witness her First Communion in Rome, where she and her husband had been living for several years and where their second child, Harry, was born. Dietrich was dumbfounded at the news because Lisl, whom he had seen very little since her marriage in 1903, was the last of his five sisters who would seem to have had religious inclinations. But one day, while Lisl was contemplating the beauty of a tree, God's grace mysteriously touched her soul. Providentially, at that same time her husband, who was a complete agnostic, happened to give her Johannes Jørgensen's life of Saint Francis of Assisi, which he considered a nice, entertaining "novel". Saint

Francis immediately won Lisl's heart. She found Christ. She found the Church. And all the beauty that had enchanted her for thirty-four years now found its fulfillment in Him "in whom are hid all the treasures of wisdom and knowledge" (Col 2:3; Litany of the Sacred Heart).

In the spring of 1913, shortly after the harrowing car trip, Lisl and her husband, Christopher, drove to Florence to see Dietrich and Gretchen. A few days later—little Franzi being left in the care of his nurse—the four of them drove to Rome in Christopher's car. Although born and raised in Italy, Dietrich had never been farther south than Siena, and both he and Gretchen were overwhelmed by the beauty of the Italian landscape from Florence to Rome. This enchantment climaxed when they entered the Eternal City through the Ponte Molle.[36] The Brewsters were living in the Palazzo Antici Mattei. It was an enchanting Roman palazzo, with a fountain, in the center of the courtyard, whose waters sang a gentle song day and night.

Dietrich and Gretchen were present in the catacombs when Lisl received her First Communion there. How moving it must have been to see the beautiful and proud Lisl humbly kneeling down to receive the Body of Christ in the Eucharist. Unfortunately, Christopher never understood his wife's conversion. To the end of his life, in 1928, religion remained foreign to him.

On the way back to Palazzo Antici Mattei, Lisl shared a carriage with her brother and, with great seriousness, urged him not to delay his own conversion. "Grace knocks at the door of one's soul," she said solemnly, "and if one does not answer the knock, it may never be repeated. Promise me that when you go back to Munich, you will take instruction." Her

[36] To Dietrich, Rome was a spiritual magnet; he revisited the city more than forty times.

brother, deeply moved, gave his promise, and soon afterward husband and wife went to a Franciscan friar, Father Heribert Holzapfel, in the Franciscan church in Munich, who prepared them for the great day of their own *Abjura*.[37]

While Dietrich was taking instruction, to his great delight Siegfried Hamburger, whom he had met in Göttingen in 1910, came to Munich. Their mutual attraction, evident from the beginning of their acquaintance, had matured into an exceptional friendship that was to last for life. Their personalities were vastly different. Siegfried was shy and reserved, and he tired easily; Dietrich was exuberant, outgoing, warm, robust, and very Italian in his ways. Yet, different as they were in background and temperament, there was a preestablished harmony between them, a synchronization of their minds and souls that was bound to bear rich fruit. Each found in the other the ideal philosophical and human counterpart. A hint given by one was immediately grasped and enriched by the other. Now that Hamburger was in Munich, the two friends could spend hours pursuing philosophical problems. Dietrich called these endless philosophical exchanges "philosophical banquets". The friends grew wings and became intoxicated by their common love for truth.

The result of this symbiosis between Dietrich and Siegfried was the deepening and development of a torrent of philosophical questions that had accumulated in Dietrich's mind since his doctoral thesis. They started investigating the nature of forgiveness, and that led them to the discovery of the different "levels" existing in the mysterious being called man, from the superficial and worldly to the spiritual. That discovery led them further to the question of "purity of heart" and to an analysis of the hearts of saints. For several weeks, they

---

[37] The *Abjura* was a solemn renunciation of heresy.

worked with such intensity that they learned more in that brief period than one normally does in months or even years of lesser concentration. When Dietrich told Reinach about their common work, the latter exclaimed, "You are pursuing the most beautiful of all philosophical questions!"

Not only did Hamburger fully share his friend's longing for truth, but there was nothing in his beautiful, transparent soul that stood between himself and truth. He was exquisitely reverent and deep. There was a note of sublimity about his being that struck everyone privileged to make his acquaintance. It was now clear to Dietrich that he had found in Siegfried Hamburger a most wonderful collaborator, one who, he was convinced, was a philosophical genius. He often said to me that Siegfried Hamburger was the most intelligent man he had ever met. His love for truth and his reverence were expressed in his noble Jewish face. He literally radiated reverence, and this reverence enriched the outstanding mind God had given him. Moreover, he exemplified graciousness and selflessness. He was always ready to serve, always desirous of helping others. Throughout his life, Hamburger remained for Dietrich the incarnation of the true friend, a person whom he could trust unconditionally, a person who *understood* him in the deepest sense of the term. In some way, Siegfried had the same devotion to Dietrich that Dietrich had had to Scheler. He shared his life, his work, his experiences in a unique way. He truly became Dietrich's "alter ego". This friendship was one of the great gifts of Dietrich von Hildebrand's life.

By the spring of 1914, Dietrich, Gretchen, and Hamburger were all moving rapidly on the path to conversion. In order to be received into the Church at that year's Easter Vigil, Dietrich and Gretchen had first to break their formal ties to the Protestant Church. At that time, a person converting from one religion or denomination to another had to give formal notification that he no longer subscribed to that particular creed. Dietrich and Gretchen had to present themselves to a Protestant minister and inform him of their decision to enter the Roman Catholic Church.

Because Dietrich had never attended a Protestant service in his life, he and Gretchen first went to the wrong parish. The pastor there was a very liberal Protestant who, without further ado, took a sheet of paper on which he indicated that they were renouncing Protestantism. He asked for their address, and when he found out where they were living, he told them that they had come to the wrong parish and that this proved that they had been very bad Protestants. "That is true," answered Dietrich, "but we both hope, with God's grace, to become good Catholics." Crestfallen, the young couple had to go through the unpleasant ritual all over again. This time they went to the right pastor, who was a convinced Protestant. For a full hour he earnestly tried to change his visitors' minds. Needless to say, he discovered he had no chance of success. Whereupon he said nobly, "I hope that you will be better Catholics than you have been Protestants."

We arrive now at the most important and the most decisive moment of Dietrich's life—his conversion to the Roman Catholic Church. Every time he mentioned this event, his face lit up with joy, and yet, usually so ebullient in speaking about his experiences, he was reserved about what took place in his soul. There are things between a soul and God that are a man's secrets.[38]

One thing stands out clearly, however. Beautiful and rewarding as his life had been, enriching as had been his contact with natural truth and beauty, he was now entering into a

---

[38] When questioned about her conversion, Edith Stein would answer graciously: "*Secretum meum mihi*"—intimating that she could not reveal her secret.

radically new world, the world of the supernatural, whose radiance, sublimity, and beauty were such that all his previous experiences paled by comparison. He was overwhelmed by a light the existence of which he had never suspected previously. He could not learn enough; he could not read enough. Every day brought new discoveries; every day was more uplifting than the preceding one. Every instruction was received with attentiveness and gratitude. The brilliant student of Edmund Husserl became the humble recipient of the Church's teaching.

One crucial factor in Dietrich's conversion was the discovery of authority. Up to that time, his opinions, his wishes, his outlook had been the decisive factor in the decisions he made. He had been his own ultimate authority. Through God's grace, he discovered that every true authority comes from Him, the Master and Creator of all things, and that Christ, the Son of God and the Redeemer of the world, had delegated this authority to His Holy Bride, the Roman Catholic Church. Just as Christ had taught authoritatively "and not like the scribes and the Pharisees" (Mk 1:22), now the Church, and she alone, who had been given the keys of the kingdom, was to teach erring man the path leading to salvation. Her teaching was infallible in matters of dogmas and morals, and all that he was called upon to do was to be receptive to her teaching and gratefully accept it.

It is remarkable how easily he gave up the intellectual sovereignty that he had enjoyed until then. So many people would have rebelled at the thought that they were being intellectually "deposed", that they should humbly accept in faith any teaching that was not luminous to their mind. Dietrich certainly did not lack intellectual self-assurance, and when he saw a truth he would defend it vigorously and tenaciously, for he knew that God had given him a powerful mind. But he also learned that man's mind is fallible and that the best and the greatest have fallen into errors and ambiguities. No human being can boast of never having made a mistake. What a gift it was for the young man, deeply enamored of truth, to accept the Church's authority and submit to it joyfully. On the one hand, to the very end of his life, he held fast to the conviction that man's mind can reach absolute truth.[39] On the other hand, he never had difficulties accepting the dogmatic and moral teaching of the Church.[40] It was so evident to Dietrich that the Catholic Church does not speak in her own name, but in God's name, and for this reason it was incomprehensible to him that a Catholic should oppose any of her solemn pronouncements. Shortly before his death, when he confided his literary bequest to me, he solemnly said, "If, after my death, you find any manuscript of mine, or even any statement, which is not in total harmony with the teaching of the Church, do not hesitate to burn it." He never, absolutely never, was exposed to the temptation to reject the Church's dogmatic and moral teaching because his mind could not see its truth. To him, it was crystal clear that this intellectual submission belonged integrally to being a Catholic; he was Catholic, and he wanted to be Catholic.

One day, Father Holzapfel, instructing the two catechumens, touched upon the question of artificial birth control, informing them that this practice was condemned by the Church. The young philosopher was baffled. He knew that

[39] See his book *What Is Philosophy?* (London: Routledge, 1991).

[40] I recall his joy when Pius XII declared the dogma of the Assumption of the Holy Virgin into Heaven (1950), and his profound sadness that some of his Catholic acquaintances opposed this "new" teaching. In a restaurant in Paris, conversation on this declaration became so heated that the disputants, Dietrich included, lost sight of the time. At one point the waiter actually begged his customers to leave: the restaurant was closing.

God had given him a keen moral sense. He rejected moral relativism and subjectivism in all its forms. Yet to him it was incomprehensible that the prevention of a not yet existing human life should be viewed as a serious sin. That artificial birth control should be a morally relevant question puzzled him. Father Holzapfel was adamant. "This is the Church's doctrine. You must accept her teaching in its totality. It is not a matter of picking and choosing; I cannot take you into the Church if you refuse to give your assent to the whole of Catholic doctrine." The young man's response was immediate and unequivocal submission. The Church had spoken; that was enough. Who was he to dare contest her holy teaching? He truly lived the words *"Credo ut intelligam"* (I believe in order to understand), the famous phrase of Saint Augustine, repeated and developed by Saint Anselm of Canterbury. Shortly afterward, to his amazement, he had such deep insights into the immorality of artificial birth control that he could no longer understand how it was that he had not perceived them before. But he learned a deep lesson, namely, the importance of humility in intellectual life. It convinced him that philosophical errors are often caused by a proud and arrogant intellectual posture, but they are rarely due to a lack of intellectual acuteness. In fact, he maintained that the most devastating intellectual errors have been made by remarkably intelligent people, for mediocre minds do not produce major errors. This same conviction led Chesterton to write: "We say that the dangerous criminal is the educated criminal. We say that the most dangerous criminal now is the entirely lawless modern philosopher. Compared to him, burglars and bigamists are essentially moral men; my heart goes out to them." [41]

[41] *The Man Who Was Thursday*, in *The Collected Works of G. K. Chesterton*, vol. 6 (San Francisco: Ignatius Press, 1991), p. 509.

Once again, the catechumen's mind was fecundated by new insights into the mystery of the sexual sphere, which, up to then, he had deeply respected, but the full sacredness of which had escaped him. Now he saw with blinding clarity that the union taking place between husband and wife should take place *in conspectu Dei* (in the sight of God), for in this moment an amazing collaboration takes place between God and potential parents. From that time on, the young philosopher was to become a champion of the Church's doctrine with regard to artificial birth control.[42]

He was granted the key insight that humility plays a crucial role in truth-centered intellectual work. In other words, man's appropriate attitude toward God and His ethical teaching is essential in order to reach deep philosophical truth (let alone theological truth). Without this cardinal Christian virtue, the most brilliant mind is bound to err, to assume it is infallible and forget, to his woe, that if man's mind is made for truth and can find certainty in knowledge, not only has this mind been obscured by original sin and needs to be purified in order to see certain "sensitive" truths, but also that there is an infinity of things that transcend reason, which man's limited intellectual capacities cannot perceive. The young man, who was a passionate knight of the objectivity of truth and a

---

[42] See Dietrich von Hildebrand's criticism of the Lambeth Conference, written in 1930, soon after this conference had taken place. For the very first time in Protestant history, a convocation of Protestant ministers declared that there were cases and instances in which artificial birth control was permissible and legitimate. That was a total reversal of the position Protestantism had defended from the very moment of its birth in the sixteenth century. See *Die Menschheit am Scheideweg* (Regensburg: Habbel, 1954), pp. 146–57. When Pope Paul VI published his encyclical *Humanae Vitae* in July 1968, Dietrich von Hildebrand was the very first Catholic thinker to defend it publicly against a very antagonistic press. See *The Encyclical Humanae Vitae: A Sign of Contradiction* (Chicago: Franciscan Herald Press, 1969); also *Man and Woman* (Chicago: Franciscan Herald Press, 1966; repr. Manchester, N.H.: Sophia Institute Press, 1992).

defender of man's capacity to reach certainty in knowledge, now saw that—to quote Pascal—"The last proceeding of reason is to recognize that there is an infinity of things that are beyond it" and that therefore two extremes are to be avoided, namely, "to exclude reason, or accept reason only" (*Pensées*, section 4, no. 267). It became luminously clear to him that "there is nothing more conformable to reason than to disavow reason" (ibid., no. 272). With immense gratitude he realized that his mind's grasp of philosophical questions had been both purified and deepened by the gift of faith, and from that moment on, this insight marked his philosophical work. He must have meditated upon the profound words of Psalm 131:

> O Lord, my heart is not lifted up,
>   my eyes are not raised too high;
> I do not occupy myself with things
>   too great and too marvelous for me.

Before being received into the Church, Dietrich and Gretchen were told that their Protestant marriage was not valid and that they could still part if they wished, a proposal they both rejected vigorously. They rejoiced to know that, as a result of their conversion, their union would now have a sacramental character, that the beauty of their natural love would be elevated to a higher and more sublime plane, unreachable by natural lovers.[43]

From then on, Dietrich's life was changed. His passionate love for beauty and for natural truth in no way waned. But he had found a beauty that was infinitely more ravishing—the face of Christ and His Church and the supernatural

[43] See Dietrich von Hildebrand, *Marriage* (1929; English edition, Manchester, N.H.: Sophia Institute Press, 1984); also *Man and Woman*.

message they convey, the path of humility and love leading to holiness.

Then came the great day—Holy Saturday, April 11, 1914—when, in the Franciscan church of Munich, both Dietrich and Gretchen, after going to confession, solemnly pronounced their *Abjura* and became grateful members of the Holy Catholic Church. The experience was overwhelming. Dietrich was keenly aware that, through God's infinite mercy and goodness, he had been permitted to enter into a world of holiness for which he had unconsciously longed. Dietrich now was a member of the Holy Catholic Church, the Bride of Christ, and, through her, could achieve an intimate communion with God that had never before been possible. He was "home" in the deepest and most sublime sense of this term. How often did he tell me that there never was a convert more radiant and jubilant than he. (It is interesting to compare Dietrich's response to that of C. S. Lewis, who wrote that he was "the most dejected and reluctant convert in all England".)[44] Gretchen also shared in her husband's bliss, but, reserved as she was, she did not manifest it in the same exuberant way. They both received the sacrament of confirmation a month later.

Dietrich's joy and enthusiasm over his conversion were such that Father Holzapfel felt it his duty to dampen his ebullient feelings. He warned him repeatedly that such a state of "exaltation" does not last and that it was typical of those who had just entered the Church to be carried away by a wave of enthusiasm. But for once this good priest was mistaken. Down to the last day of his life, the mere mention of Holy Church or of a conversion filled Dietrich with such joy that one would have sworn he had just entered the Church

---

[44] *Surprised by Joy*, pp. 228–29.

himself. But Father Holzapfel had an important mission to fulfill. In very outspoken words, he reminded Dietrich that beautiful as his response was to the Church, whom he saw so clearly as the Bride of Christ and the custodian of supernatural treasures, he should not forget that he, the sinner, desperately *needed* the Church for salvation, while she did not need him. In Dietrich's own terminology, his "response to value" was totally appropriate, but Father Holzapfel's remark was crucial, for it drew the young man's attention to his spiritual poverty and his dire need of personal redemption. He had to acknowledge that, beautiful as his background had been, rich as were the talents God had given him, he had to humble himself to enter into the world of Holy Church; he had to say in all humility: "Save me, lest I perish." His eyes were opened to an overwhelming truth that his talented mind had not perceived: "Without me, you can do nothing."

When, in 1915, Dietrich asked Father Holzapfel what he should do for Lent, the latter answered without a moment's hesitation: "Refrain from speaking about religion until Easter." It was a terrible sacrifice for the ardent convert. A man in love wants, after all, to speak about his beloved.

Like Edith Stein seven years later, the young doctor of philosophy's love for wisdom never abated. Now, however, philosophical truth, important as it was and as it remained throughout his life,[45] was infinitely transcended by a wisdom that had never entered man's head. Truth was no longer to be found only in judgments and propositions: Truth was a living Person, the second Person of the Holy Trinity, the Savior of the world, whom he could adore. From his youth, Dietrich had revered natural truth. Now he learned to adore Truth

---

[45] See his *The Trojan Horse in the City of God* (Chicago: Franciscan Herald Press, 1967; repr. Manchester, N.H.: Sophia Institute Press, 1993), in which he discusses this problem.

itself, and on his knees, for "God has highly exalted him [Christ] and bestowed on him the name which is above every name, that at the name of Jesus every knee should bow, in heaven and on earth" (Phil 2:9–10). Every man is bound to respect natural truth, but no one is called upon to bend his knee in front of it. From that moment on, Dietrich's special calling, his mission, was to proclaim and confess "the New World of Christianity", which made all things new.[46] Much as he continued to be fascinated by purely philosophical questions, his delight now was to contemplate (and later to write about) the transformation that takes place in man's life when illumined by the radiance of revelation.[47]

Dietrich knew full well that this passion for the supernatural could jeopardize his philosophical career. Even in Catholic Bavaria, it was neither scholarly nor "professional" to hint at the reality of the supernatural on "sacred" university grounds. There was a sad dichotomy in the lives of most university professors: their faith was one thing, their intellectual pursuits another. Dietrich soon took note of this fact and was grieved by it. He considered this attitude to be deplorable. He firmly decided not to conform to secularist norms. He knew that a light is not to be hidden. It is to be put in a place of honor so that it can illumine those around it. He certainly intended to

[46] It was highly significant that the first article he wrote after his *Habilitation* was entitled "Die Neue Welt des Christentums" (The New World of Christianity), published in the periodical *Seele* 2 (1920): 2–11; repr. in *Menschheit am Scheideweg*, in which he speaks eloquently about the discovery of the supernatural and at the same time, in a truly prophetic vein, warns Catholics not to allow its progressive erosion in their lives.

[47] This theme is splendidly surveyed in his masterpiece, *Transformation in Christ: On the Christian Attitude of Mind*. This book was first published under the pseudonym Peter Ott in 1940 by Benziger in Switzerland, because it could not have been sold under the author's name in Nazi Germany, where he was condemned to death *in absentia*. English edition: New York: Longmans, Green, 1948; San Francisco: Ignatius Press, 2001.

teach philosophy and not theology, but it was to be a philosophy open to a higher reality, not a philosophy systematically
cut off from it. He knew that faith not only did not contradict
reason but transcended it. It also shed light on "sensitive"
domains of human reason obscured by sin.

But human life is no paradise. In all this joy, there was a sad
note—the opposition of Adolf and Irene von Hildebrand to
their son's conversion. Dietrich loved his parents, and he had
a particular closeness and devotion toward his mother. But
every time he broached the subject of the Church, he felt
their opposition. Their son had entered into a world that was
inaccessible to them, a world from which they felt "excluded"
because, in spite of all their lovable and beautiful qualities,
their outlook on life was thoroughly liberal and secular. A
chasm was opening up between parents and son.

When their son and daughter-in-law were received into
the Catholic Church in April 1914, Adolf and Irene von
Hildebrand were vacationing in Italy. They had already suspected, however, that Dietrich and Gretchen might take this
step while they were gone. Upon their return to Munich, the
very first question they asked their son-in-law Fedja Georgii
was, "Has Dietrich become a Catholic?" Fedja had no choice
but to answer in the affirmative. Adolf and Irene's response
was surprisingly virulent and bitter. They were literally beside
themselves, and they plainly refused to have any contact with
the young converts. The three von Hildebrand sisters living
in Munich had to use all their skills to mollify their parents.
As usually happens in such cases, they relented after a time,
and a reconciliation took place; but, if the wound healed, the
scar remained. Adolf and Irene were particularly resentful
because their son had made his decision without informing
them, "behind their backs". When Dietrich had decided not
to inform them of the step he intended to take, he had been

sorrowfully aware that his dear parents would feel betrayed. But what was he to do? Knowing how opposed they were to the Catholic Church (while they were totally ignorant of her teaching), Dietrich reasoned that it was better to present his parents with a *fait accompli* than to have painful discussions that could lead nowhere. It can be assumed that he and Gretchen came to this decision after discussing their situation with Father Holzapfel, their spiritual director.

Was the decision wise? There are cases in life in which two alternative solutions both seem equally unsatisfactory. Søren Kierkegaard had personally experienced these painful circumstances, and he nicely formulated the dilemma: "Do it/ or don't do it—you will regret both." [48]

Had Dietrich informed his parents of his irrevocable decision, he would most certainly have faced an angry encounter that would have stolen his inner peace. Recalling the painful and meaningless arguments he had had with his parents over his engagement to Gretchen a few years earlier, he decided not to speak, even though he knew that his parents would interpret his silence as a lack of trust. That is precisely what happened. Both his parents were deeply hurt, and, for the second time, a wedge was driven between him and them, though by this time they had fully accepted Gretchen as their daughter-in-law and had a warm, loving relationship with her. His father remarked sadly that he had done everything possible in his son's education to enable him to be "free", and not only had Dietrich chosen to bind himself in marriage at a very young age, but he had once again chosen to curtail this precious freedom by becoming a Roman Catholic. When, a year earlier, Lisl had entered the Church, her parents did not take her conversion seriously, because they had always

[48] *Either-Or*, vol. 2 (Princeton, N.J.: Princeton University Press, 1944), p. 134.

considered her a bit eccentric. "She must have fallen in love
with a priest and entered the Church to please him", her
father reasoned. He never understood how deep his daughter's
conversion was. But their son's conversion was, to his parents'
mind, very different. He was a man. His decision was to be
gauged differently, and Adolf von Hildebrand immediately
sensed that his son's commitment was radically transforming
his life.

It was profoundly sad for the young convert that people so
dear to him, people to whom he owed so much, could not
understand the step he had taken and that, instead of rejoicing (which would have been the case had they been granted
the gift of faith), they were embittered.[49] Later in life, Dietrich
frequently deplored the fact that on numerous occasions his
parents' opposition to his conversion triggered in him an
unfortunate response. He felt that he had to be on the defen-
sive, and this conviction hardened his own position. He had a
long way to go before understanding that his parents could be
won over only by a deepened affection and a greater gratitude. The young convert was so afraid that his parents would
force him to compromise with his newly found faith that he
became rigid in his position. Two incidents illustrate this new
attitude, for which he later felt deep contrition. During the
First World War, his parents spent their summers in a lovely
small town south of Munich. Dietrich, Gretchen, and little
Franzi were often invited to spend their Sundays with them.
Adolf von Hildebrand always urged them to come early so

---

[49] It is sad indeed when a person is depressed about an event that objectively
calls for a response of joy and gratitude, because of a deep, invincible misunderstanding of the situation. Seven years later, Edith Stein—another outstanding
student of Husserl--went through the same mental agony, but in a more
dramatic way: her mother wept when Edith broke the news that she had been
baptized.

that they could enjoy a long day together. But Dietrich, enamored of Gregorian chant, insisted upon going to the late-morning High Mass, which prevented their taking an early train. Once Adolf, hoping that his son had made a sacrifice for his sake, walked all the way to the station to meet them. To his great disappointment, the expected guests were not on the train. A similar episode took place in Lugano in April 1919, when Adolf and Irene visited their son, who had been vacationing in Switzerland for a number of months after the armistice. After several months of separation, Dietrich's parents were looking forward to a long visit with him. But shortly after their arrival and to their bitter disappointment, he decided to return to Munich for Holy Week services, fearing that if he attended the lengthy services in Lugano, his parents would object and put pressure on him to shorten his stay in church for their sake.

In hindsight, Dietrich later saw how wrong his attitude had been, and he deplored it. He who so ardently wished to share his faith with his parents actually put stumbling blocks in their path. The supernatural was so inaccessible to them that only God's grace and patient love could have removed the veil covering their eyes. Intellectually speaking, Dietrich understood that we are called upon to become "new creatures" in Christ, but he did not see clearly how to relate this truth to his daily life. It always remained difficult for him to give up something beautiful, and his longing for noble enjoyments was such that it often prevented him from seeing a moral call issuing from another source. Sadly enough, even though there never was a break between Dietrich and his exceptional parents, their relationship never regained its pristine warmth. Throughout his life, he continually prayed for the two very remarkable people who had given him life and to whom he owed so much.

Dietrich loved all his sisters with the deepest fraternal affection and burned to share with them the source of his newly found joy. He lent them Catholic books. He talked to them about the supernatural. He radiated such happiness and joy that his sisters were struck by his demeanor. Soon Nini, Zusi, and Bertele, who were living in Munich or close by, became powerfully attracted to the Church and wished with all their hearts to enter into this sacred ark, but their husbands were fiercely opposed to their conversion. As a matter of fact, Nini's husband, Carlo Sattler, fearing his brother-in-law's influence on his wife, forbade her to see her now passionately Catholic brother. From time to time brother and sister would meet secretly in the lovely cemetery surrounding the church of Sankt Georg, close to the Maria Theresia Strasse. Eventually, in 1916, Zusi and Bertele's husbands relented and gave their consent to their wives' conversion. Nini's husband yielded to his wife's ardent wishes in 1917. Bertele's husband, Dietrich's dear friend Walter Braunfels, entered the Church in 1918. Bernhardt, Nini's eldest son (born in 1903), converted in 1919. Zusi's husband, Fedja Georgii, entered the Church in 1921 and became an ardent Catholic, a daily communicant, and a close friend of Pius XII. By the early 1920s, all of Adolf von Hildebrand's children, three of his sons-in-law, and his daughter-in-law had converted to the Church. All his grandchildren were brought up as Roman Catholics.

The religious and moral duel that had been initiated between Adolf and his son years before terminated in an overwhelming victory for the son. Interestingly enough, when Nini, Zusi, and Bertele converted, their father showed no sign of displeasure. As a matter of fact, being close to the royal family in Munich and knowing what an ardent Catholic the Infanta Maria de la Paz was, Adolf immediately informed her each time another of his daughters became Catholic.

Vivi Hildebrand-Baltus was the only one who converted after her parents' death in 1921. Not only had this gentle creature always had great difficulty making up her mind, she actually majored in procrastination. It is possible also that her extraordinarily deep attachment to both her parents explained her hesitancy. Her devotion to them was so deep that, no doubt, she suffered living away in Belgium, and she used every possible occasion to go back to Munich. She was the only one of the six von Hildebrand children who was married in a Catholic Church (Sankt Georg in Munich) because her husband, Georges Baltus, a lapsed Catholic, insisted on being married by a priest—to please his Catholic family, because he liked the idea of a solemn commitment for life, or for purely conventional reasons—it is hard to say. (Belgium is a Catholic country, so to be married in a Catholic church was the proper thing to do. Georges Baltus' case is not infrequent in Catholic countries.) Georges also flatly refused to sign a paper promising Vivi her freedom in case the marriage proved to be unhappy. Such a written promise had saved Irene from her bond with Franz Koppel. For this reason, she talked her older daughters into requesting the same from their fiancés, but Georges would not hear of it. His Catholic education had left traces in him.

Apart from his beloved sisters, there was one person whom Dietrich ardently wished to see enter the Church—the man who was now his alter ego, Siegfried Hamburger. The two students of Husserl had become so close to one another that it was inconceivable that Siegfried not follow in the footsteps of his friend. Siegfried's openness to truth, his reverence, and his spiritual longing must inevitably lead this exceptional man to the Gospel. As we shall see soon, this great wish was going to be fulfilled.

Understandably, Dietrich was now eager to share the news

of his conversion with his dear friend Scheler, who, through his courses, his writings, and his endless conversations, had been a spiritual signpost for his young admirer. Whether or not Scheler ever intended to be instrumental in his conversion is a question I leave open. And it is not important. God can use anyone or anything to draw souls to Himself. No man can convert another man; God's grace accomplishes it. Scheler was intellectually convinced of the truth of Catholic teaching, but he had not let her light filter into his personal life to change and transform it. He was definitely not an apostle, as Dietrich was to become, for the latter continually hoped that God would use him—imperfect as he was—as an instrument to help others to share his faith and the source of his joy.[50]

A few days after their reception into the Church, Dietrich, Gretchen, and little Franzi took the train to Göttingen, where Scheler happened to be at the time (although his home was still in Berlin). As soon as he saw his friend, Dietrich informed him of the earth-shaking event that had changed his life. He was hoping that Max would give an appropriate response of joy. To his disappointment, the latter took the news quite casually, treating it more as an interesting piece of information than as an overwhelming fact. He was cordial and friendly, but his response fell far short of what was called for. It saddened the young man, but he knew that Scheler, although he had married Märit in a Catholic church, had not

[50] How very different Scheler was from Léon Bloy, the French writer who played a crucial role in Jacques and Raïssa Maritain's conversion: whereas Bloy was an ardent Catholic whose great wish was to see these two truth-loving, talented, and lovable young people enter the Church, Scheler was, alas, not practicing his faith; and I doubt that he ardently wished his young admirer, Dietrich, to enter the Church. God had given Scheler extraordinary insights into the "spirit of Roman Catholicism"; speaking, he was convinced of its divine origin and of its truth, and he was fascinated by the wealth of ideas her teaching presented to the human mind; but this beauty never penetrated into Scheler's personal life, never transformed his soul.

come back to the sacraments, as his friend had fervently hoped he would. Dietrich had convinced himself that, once married to someone he loved, Scheler would establish a harmony between his ideas and his life. Alas, it did not seem to be the case.

Dietrich begged Max to keep the news quiet, because he himself wanted to share it with his other friends. So, the very next day, Dietrich paid a visit to Adolf Reinach, who was for him, as we know, the absolute intellectual authority. Taking into account that his revered teacher was liberal in his views, the young convert was apprehensive about sharing the news of his conversion with someone he respected so deeply. He sensed how painful it would be for him if Reinach's response duplicated that of Adolf and Irene von Hildebrand. Had Reinach raised an objection, it would have been deeply upsetting to him, although it would not have shaken his faith. (Interestingly enough, had Scheler made negative comments, they would have left him indifferent. Dietrich, while continuing to admire his friend's genius, was by now intellectually independent of Scheler's views.)

Consequently, upon entering Reinach's library, Dietrich fumbled for words, stammered, and finally managed to inform his revered teacher that he had become a Roman Catholic. Reinach was kind, as always, but obviously, given his personal stance, he could neither understand nor fully appreciate the importance of this step. He told the nervous young man that Scheler had already hastened to share this information with him, and that he felt bad when he witnessed how ill at ease his student was. Reinach's purity of heart was such that, Dietrich, deep down, was convinced that he, too, would find Christ. His intellectual honesty and his love for truth were so deep that he was bound to move closer and closer to the *lumen Christi*. But it would take a while before this noble mind turned from a burning love of truth to a burning love of Truth itself.

During his brief stay at Göttingen, Dietrich attended a psychological congress. It depressed him greatly. The intellectual climate was overwhelmingly relativistic and positivistic. It was followed by another congress in Halle that was no better. What a contrast between the world of beauty, sublimity, and truth, of which he had now become a citizen, and the "spirit of the time"! Dietrich von Hildebrand found the talks delivered by the speakers empty, intellectually pretentious, and vain.[51] Together with Scheler, he then went to Berlin, where Märit was expecting them. It was the first time that he had visited them as husband and wife.

Scheler suggested that they go to the theater with some of his bright but highly sophisticated friends. They were all very worldly, and Scheler's proposal did not appeal to Dietrich at all. He feared that Scheler would purposely choose a play that was risqué to enjoy his friend's embarrassment, thinking it would be fun to make this young Catholic blush. Since his conversion, Dietrich had developed a still deeper horror of anything that touched on sexual immorality, let alone pornography, and Scheler and his friends probably assumed that the young convert was in danger of becoming straitlaced and puritanical. In fact, the play turned out to be both stupid and harmless. In his relief, Dietrich kept laughing, which irritated Scheler intensely, for he was bored and could not see what was funny about the performance.

While in Berlin, Dietrich made the acquaintance of the great Jewish thinker Martin Buber. A friend of his, a Herr Süssmilch, was also present. The latter had the rather fantastic idea of founding an association of "important people". In

[51] He must have thought of St. Augustine's judgment on the teaching of the Manichees: pompous words and no spiritual food whatever.

recruiting candidates no attention whatsoever was to be paid to a person's philosophy; the only requirement was that he be "important". One can readily imagine how many candidates applied to the association, convinced that they had the necessary qualification! The organization was to have "twelve apostles" and a *Kulturpapst* (culture pope). Scheler rightly remarked that an organization should have a definite purpose toward which people might gravitate but that an organization without any purpose was senseless. This objection made no impression upon Herr Süssmilch, who insisted that such an organization was meaningful in and by itself. Buber then read a letter from a Herr Barlach, who had received an invitation to join. He regretfully declined, because, as he wrote, this was not his "cup of tea". The tone of the letter, however, indicated that he took the whole thing seriously. Such was the intellectual mentality prevalent at the time—brilliance, wit, and sharpness of mind rated higher than reverence for truth.

The conversation then turned to the topic of miracles. Much to Dietrich's surprise and disappointment, Buber defended the thesis that there was absolutely no difference between magic and miracle—a position that struck Dietrich as unorthodox for a Jew. Needless to say, he challenged Buber's views vigorously, but none of his arguments made any impression.

As this unsatisfactory visit drew to a close, Dietrich was happy to leave Berlin and go back to Göttingen to pick up Gretchen, who had proudly presented her son, now aged twenty-seven months, to her dear grandmother. The trio then went back to Munich, where Dietrich was planning to start working on his *Habilitation*.[52]

---

[52] The *Habilitation* involves a major written work (in a sense, a second Ph.D. dissertation), an oral examination, and a "trial lecture". The degree awarded, that of "Dozent", confers the right to lecture at any German university.

CHAPTER 3

World War I and Its Aftermath
1914–1920

After his trying sojourn in Berlin, Dietrich was overjoyed to be back in Munich, in a truly Catholic atmosphere, the only atmosphere in which he could now breathe freely and be happy. He spent every free moment in the library, devouring Catholic literature—the Fathers and Doctors of the Church, the history of the Church, lives of the saints and the founders of religious orders. In a short span of time, he acquired a formidable knowledge of his faith. It was exhilarating for him to discover intellectual and spiritual treasures the existence of which he had not even suspected a few years earlier. Thanks to his phenomenal memory, all these readings were imprinted on his mind and soul, and they remained his possession for life. The more he read, the greater was his gratitude that he had been granted the grace to enter the blessed Ark of the Church. He could not get enough of the spiritual food of which he had been deprived for so long. He developed an ardent desire to see all people find the plenitude of truth that to him was a source of such bliss. He became a "confessor", and he was to remain one for the rest of his life. He longed to share with others what he himself had received. The more he loved them, the greater his longing to share these treasures with them. God rewarded his longing to see others share in his joy. In the course of his life, more than a hundred friends and acquaintances entered the Church.

But the joyful weeks following Dietrich's and Gretchen's conversion were suddenly darkened by political events. On June 28, 1914, the heir to the Austrian Empire, the Archduke Franz-Ferdinand, and his wife, Sophie, were brutally murdered by a Serbian fanatic in Sarajevo. On that very day, Dietrich had accompanied his father to the burial of the Duke of Meiningen, whose wife, the Baronin Heldburg, was his Protestant godmother. While waiting for a train connection in Stuttgart, Dietrich happened to hear the dreadful news that was to shake Europe to its foundation. Both father and son were stunned. Dietrich feared that Europe would enter into a hideous conflict, the consequences of which would be incalculable, and, indeed, the assassination triggered a chain reaction that led to World War I.

At first, his sympathies were with Austria. After all, that great Catholic country had been insulted politically, and such an insult could not be passed over lightly. It was a typical *casus belli*. On the other hand, he hated Prussian militarism, with its cult of brutal force. When on August 4, 1914, German troops invaded neutral Belgium, Dietrich was horrified. Although the invasion was justified at the time by the famous phrase *"Not kennt kein Gebot"* (Necessity knows no law), it was precisely an example of the pragmatism in moral matters that was repugnant to him. To grasp the immorality of the violation, keep in mind that the treaty guaranteeing the neutrality of Belgium had been signed by several nations, including Germany, in the name of the Holy Trinity.

At first, the response to the declaration of war triggered a wave of enthusiasm in Munich. Thousands of people flocked downtown to manifest their solidarity with Austria. One day Dietrich and a friend of his named Rupé happened to find themselves in front of the central post office, where they met by chance a Pole they knew, by the name of Rosenblum. The three men immediately started a philosophical discussion. Soon they became so absorbed by their topic that they did not notice that they were surrounded by a crowd of shouting people. Their discussion was suddenly interrupted when a friend of Rosenblum's, another Pole, was arrested by the police. Dietrich, typically, went over to Rosenblum's friend and said, "Don't worry; this is clearly a mistake. You will be released immediately." At that moment, a hand was clapped on his shoulder, and a policeman said to him, "You too are under arrest." When the astounded young man asked him why, he was told curtly, "You will soon find out." The two Poles, Rupé, and Dietrich were taken to the police station. Fortunately, the police protected them, for the raging mob would have torn them to pieces. "They are spies! Down with the Russian spies! Finally we have caught them. They should be hanged!" [1]

The young men were grateful to find themselves behind the walls of the police station, separated from the menacing mob. They were questioned by the police. When Dietrich gave his name, the policeman was stunned. Everyone in Munich knew and revered Adolf von Hildebrand, and the police could only offer profuse apologies for Dietrich's arrest. Dietrich and his friends were immediately released but through a back door, lest they suffer injury at the hands of the mob. It was a fearful experience, but a valuable one. It taught

[1] False rumors spreading in Munich at the time, that the water had been contaminated, and that dynamite had been put in the central post office, caused widespread hysteria.

him about the fierce irrationality of mobs and the danger of being exposed to their fury. In such cases, reason is so completely dethroned that there is nothing one can do to protect oneself.

The onset of war presented Dietrich and his contemporaries with a dilemma—to volunteer for the army or to wait to be drafted. Siegfried Hamburger, knowing that he would be drafted soon because he was unmarried, decided to volunteer so that he could choose the field in which he would serve. He chose the infantry and eventually spent four years at the front. This decision immediately precipitated a spiritual crisis for him. Knowing the danger to which he would inevitably be exposed, the question of his conversion became urgent. He had firmly decided to enter the Church, but before he could be baptized, he had to renounce his purely formal allegiance to the synagogue. Hamburger wished to do this in Munich, because he had only a few days before reporting to his unit. He went to the local rabbi, who refused to have anything to do with him. "You come from Kattowitz", he said. "You must go back to your hometown." [2] Hamburger was running out of time, and to go back to his birthplace was simply not feasible. As soon as war had been declared, the trains had become slow and unreliable. He discussed his situation with his friend, who found out that what was needed was simply a formal act of recanting in front of a rabbi and two witnesses. So Hamburger, along with Dietrich and Gretchen, went back to the local rabbi. Even though the rabbi tried to avoid seeing them, they managed to confront him at home, and Hamburger informed him clearly and decisively, in front of Dietrich and Gretchen as witnesses, that he renounced Judaism. He could then be baptized, and the ceremony took

[2] Kattowitz (or Katowice), a city in south-central Poland, was at the time part of the German territory.

place in the lovely church of Sankt Georg in Munich.
Dietrich and Gretchen were his radiant godparents.[3]

Adolf Reinach also volunteered for the army. Like many
other Jews at the time, he was an ardent German patriot and
wanted to prove his love for his country by immediately
offering his services. However, as he was over thirty and very
nearsighted, he had difficulty being accepted. It was only
through the intervention of his younger brother Heinrich,
who was an officer, that his wish was fulfilled. As soon as his
training was completed, he was sent to the front, where he
fought until 1917.

Like his friend Hermann Solbrig and two of his brothers-
in-law, Carlo Sattler and Fedja Georgii, Dietrich, who had
not been mobilized (he was married and had a child), opted
to work for a Red Cross unit, which was, early in the war, an
acceptable substitute for military service. The men attended a
training course, and then they started planning to go to the
front as stretcher-bearers and ambulance helpers. Adolf von
Hildebrand put his car at their disposal, but, just as they were
about to depart, Dietrich developed a problem with his is-
chium that paralyzed him so completely that it was impossible for him to move for several days. The others left without
him. When he recovered, he started to look for work in
which he could contribute to the all-out efforts of his compatriots. He found out that he could enlist in an army corps
that went close to the French front in southern Germany to

---

[3] Not everyone was so delighted. When Hamburger's mother heard the
news of her son's conversion, she became so distraught that a doctor had to be
called. Placing all the blame for Hamburger's decision on his friend von Hildebrand, she forbade Hamburger's sister Stephanie to associate with him again.
These efforts were in vain; Stephanie later converted and became a Benedictine
nun in Belgium. Hamburger's brother Heinrich also converted, and he too
became a Benedictine, first in Austria, and then in Belgium, where he died at a
ripe old age.

bring wounded soldiers back to hospitals. The train usually went to Freiburg im Breisgau and waited there for several days until the wounded (both French and German) arrived. While waiting, Dietrich spent time in the cathedral, praying, or in a café, writing long letters to Gretchen of his longing to see her and little Franzi. Once he paid a visit to Husserl, who had received a professorship at the University of Freiburg im Breisgau. One day the train went as far as Colmar, where one could hear the rumbling of guns and cannons.

At night, Dietrich shared a heated wagon with other Red Cross helpers. Before going to sleep, his comrades would entertain each other by relating their romantic "adventures". Needless to say, these were not edifying. Saddened and shocked, Dietrich tried to silence them, but his objections were received with scoffing and laughter. He was labelled a "sissy" and was made the laughingstock of the company. He tried to block his ears so as not to hear the unsavory details related with gusto, but his comrades yelled all the louder. Finally, Dietrich took his cot and blanket and moved to another compartment (one that was not heated; the thermometer registered forty degrees Fahrenheit!), so as not to expose himself to salacious talk. He might have caught pneumonia, but he preferred to take that risk rather than to have to hear offensive stories. He had always hated sexual filth, but now, thanks to his discovery of the sublimity of married love and his deepened love for Gretchen, he was spiritually nauseated by what those unfortunate young men thought to be "good jokes".[4]

Another episode is just as typical of him. One day, the commander announced that the company had received a large

---

[4] See *Reinheit und Jungfräulichkeit* (Cologne: Oratoriums Verlag, 1927). A recent English edition is *Purity* (Steubenville, Ohio: Franciscan University Press, 1989).

shipment of wine that was to be given to the wounded soldiers. Immediately, a German soldier remarked that this wine
should be given exclusively "to our gallant German soldiers",
and not to the "dirty French". Dietrich raised his voice and
said, "A wounded man is a wounded man and therefore
sacrosanct, and to me it is totally irrelevant whether he is
German or French. He is a person and should be respected as
such. I shall personally take care of the distribution of the
wine, serving the German soldiers first. There is plenty for
everybody." Such an appeal to fairness was risky. Nationalism
was at a peak, and some fanatic might have considered
Dietrich a potential traitor. In any case, the courageous young
man did take care of the distribution of the wine. When he
came to the French soldiers, he was able, with his fluent
French, to give those poor wounded men some words of
kindness and encouragement.

On another occasion, working in the hospital, Dietrich
heard a medical assistant, upon being informed that a French
soldier's legs were to be amputated, exclaim, "Why should
French soldiers have legs?" The remark infuriated Dietrich,
yet it gave him an insight into the abyss of wickedness normally hidden in the human heart until it is released when
armed conflict seems to justify it.

Dietrich worked in the Red Cross transport operation
until the end of February 1915. Then, instead of going back
to Munich, the sick transport went to Augsburg. He was
given a three-day leave. Suffering from an inflamed wisdom
tooth, he went to his dentist, Dr. Cecconi, who extracted the
tooth. For days after what should have been a minor surgical
intervention, Dietrich suffered such agonizing pains and swell-
ing that he could not open his mouth. Totally incapacitated
for days, he could not return in time to the Red Cross
transport, which was leaving Augsburg for the front. He re-

quested permanent leave from this operation, but he offered
to continue to work for the Red Cross in another capacity.
His dentist told him that he was doing volunteer work in a
hospital in Munich, assisting the main surgeon, a Dr. Luxemburger. Feeling the press of work as the casualties of war kept
mounting, Dr. Cecconi asked Dietrich to become his assistant, and he offered to train him. Dietrich, who had always
had a keen interest in medicine even though he had had no
interest the natural sciences, gratefully accepted his offer. He
started doing hospital work the very next day. Later in 1915,
when war broke out between Germany and Italy, Dr.
Cecconi, who was an Italian citizen, had to leave Germany.
Dr. Luxemburger, who had observed Dietrich's reliability and
devotion to his work of *médecin malgré lui* (the title of a play
by Molière) asked him to replace Cecconi as his surgical
assistant. From 1915 until he was mobilized in the spring of
1918, Dietrich worked long hours in the hospital, assisting at
innumerable operations. Although he refrained from acting
on his own or without supervision, he acquired much practical knowledge, and Dr. Luxemburger began to depend on
him more and more. In fact, he preferred to have an assistant
"who knew that he knew not", to quote Socrates, than a
young medical student who might overestimate his knowledge and act on his own.

All during his life, Dietrich enjoyed talking to medical
doctors and trying to deepen his familiarity with their field.
Not surprisingly, the combination of his academic title and
his being an assistant to the principal surgeon in a large hospital led some people to think that he actually was a medical
doctor. A doctor pulled him aside one day to advise him not
to care overmuch about his patients and to be concerned
primarily about his own welfare! He did not know that he
was addressing someone who might someday be his patient.

Dietrich von Hildebrand in his late seventies.

Dietrich von Hildebrand at age 83.

Dietrich von Hildebrand in his late forties.

Siegfried Hamburger.

Edmond Michelet, who saved Dietrich von Hildebrand from the Nazis, with his wife (1946), in Chartres.

The composer Walter Braunfels, Dietrich's brother-in-law.

*Franzi von Hildebrand
as a small child.*

*Gretchen and Franzi
(1915).*

Gretchen von Hildebrand as a young woman.

Dietrich von Hildebrand at age 20.

Dietrich at age 13, with his private tutor, Ludwig Curtius.

Photo taken at the May 29, 1909, wedding of composer Franz von Hösslin and his bride, Hela Pflaun (at left). Dietrich von Hildebrand is third from left, followed by Wilhelm Furtwängler, Märit Furtwängler, Giulietta Bulle, Marguerite Ottenheimer, and her fiancé, Hermann Solbrig.

San Francesco, the von Hildebrand home in Florence, Italy.

San Francesco.

Irene von Hildebrand, Dietrich von Hildebrand's mother.

Bertele von Hildebrand, sculpted by her father.

Vivi von Hildebrand, sculpted by her father.

Vivi and Bertele, bust by Adolf von Hildebrand.

Left to right: Bertele, Dietrich, and Silvia von Hildebrand (1893).

Adolf von Hildebrand (right) as a young man.

"Father Rhine" fountain in Munich, by Adolf von Hildebrand.

The Wittlesbach fountain in Munich, by Adolf von Hildebrand, is considered his masterpiece. The artist was knighted upon completion of this work.

Adolf von Hildebrand. Painting by Hans von Marées.

Pinacothek (Museum), Munich.

Needless to say, the initial outbreak of war and the turmoil it created prevented Dietrich from doing serious work on his *Habilitation*. Nevertheless, he kept thinking about his thesis, and it was maturing in his mind. By late 1915 or early 1916, he was eager to commence the work, even if only on a part-time basis because the greater part of his day was spent at the hospital. His hospital work was both exhausting and time-consuming.

In order to begin the *Habilitation*, Dietrich had to find a mentor who would agree to supervise his work. Throughout his life, he suffered from severe inhibitions as far as his career was concerned, and he often refused to take the steps that could further his professional prospects. I do not think I have ever met anyone more helpless when it came to promoting his own career. Only those who knew him well were aware of this baffling contrast between his usual self-assurance (he was in no way shy) and his total helplessness in certain situations.

Father Heribert Holzapfel, who had instructed Dietrich and Gretchen in the faith, soon noticed this weakness and convinced him that he should overcome it. He urged him to choose as his adviser F. W. Foerster,[5] the famous professor of education (or "pedagogy", as it was then called). Obediently but reluctantly, Dietrich followed his advice and returned to the University of Munich to register for one of Foerster's courses.

Dietrich's impression of his mentor at their first meeting was completely negative. Foerster had a Prussian accent, which to someone living in southern Germany sounded unattractive. His way of expressing himself was foreign to the

[5] Friedrich Wilhelm Foerster (1869–1966), an important name in the field of education, was the author of many books.

young man. Moreover, that day the sun was shining on Foerster's face, and it distorted his noble features. Although Dietrich was usually very objective, on this occasion he let himself be guided by a purely subjective impression, triggered by his deep-seated inhibition. Swayed by this subjective attitude, Dietrich went home and told Gretchen that he would never get his *Habilitation* under Foerster.

Nevertheless, pressed by Father Holzapfel, he overcame his misgivings and returned to Foerster's course. Soon he had to acknowledge that his first impression had no validity. As a matter of fact, he discovered how lovable a personality Foerster was—trustworthy, honest, courageous, and witty. Soon afterward, Dietrich also made the acquaintance of Foerster's wife, and he introduced Gretchen to the couple. They met frequently in restaurants or in Foerster's apartment and spent delightful, enriching evenings, animated by serious discussions, peppered by much wit and banter. Foerster had a unique sense of humor and was a wonderful conversationalist.

Encouraged by this personal contact, Dietrich asked Foerster to accept the supervision of his *Habilitation* and told him that he was planning to work on the concept of authority. His conversion had brought about a sort of "revolution" in the young philosopher's thinking. Upon becoming a Catholic, he had discovered the gift that authority is for weak and erring human beings (the best and most intelligent of whom make mistakes). He also recognized that all authentic authority derives from God. He found it a blessing to know that there is a voice speaking from above that informs man how to serve God as He wants to be honored and gives him guidelines for salvation. Dietrich submitted his proposal to Foerster and told him what had determined his choice. The latter approved of his topic and agreed to supervise his thesis. He expressed his sympathy for Roman Catholicism, telling

Dietrich that his younger sister had recently entered the Church in Berlin.

Foerster exerted a great deal of influence on Dietrich's political views, for he opened his eyes more and more to the dangers of Prussian militarism and the threat that the cult of brutal force constituted for the moral fiber of Germany. Foerster had long before made himself notorious because of his stand against Prussian militarism as incarnated in the "Iron Chancellor", Otto von Bismarck.[6] Because of those views, Foerster was extremely unpopular among German nationalists, whose basic tenet was *Deutschland über alles* (Germany above everything else). He had left Prussia, where he was persona non grata and, after teaching for a few years in Vienna, had been named professor at the University of Munich in 1914. Aside from his political views, Foerster deserves special mention for his monumental work on education. He can rightly be considered one of the great educators of the late nineteenth and the twentieth century.

However, in 1916, soon after taking Dietrich under his wing, Foerster took a leave of absence from the university and went to Switzerland, where he had a house in Zürich. He had a high regard for Swiss democracy, and he felt very much at home in this small country, where the rights of minorities were rigorously respected.

With the departure of Foerster, Scheler, whose influence on Dietrich remained strong, convinced his friend to change mentors for his *Habilitation* from Foerster to Professor Baeumker, a Catholic who was professor of philosophy at the University of Munich. Scheler argued that it would be wiser for Dietrich to study for his *Habilitation* under a philosopher than under a professor of education. The argument was convinc-

---

[6] Otto von Bismarck (1815–1898), Prussian statesman, became the first chancellor of the German empire.

ing, and Dietrich followed his counsel, a sound one this time. Once again, he had to overcome his inhibitions and make the acquaintance of Baeumker, by registering for the latter's courses. As Scheler had predicted, this kind and lovable man agreed to be Dietrich's mentor and approved the subject that he had chosen: "Morality and the Knowledge of Moral Values". He planned to examine the Socratic problem of whether knowledge guarantees virtue and to deal with the different sources of moral blindness. He also intended to show that morally blind persons cannot be exonerated from all responsibility. It turned out to be a powerful work, which went further and deeper than his Ph.D. dissertation. Unfortunately, according to Karl Schumann, Husserl did not show any interest in this book. It is even doubtful that he read it.[7]

The war years witnessed significant improvement in Scheler's professional prospects. His great work *Der Formalismus in der Ethik und die materiale Wertethik* (Formalism in ethics and material value ethics) was published in 1916. In 1915, he published *Der Genius des Krieges und der deutsche Krieg* (The genius of war and the German War), a book that enjoyed enormous success and made Scheler famous. Because of this book, during the years 1917 and 1918 the German foreign office sent Scheler to both Holland and Switzerland as "an ambassador of good will". The scandal of the past was forgotten, and Scheler's talent now received full recognition. *Der Genius des Krieges* contained some brilliant insights. He highlighted the important role that Germany was to play in Europe and expressed his critical views about England and its philosophy as witnessed in the theories of men such as Thomas Hobbes, Roger Bacon, David Hume, John Stuart Mill, Herbert Spencer, and Charles Darwin. Given the political

---

[7] Dietrich's *Habilitation* thesis was published in the *Jahrbuch für Philosophische und Phänomenologische Forschung* in 1921.

climate at the time the book was published, its pro-German stance made it enormously popular. It was also a valuable tool of German propaganda.[8]

At first, Dietrich responded positively to this work, in which Scheler claimed that the archenemy of Germany was England, not France. Later, however, as his political views took shape under the influence of Foerster, he found the book not only too nationalistic but also tainted with an opportunism that repelled him.

Dietrich rejoiced deeply in 1916 when Scheler, after a visit to the Benedictine Abbey of Beuron, decided to return to the Church, from which he had been away for so long. His wife, Märit, soon followed suit, and once again Dietrich and Gretchen rejoiced. Scheler's conversion was a personal gift for Dietrich. The latter was conscious of the intellectual debt he owed to Max and had for years grieved deeply that the man who had played such a role in his own conversion was himself outside the fold. He had prayed ardently for this event.

But Dietrich soon noticed that Scheler's second conversion had not struck very deep roots in his soul. Once, when Scheler and his wife were visiting the von Hildebrands in Munich, they went to Mass together. Dietrich noticed that Max was restless, fumbling through his missal, giving the impression that he did not know what to do or that he was bored. All of a sudden, someone fainted, and Scheler's eagerness to help carry the person outside betrayed the sort of

[8] See *Aletheia* (1992), pp. 4–33. John R. Staude wrote of Scheler's *Der Genius des Krieges*, "War was thus both natural and good. . . . Germany had a spiritual world-historical mission not simply to purify and revivify herself, but to insure the very survival of human civilization": *Max Scheler, 1874–1928* (New York: Free Press, [1967]), pp. 71–72; and further, "Scheler considered German militarism to be a work of art, the highest cultural expression of the German soul" (p. 81).

liberation a person experiences when he has a valid excuse for leaving. Scheler was the sort of person for whom knowledge was everything. Once he knew a topic, or thought he knew it, he was likely to lose interest in it. He would read the Liturgy and then somehow conclude that he had exhausted the plenitude of its content. He seemed to have but little understanding for the "contemplative" dimension of knowledge, the happy dwelling in its depth and sublimity, a dimension that was integral both to Dietrich's life and to his philosophy.[9]

The following week, Märit came alone to Mass with Dietrich and Gretchen, saying that her husband had a toothache and was therefore excused. The profound joy Dietrich had experienced upon hearing that his prayer had been answered—and that the friend to whom he was so indebted had found his way back into the Church—was now dampened by the fear that Scheler's conversion was not leading to a new life, to a transformation of his soul. Dietrich's presentiment turned out to be justified: Scheler's faith lacked deep roots and was not forming his life.

Scheler's religious state of mind continued to perplex and concern Dietrich throughout 1916 and 1917. On the one hand, in 1917, Scheler published his beautiful book *Vom Umsturtz der Werte* (The toppling down—or the overthrow—of values). On the other hand, he baffled Dietrich by his response to the personality of Father Lippert—an outstanding Jesuit whom Dietrich had met after his conversion and who had deeply impressed him. Since he had entered into the Church, Dietrich had been eager to make the acquaintance of Catholics who truly lived their faith, and he was blessed by meeting quite a few of them. Father Lippert combined a

---

[9] See *What Is Philosophy?*, chap. 6.

brilliant mind with a great humility and goodness. He was known to have helped many souls on their way to God through his deep faith and boundless charity. For this reason, Dietrich looked forward to bringing Scheler into contact with him. But to Dietrich's amazement and grief, Scheler declared categorically that his impression of Father Lippert was definitely negative. His friend was stunned. How was it possible that this outstanding man, radiating a supernatural spirit, should be disliked by anyone? Scheler justified his antipathy by saying that Father Lippert exuded a typical "Jesuitic, icy coldness". Dietrich hotly challenged this unjust assertion, telling his friend that he had seen Father Lippert in many situations and that every new encounter had deepened his conviction that he radiated true supernatural love. But Scheler, who was enamored of his own subjective impressions, refused to listen.

At about this time, Scheler published an article on Eastern and Western Christianity. In it, he put such emphasis on the differences between the two—placing greater emphasis on cultural differences than on dogmatic ones—that, implicitly, it sounded as if Roman Catholicism was closer to Protestantism than it was to Eastern Orthodox Christianity. Once again, Dietrich challenged this position and raised several objections. A heated discussion followed, which Scheler ended by saying defensively, "You talk as if you alone were a Roman Catholic. I too am one." The position Scheler was defending, however, proved conclusively that his approach to Christianity had become more sociological than supernatural.

Throughout 1917, Dietrich continued to work in his free time on his *Habilitation*. His new mentor, Professor Baeumker, although a good and kind man, was not cut of the material from which heroes are made. He was as prudent as Foerster had been daring. He wanted to play it safe during the period of turmoil in Germany. He also wanted to protect the young man whose *Habilitation* he had agreed to guide. Baeumker was worried (and rightly so) because he knew he was dealing with an *enfant terrible* whose convictions were so firm that he was willing to put his head on the block in order to live up to their demands. Motivated by a sincere desire to smooth the way of the young man's career, Baeumker advised him never to mention the word "religion" on university grounds. He suggested he should replace it with "metaphysics", which sounded more "professional"! In addition, Baeumker begged his protégé not to make himself conspicuous by taking sides in the dispute that Foerster's political views had triggered at the University of Munich. Although Foerster never discussed political themes in his courses, when he returned to Germany from Switzerland he had given an extremely daring lecture, outside university halls, in which he did not mince words and publicly denounced German militarism, particularly the crimes the German army had committed in Belgium. Early in the conflict, in an act of iconoclastic brutality, the Germans had burned the invaluable library at the University of Louvain.[10]

One of the plans nurtured by German militarists and nationalists was the annexation of Belgium. In their eyes, such a move was justified on the ground that Germany needed more *Lebensraum* (living space), a claim reiterated by Hitler a few years later. On one occasion, Dietrich had a very heated discussion with his dear friend Günther Jachmann concerning the war aims. Like most intellectuals, Jachmann was tainted with a nationalism Dietrich could not abide (the question of right and wrong was infinitely more important to him than

[10] The library was rebuilt after the war, thanks to the generosity of the U.S. government.

national considerations). This position led him also to a serious conflict with an acquaintance named Heimsöth, whom he tried to convince that the annexation of foreign countries was not only an injustice but political madness, because the populations whose territory had been annexed would understandably create constant conflict and unrest. True peace would be unthinkable under such conditions. To this, Heimsöth replied, "But there is no need whatever for Belgians to remain in their territory. Their soil is excellent and could be given to our own peasants. The Belgian population could systematically be stamped out [*evanouieren*]." This shameful remark triggered Dietrich's holy wrath.

Dietrich had promised Baeumker that he would be prudent and not get involved in the conflict that Foerster's stance on the war had triggered. Unfortunately, he chose to be present at the first lecture Foerster gave when he came back to the University of Munich in 1917. Wisdom teaches one that the best way not to fall into temptation is not to expose oneself to it. One "temptation" against which the idealistic young man should have known that he was powerless was to see evil or an injustice take place while trying to remain a passive spectator. He reasoned that to remain passive actually means to condone the evil action. When Foerster arrived at the lecture hall, the nationalist students started shouting, "*Nieder*, down with Foerster!" Dietrich, forgetting his promise to Baeumker, began shouting at the top of his powerful voice, "*Hoch, Foerster!*" (Long live Foerster!) The sincerity and ardor of his commitment was such that in no time he rallied to his side many students who started chiming in. The young philosopher then learned a lesson he would never forget. He discovered that most people are sheep who follow the lead of whoever they think is on the winning side, with no clear knowledge of whom or what they are following. Within minutes, Dietrich noticed that his courageous leadership had gained such ascendency over the student body that most of them were now shouting, "Long live Foerster". Indeed the uproar ended in a sort of apotheosis of the professor. Foerster was a man of outstanding courage and self-control. He could face a mob without batting an eyelash, and his self-discipline was extraordinary. When booed, he could remain absolutely calm because of his deep-set conviction that he was standing for truth and justice.

Indeed, Foerster's unshakeable commitment to the anti-nationalist cause provided another startling contrast to the wavering Scheler. Dietrich brought them together, at Scheler's request, and one cannot imagine two more ill-paired men. Foerster was disciplined, conscientious, reliable, systematic, scrupulously honest and trustworthy, and outstandingly courageous. Scheler was undisciplined, erratic, and unpredictable; a genius who had never tried to improve himself and did not wish to do so, who lied to himself and to others when convenient. Scheler, in spite of his brilliant insights, had remained infantile in many ways. Nevertheless, he was the more profound thinker of the two; he had a richer outlook, more fertile insights, and a broader cultural background.

When they met, Scheler had come back to the Church, whereas Foerster, in spite of his sympathies for Christ's bride, had remained Protestant. Foerster's attraction to the Roman Catholic Church was grounded less in her divine origin than in her profound pedagogical insights. He saw clearly that the principles of Roman Catholicism, applied to education, were clearly the wisest and soundest for which an educator could wish. That was not enough, however, to convince him that a personal commitment was necessary.

As far as political matters were concerned, Scheler saw many interesting phenomena about the war that had escaped

Foerster's attention, for the latter was exclusively absorbed by one theme—his fight against German militarism and nationalism. Foerster's aim was to have Germany steer once again toward the federative direction that had been hers until Bismarck. Scheler never committed himself totally to any one program of political action. He observed everything with keen interest but remained a spectator and avoided the implications of what he perceived. Foerster, on the other hand, took a clear position and accepted all the implications flowing from it. He was a fighter, a passionate defender of right.

It was fascinating to watch these two contrasting personalities, but it was clear from the very first moment that no deep or lasting understanding was possible between them. Foerster mistrusted Scheler from the start. He tried to force him to take a clear stand on political issues, which Scheler refused to do, fencing cleverly to prevent Foerster from pinning him down. It was obvious that he had scant sympathy for Foerster.

Although 1917 witnessed the return of Professor Foerster to Bavaria and the conversion of Dietrich's eldest sister, Nini, the year also brought Dietrich one of the great sorrows of his life. Märit Scheler informed him that Adolf Reinach, his beloved and revered teacher, had been killed in Flanders on November 16, 1917. Dietrich was stunned. Was it possible that this extraordinary, noble, talented man, whose life could have benefited so many people, was no longer on this earth? [11]

Dietrich soon heard the details of Reinach's death. His commanding officer had asked for a volunteer to lead a

---

[11] Adolf Reinach was not the only Göttingen victim of this bloody war; several of von Hildebrand's acquaintances from the university also lost their lives: Kaibl, Staiger, Clemens, Frankfurter, and Wolfgang Husserl, one of Edmund Husserl's two sons.

dangerous patrol, and Reinach had immediately stepped forward. Trying to accomplish the mission given him, he was hit
in the eye by a bullet and died instantly.

When Reinach had volunteered for military service in
1914, Dietrich had sent him *The Confessions* of Saint Augustine, which he always considered the most beautiful of all
books after the Bible. This conviction led him to declare,
"Beloved Saint Augustine, what an overwhelming experience it was for me to get to know you, to have the privilege
of dwelling in your spirit; what a crucial role you have played
in my life." This work made a deep impression upon Reinach.
Early in 1916, Adolf wrote Dietrich a letter that filled the
latter's soul with joy and gratitude. He told him that he had
found Christ, and that he now felt much closer to Dietrich
than before. He wrote further that the terrible sufferings that
the two warring sides were experiencing had clearly the
meaning of calling men back to God. This letter had a totally
new "ring", echoing the depth of his religious experience.

Dietrich had by then become certain that his beloved
teacher was "on the way" to embracing Catholicism. Moreover, in the same letter, Reinach suggested that his former
pupil abandon the formal *Sie* address and turn to the familiar
Du, a step that is so meaningful in languages in which these
subtle distinctions are made. This offer on Reinach's part
indicated how close the two men had become. Soon afterward, Dietrich sent Reinach a Roman missal in Latin and
German, hoping that his revered teacher would find the fullness of revealed truth.

A few months later (May 1916), Reinach's wife, Anna,
came to Munich. She told Dietrich and Gretchen that both
she and her husband had been baptized. Upon hearing this
news, Dietrich's joy was boundless, but it was dampened
when Anna told him that they had become Protestants and

added that, after all, confessional differences do not have much meaning.

Great as his joy was that Reinach had now found Christ "in whom resides the plenitude of divinity", he was grieved that someone for whom he had such a deep respect had opted for (what Adrienne von Speyr, a convert from Protestantism, was to call) a truncated Christianity.[12] The news caused him to lie awake an entire night.[13]

And so on a cold, wintry day at the end of December 1917, Dietrich went to Göttingen once again to pay his last respects to a man to whom he was so indebted, whom he revered so deeply, and who had become a very special friend. He delivered a brief eulogy at the grave at the request of Reinach's widow. The dead man's father was present. This noble elderly man had received the terrible news of his son's death late one evening. He decided to postpone telling his dear wife the dreadful news until the next morning, saying to himself, "Why should I ruin her night's sleep?" Deeply moved, Dietrich said a few words about Adolf the man and Reinach the philosopher, and the sobbing father thanked him through his tears, murmuring, "You truly have succeeded in painting his personality."

[12] Adrienne von Speyr, *Aus meinem Leben: Fragment einer Selbst biographie* (Einsiedeln: Johannes Verlag, 1984), p. 162; English edition: *My Early Years* (San Francisco: Ignatius Press, 1995), p. 191: "the narrow God of Protestantism".

[13] A few years later, in 1923, Anna Reinach converted to Roman Catholicism and then related to Dietrich and Gretchen the details of her own and her husband's conversion. Both had become convinced of the divinity of Christ; and when Adolf came home for a brief furlough in 1916, husband and wife discussed together their newly won faith. Anna suggested that they should immediately be baptized. Adolf objected that he was not yet ready because he had had no time to examine the doctrinal differences between Roman Catholicism and Protestantism. Anna replied that such differences were not important. She had been befriended by an Evangelical Lutheran clergyman, who had assured her that faith in Christ was all that was necessary for baptism. Reinach yielded to his wife's wishes.

It was on that occasion that Dietrich made the acquaintance of Edith Stein, who shared Dietrich's devotion to his
teacher. For her too, Reinach had been a light and had become a great friend. She, of course, knew about Dietrich, for
he had founded the Philosophical Association in Göttingen
that she had joined in 1913, and everyone in Göttingen had
heard much about Husserl's favorite student.[14] No relationship developed between them on this occasion.[15] Edith Stein
was extremely shy and very reserved. On the other hand,
Anneliese Scheunemann, the friend who had accompanied
her to Reinach's funeral, attracted Dietrich's attention because he knew that his friend Heinrich Reinach was in love
with her.[16]

To all those who loved and revered Adolf Reinach, his
death was a terrible blow, and Dietrich's detestation of meaningless war was deepened by this loss. In addition to viewing
the war from the anti-militarist stand he had acquired from
Foerster, Dietrich now also saw it from a Catholic point of
view. He knew that, behind the scenes, Pope Benedict XV
was working tirelessly to bring about peace. He also knew
that Foerster had personally spoken to Emperor Karl of Austria.[17] He was a fervent Catholic, anxious to follow the guide-

[14] See Edith Stein, *Life in a Jewish Family*, trans. Josephine Koeppel (Washington, D.C.: ICS Publications, 1986), p. 253.

[15] They later met again in Salzburg in 1930, at a Summer Conference of the
Union of Catholic Intellectuals.

[16] Later Dietrich, as *Doctor Amoris*, played an important role in their engagement. Subsequently, to his great joy, both Heinrich and Anneliese converted to
Roman Catholicism. They wisely emigrated to Brazil to escape the terrible
persecutions of the Jews that were raging in the Third Reich. They died in their
adopted country.

[17] Emperor Karl I (1887–1922), Emperor of Austria and King of Hungary
from 1916 to 1918, became heir presumptive after the assassination of his uncle
Archduke Franz-Ferdinand at Sarajevo in June 1914, but he was forced to
abdicate in 1918.

lines of the Pope—who was advocating a truce with no victor. Unfortunately, German spies planted by General Ludendorff[18] in the emperor's entourage had informed him of these plans and had enabled him to foil them.

As the war progressed, Germany encountered more and more military problems. The number of casualties was fearful and continually rising. It was becoming increasingly difficult to avoid mobilization, for everyone capable of serving in the armed forces was being called to military duty. Substitute work was no longer accepted. There was an inevitable tug-of-war between hospitals, which were terribly understaffed and more and more inundated with wounded soldiers, and the army, which urgently needed more soldiers at the front to replace those who had fallen or been wounded.

By then, the futility of the war, which Dietrich hated with every fiber of his being, had become so evident to him that, in spite of his strong Austrian sympathies, he began to hope that the Allies would be victorious. Under Foerster's tutelage, Prussian militarism had become more and more repugnant to him. The volunteer work he was doing in a Munich clinic had relieved him of the duty of military service. In the spring of 1918, however, to his distress, Dr. Luxemburger's request that Dietrich be permitted to continue assisting him—a post in which Dietrich had become more and more indispensable—was turned down. Early in April, he was ordered to report to New Ulm for military training on the first of May.

As soon as he received this piece of news, Dietrich rushed to Professor Baeumker and told him that he would deliver the completed manuscript of his *Habilitation* by the end of the

---

[18] Erich von Ludendorff (1865–1937), a general in the German army from 1904 to 1933, was also a leader of the Hitler *Putsch* in 1923 in Munich, but later was acquitted of treason.

month. The title Baeumker had approved was *"Sittlichkeit und ethische Werterkenntnis"* (Morality and the knowledge of moral values). Dietrich stopped working at the hospital, and for a whole month he concentrated completely on his dissertation. He had to work with incredible intensity to finish it in such a short span of time. A secretary was appointed to type the manuscript, which Gretchen dictated (for Dietrich's handwriting was often illegible). By a sheer tour de force, he managed to finish the dissertation on time and give it to Professor Baeumker for final approval. Dietrich then had to face the inevitable, to go to New Ulm for military training. He was very unhappy about this new turn of events. Whereas he had a great interest in medicine and knew that he was doing good and meaningful work at the hospital, he knew that he was not cut from the material that makes good soldiers. He was unusually helpless in practical matters, and there was hardly anyone less suited for the military's rules, its impersonalism, its inhumanity. He hated brutality, he hated violence, and, to top it all, he hated the meaningless war that was bleeding Europe to death. He had a dark presentiment that Europe would never recover from a conflict that, to his mind, should have been avoided at all cost and for which there was only one possible Christian solution—peace without a victor. And now, against his moral sense, he was going to be forced to kill and possibly to die for a cause that was not worth it.

For several months, Dietrich underwent military training in New Ulm. Gretchen and little Franzi accompanied him there. He had to don a filthy uniform and a cap with a thick crust of dirt that disgusted him. When Gretchen saw him in this attire, she started to cry. The months spent in New Ulm were in a sense tragi-comic—tragic because of the pain he endured; comic because of the contrast between the military world and his personality. What the *soldat malgré lui* suffered during those months is hard to put into words. He tried his best to adapt himself to the circumstances and deserves commendation for mastering the art of greeting his superiors, clamorously clicking his heels! He never had difficulty submitting to authority, whereas many of his comrades would remark in very vulgar language that the commanding officer was "made of the same dung as they were made of", and they could not see why they should show him respect.

Dietrich wrote of his friend's visit at this time. "To my great joy, Hamburger came to New Ulm while I was having my training. It was clear that his spiritual life was blossoming more and more. Already in 1915, when he came to Munich for a brief furlough, he had shared with me his joy upon reading the autobiography of Saint Thérèse of Lisieux, which I had also read. Clearly, through God's grace, the sufferings he had gone through at the front had brought him still closer to Him."

Now Hamburger was in New Ulm for additional training as an officer. "We happened to find ourselves in the same course. It was truly incredible that he who had been in the army for almost four years and I who had been drafted for only a few months were receiving the same instructions! Even though his main duty had been a paymaster substitute, he had been exposed to many dangers and had suffered much. It was touching to hear that while watching telephone connections, and facing the enemy, he would sit down, leaning against a cannon, and read *The Imitation of Christ*. He also told me about an episode which enchanted me. His comrades had started affairs with French women, and, as Hamburger was fluent in French, they asked him to write letters to confirm the hour of their trysts. Hamburger, who wanted to prevent these sins, wrote notes cancelling the immoral rendez-vous, much to the surprise and disappointment of the soldiers whose 'friends' did not show up."

It soon became clear to Dietrich that things were not going well for Germany; the soldiers' morale was very low. They were sullen and discouraged, without enthusiasm for what they rightly viewed as a lost cause. Some, who had been at the front for more than three years and had come to New Ulm for additional training, often protested when they were sent back. One day the soldiers in training were told to shoot those who were refusing to enter the train returning them to the front. The next day, Dietrich was assigned this horrible task. He had firmly decided to let himself be shot rather than do something he considered immoral. But on that very day, he thanked God, for no soldier rebelled.

In spite of his efforts to adjust, Dietrich found the world of the military so totally foreign that he proved to be a hopelessly difficult soldier to train, having a strange propensity to turn left when the sergeant yelled "Right". One day, he was ordered to man a cannon, but his performance was pitiful. His superior, considering him a perfect idiot, asked him what he was planning to do later in life. When the unhappy soldier answered that he was working on his *Habilitation* and intended to teach at the university, the sergeant exclaimed, with a voice loaded with irony, "You want to teach!" and guffawed.

In the meantime, he received a letter from Baeumker informing him that his *Habilitation* thesis had been accepted and that he had to come to Munich to pass the Colloqium—an interrogation during which several professors challenge the thesis. He needed permission from his sergeant to get a three-day leave. When he asked for it, the answer was: "Do you want to be an academic or a soldier?" The question was not a difficult one . . . but, for once, Dietrich wisely controlled his tongue. He did get permission to go to Munich for a brief furlough at Pentecost 1918. It was a great relief for him to be away from what he considered a spiritual jail.

The Colloqium went extremely well, and he was congratulated on his performance. This time, he was not questioned about frogs and insects. He was truly in his element, dealing with the field that he loved passionately. He had worked on his *Habilitation* under the most adverse circumstances, and, had it not been for his outstanding gifts, he could never have written a book of this depth. Since the very beginning of the war, he had had hardly any time to devote to philosophy, but as he continued to think about his topic, it had matured more and more in his mind.

He had to meet one more requirement before officially joining the faculty at the University of Munich—to give a public lecture on a topic of his choice. It was customary for the whole faculty to assist at this great event, and again, they could challenge the speaker's position. Dietrich chose to speak on the "Essence of Punishment", and, by curtailing his sleep to the bare minimum, he managed to complete work on the lecture. It was delivered in Munich in August 1918. Unfortunately, his parents were out of town and could not be present, but of course Gretchen came, accompanied by his sister Nini. Once again, his performance was flawless. Alexander Pfänder congratulated him and welcomed him as a new faculty member. The kind Baeumker made some laudatory remarks and complimented the new professor for having had "the courage to mention God's name"! Finally, Dietrich was officially allowed to teach and to enter into a profession for which he knew he was made and which was going to give him so much joy.

It is was customary in Germany that young men who had an academic degree would—after their basic military training—receive an officer's training course. Dietrich certainly qualified, but a sergeant (whom he called Pizarro—a vicious character in Beethoven's opera *Fidelio*) had, for some purely subjective reason, developed a dislike bordering on hatred for this soldier *malgré lui*. One comrade overheard him say that, even though Dietrich's training had lasted only a few weeks, he was planning to send him to the front, adding viciously, "There is a spot I know of from which he will never come back." Dietrich was horrified when he heard this piece of brutal news. He was physically exhausted; he had lost a great deal of weight, and he was terribly low in spirits.[19] Before going to the front, he had to undergo a medical examination; so while he was in Munich he had himself examined by Dr. Luxemburger. The doctor suspected that he was suffering from chronic appendicitis and had his ex-assistant hospitalized for several days for observation. Dr. Luxemburger then certified that Dietrich was not fit for active duty but could serve his country in other capacities. When Dietrich brought this certificate back to New Ulm, through a sheer piece of luck or providence, "Pizarro" was on a brief furlough, and the medical certificate was relayed to a higher authority. Soon afterward, to his relief, Dietrich was discharged. He returned to the hospital, where he worked until the war was over. As it happened, he received this happy news on October 7, his father's seventy-first birthday. The date of the official discharge was October 10, 1918, thirty-two days before the armistice. Adolf von Hildebrand declared that that discharge was for him the best birthday gift he could have hoped for; he had been very worried about his son. The nightmare was over.

*

[19] In spite of his robust health, Dietrich was often very sick, and more than once his life was in danger. But he usually recovered surprisingly fast. Gretchen, on the other hand, looked frail but was hardly ever sick.

Husserl had called Dietrich's Ph.D. dissertation a masterpiece (an *opus eximium*) and had written many comments in the margin to express his appreciation. There is no doubt that he considered von Hildebrand a talented student, if not his most talented. Yet when Dietrich converted to Roman Catholicism, in 1914, Husserl's response had been far from supportive. He gave expression to his disapproval by stating that "a great talent has been lost for philosophy—Dietrich von Hildebrand has become a Roman Catholic." He seemed to assume that faith has a blinding effect on reason.[20] When Dietrich's Ph.D. dissertation was published in the *Jahrbuch* in 1921, with a section added to the original thesis in which he illustrated a morally noble action by referring to Saint Stephen, who, while being stoned, prayed for his murderers, Husserl's comment (written in the margin of the galleys) was "Catholic propaganda".[21]

Dietrich was deeply chagrined both by Husserl's response to his conversion and, later, by his unwarranted allusion to Catholic propaganda. He had a profound affection for his teacher, thought highly of his genius, was touched by his lovable personality, and was indebted to him for the courageous fight

[20] See Schumann, *Husserl und Hildebrand*, pp. 4–33, for a more detailed presentation of this theme.

[21] Ibid. Mrs. Husserl was under the sway of anti-Catholic prejudices, but God had His ways of opening her eyes. When her husband died in Freiburg in April 1938, a Belgian Franciscan, Father Herman van Breda, went to Germany, collected the Husserlian Literary Bequest, brought it to the Catholic University of Louvain, and convinced Mrs. Husserl to leave Germany, where she was clearly in danger. When the Nazis invaded Belgium in 1940, Mrs. Husserl was hidden in a convent. Witnessing the charity of Catholics living their faith, she converted and was received into the Catholic Church. As Father Österreicher later wrote, very beautifully, "Thus the Church has taken under her protection what Husserl left behind, his thought and his love": *Seven Jewish Philosophers Discover Christ* (New York: Devin Adair, 1952), p. 97. God's ways are mysterious and overwhelming.

his mentor had put up to try to persuade his science professors to award him a *summa cum laude* at the completion of his doctorate. But regrettably, after Dietrich's conversion, there was hardly any contact between himself and the founder of the phenomenological school.[22]

It was typical that, in the face of his esteemed teacher's unfriendly response to his conversion, Dietrich avoided any frank discussion of their strained relations. In such situations, he was terribly inhibited. Whereas Edith Stein, who was so reserved, continued after her conversion to remain in contact with her teacher, Dietrich, who was so outgoing, withdrew within himself, felt terribly helpless, and as a result gave Husserl the impression that he was ungrateful and no longer appreciated him. No doubt, Edith Stein's attitude was wiser. Had Dietrich adopted the same attitude, it is not likely that Husserl would have refused in 1921 to recommend him for a full professorship at the University of Freiburg im Breisgau, where Husserl had been appointed professor. Although Dietrich von Hildebrand's name had been put on the list of candidates, Husserl's refusal to endorse his candidacy sealed his fate. It was not the only case in Dietrich's life in which this "sin of omission" had dire consequences. Nevertheless, his inner attitude toward Husserl remained one of respect and gratitude, and he deeply regretted the sad ending of the relationship.

In November 1918, the war came to an end, with a crushing defeat for the German army. The defeated country found itself in a state nearing collapse. Inflation rose to unimaginable rates. (Adolf von Hildebrand had bought a beautiful piece of property south of Munich, which, very unwisely, his

[22] As previously noted, Dietrich briefly visited Husserl in Freiburg in 1915; the very last time he saw him was in Vienna in 1937.

heirs sold shortly after his death. When the deal was completed and the money was paid, it was worth the price of a
box of cigars.) The German Mark was valueless on the international market. The fact that many people were totally ruined created an ideal background for revolution. Germany
was in such disarray that a handful of soldiers, under the
leadership of the socialist journalist Kurt Eisner,[23] toppled the
Wittelbach monarchy. That was an ominous sign and for the
aging Adolf von Hildebrand a terrible blow. He had been in
close contact with the royal family for years and was personally shattered by this new turn of events. It darkened the last
years of his otherwise happy life.[24]

Now that travel was again possible, Adolf von Hildebrand
offered his son a trip to Switzerland. Dietrich was so run
down, because of the physical and psychological strain he had
been under for four years, that he badly needed a rest. In fact,
he became quite sick shortly after he began to teach at the
university in the fall of 1918, and he had to cancel his course
altogether. Dietrich gratefully accepted his father's offer,
and, together with Gretchen and Franzi, now aged seven
and a half, he left for Switzerland. From late November 1918
until April 1919, the trio remained in this peaceful country.
The contrast with war-torn Germany, where even the most
elementary things were in short supply and many goods were
simply impossible to find, was amazing. It was like awakening
from a bad dream to see the sun shining and hear the birds
singing. Instead of money, as the Mark was valueless, Adolf
von Hildebrand gave his son a valuable painting by Cranach,

---

[23] Kurt Eisner (1867–1919), German journalist and politican, became a socialist leader in Bavaria. He was assassinated in February 1919.

[24] See Isolde Kurz, *Der Meister von San Francesco* (Tübingen: Rainer,
Wunderlich Verlag, n.d.), p. 83.

telling him to bring it to Brown Bovery—the Swiss million-
aire—who could either buy it or keep it as security. In exchange, Bovery was to give Dietrich a monthly allowance,
enabling him to live comfortably. Upon his arrival, Dietrich
visited the tycoon, who accepted the bargain. After a brief
stay in Zürich, he and Gretchen paid a visit to the general of
the Jesuits, who was residing in Zizers. Meeting Father
Ledochowski, S.J., was for Dietrich a particularly beautiful
experience. Since his conversion, he always considered it
a privilege to meet Catholic spiritual leaders. Father Ledochowski was an Austrian citizen, for he came from a part of
Poland that was at that time Austrian territory. Even though
he was the Jesuit general, whose official residence is Rome,
he had not been permitted to stay in the Holy City because
Italy had been at war with Austria. Father Ledochowski took
refuge in Switzerland. Dietrich found him to be a remarkable
man of superior intelligence, with a powerful personality that
radiated a deep spiritual life. During their interview, Father
Ledochowski happened to refer to Clémenceau,[25] and he told
his visitor how very anti-religious the French statesman was.
He had once said to Ledochowski, "I hate a world in which
people believe in a God who is good and just."

After this visit, Dietrich, Gretchen, and Franzi went to
Saint Moritz, a resort famous for the purity of its air and the
beauty of its landscape. There Dietrich hoped to recover his
health. It was in Saint Moritz, however, that, just at Christ-
mastime, Dietrich caught the fearful "Spanish flu". Within
hours, he was close to death.[26] Gretchen was terribly upset
and nursed her husband with great devotion. She was aware

[25] Georges Clémenceau (1841–1921) was the French prime minister during
most of World War I.
[26] This dreadful disease actually killed as many people in a few months as four
years of war had done.

of how dangerous his state was, and she even telegraphed to Munich to inform his parents that he had caught pneumonia. Dietrich, on the other hand, knowing that he could die, was full of hope and totally resigned to God's will. Like many very sick people, he saw his whole life pass in front of him—a profound experience that one does not forget.

On Christmas Eve, he was so sick and weak that he became totally passive. He heard from far away the lively music that was being played in the hotel—Strauss' waltzes, which reminded him of the time he had spent in Vienna a few years earlier. Dietrich slowly recovered, but it took a while until his full strength came back. Then the whole family left for southern Switzerland: to Ancona for a few days and then to Lugano for several weeks. There Dietrich's parents joined them shortly before Easter 1919.

The postwar situation in Germany remained desperate, and on May 1, 1919—a few short months after the fall of the monarchy—the Communists staged a coup in Munich. There was fighting and shooting in the streets. One of Dietrich's close childhood friends, Hermann Solbrig, was caught in a crossfire and severely wounded. Dietrich and Gretchen heard the terrible news only when they came back to Munich on the fifth of that month; the trip from Switzerland to the Bavarian capital took much longer than expected because of the fighting and because the trains were not running on regular schedules.

Dietrich and Hermann had been friends since they were teenagers. In 1910 Hermann had married Marguerite Ottenheimer, a close friend of Märit Furtwängler, whom Dietrich himself had met when he was fifteen, and who was to play a great role in his life. Hermann and Marguerite had a little daughter, Margarete. Hermann was a fallen-away Catholic, and when Dietrich converted his wish was to have this close friend find his way back into the Church. Hermann was lovable and handsome, had a heart of gold, and was affectionate and generous, but he was totally undisciplined and more concerned about enjoying life than turning his attention to serious questions. To his amazement and stupefaction, however, Dietrich heard that the very moment his friend was hit by a bullet he recovered his faith. Transported to his home, although suffering agonizing pains, he had become "a new man". He immediately requested that a lawyer be called and dictated a statement that his little daughter, Margarete (nicknamed Mücki), who was almost eight years old, should receive a Catholic education.

Overwhelmed by the unexpected, tragic news, Dietrich rushed over to Hermann's home, where he had gone so often during his teenage years. Hermann had just received the sacrament of Extreme Unction, and as Dietrich entered the dying man's room the latter exclaimed, "How am I to express the bliss I have experienced upon receiving the Sacrament of the Dying? All the joys I have experienced in my life up to now are just dust and ashes by comparison." One could see on his face that he was in physical agony. The pains were so severe that he was tearing his bed sheets with his teeth. And yet he radiated joy and peace. His face seemed transfigured with a totally new expression. His conversion was so deep and so radical that it immediately brought forth its fruits. In the course of recent months, he had been feuding with his mother and sisters. With Christian love, he begged them for forgiveness. His one overwhelming concern was to speak about Christ and His Church, to give vent to his longing for the supernatural and the sacred. All his thoughts were now centered on his newly-found faith. He begged Dietrich to come to him as often as possible so that he could speak with him about the greatness and beauty of the Catholic faith.

Dietrich witnessed very many conversions in his life, but Hermann's conversion stands out as bordering on the miraculous. Within seconds, like Saint Paul in Damascus, Hermann was truly "reborn". All his natural lovableness, far from being lost, was purified and elevated to the much higher plane of Christian love.

Shattered by this experience, Dietrich rushed home to share the news with Gretchen, who also was deeply moved. But it was clear that the wounded man was doomed. A severe infection developed, and on June 16, six weeks after the Communist *Putsch*, Hermann died, entrusting his despairing wife and his little daughter to Dietrich von Hildebrand.

Marguerite was in such a state of despair (she loved her husband to distraction) that everyone feared she would take her life. As a matter of fact, it was her firm intention to do so. But with God's grace, Dietrich succeeded in convincing her that if she were to take this fatal step, she would forfeit forever every chance of seeing her beloved husband again in another world. On the other hand, if she followed his example, she would one day be reunited with him in the joy of heaven. Grace conquered, and some eight weeks afterward, on August 13, 1919, Marguerite Solbrig was received into the Roman Catholic Church.

Those weeks were physically exhausting for Dietrich. He had taken up his teaching at the university, and he was working intensely on his courses. He was also instructing Marguerite in the faith and giving her every free moment that he had, even until late in the night, for she desperately needed help. Not only was he instructing her, but he was also consoling her and comforting her. He hardly got any sleep at all. But what a joy it was to be instrumental in bringing another great soul into the Ark of Holy Church. Marguerite's conversion was to bear great fruit. From that moment on, her faith became the very core of her life. There are such moments in life when grace becomes tangible, when the believer is given a taste of a reality that usually rests totally on faith. Hermann's death was a source of deep grief and, at the same time, something of a triumph. Indeed, "I tell you, there will be more joy in heaven over one sinner who repents than over ninety-nine righteous persons who need no repentance" (Lk 15:7). Although Dietrich had lost a dear friend, he had confidence that Hermann had died in an admirable disposition of faith and resignation to God's will and every reason to hope that heaven had received one more citizen.

Marguerite's gratitude toward the friend of her youth never abated. Through her devotion, her selflessness, and her faithfulness she more than repaid Dietrich, whom God had used as an instrument to bring her into the Church. She eventually became his secretary in Munich and then in Vienna, where she worked actively on his anti-Nazi newspaper from 1934 to 1938.

Dietrich's university career then began in earnest. From the very start, this vibrant young professor—so different from his conventional colleagues—attracted many followers. He was decidedly not like the typical stiff and reserved German professor. His Italian ways, his spontaneity, and his unconventional manner, however, were not always appreciated by several of his colleagues. He refused to divide his life into compartments and to yield to the "spirit of the university", which expected professors to be pure intellects once they stepped onto its sacred grounds. Moreover, Dietrich was a Catholic, and he could not understand why he should have to leave his faith at the university gates. He never used his faith as an argument for a position that he was defending, but he had discovered how deeply faith can enlarge and deepen one's intellectual horizon. It fecundates reason, enriches it, and enables it to perceive nuances and questions that remain veiled to those who have never received that unfathomable gift. Dietrich von Hildebrand was experientially convinced that faith, far from being an obstacle to intellectual pursuits, actually liberates and purifies the human mind, so deeply affected by original sin.

Dietrich made a point of honoring those of his students who were priests by giving them precedence when entering a room. One of his colleagues, noticing that he was upsetting university rules, challenged his behavior. "Why do you let a student of yours pass in front of you?" he inquired. The young professor, baffled by the question, answered, "Because this student happens to be a priest." That answer did not satisfy his colleague, who, although a Catholic, did not view the anointing of the priest's hands as giving a man a dignity superior to that of "Herr Professor", one who had earned a Ph.D. "That may be," the colleague retorted, "but he has no doctorate." To the ardent young convert, this attitude was a source of grief. He saw more and more how severely the supernatural sense of these conventional Catholics had been eroded. The concerns that Professor Baeumker had had about him were justified. Dietrich von Hildebrand was not going to conform to the conventional mold of a German professor, and this "revolutionary" attitude threatened to jeopardize his career.

After the publication of *Purity and Virginity*, a fellow professor addressed Dietrich in the following words: "Dear Colleague. May I give you a friendly piece of advice. If you want to ascend in the hierarchy of the University, do not write books on such topics as purity. I would suggest that you do some research work on Sieger of Brabant: very little has been written about him, and it would establish your reputation as a scholar. A book on purity is clearly intended for high school girls." Fully understanding that his colleague meant well, Dietrich thanked him but informed him that whereas he had scant interest in the Belgian philosopher, he considered the virtue of purity to be of great importance. The professor seemed far from convinced.

In 1919, thanks to the fame that his book *Der Genius des Krieges und der deutsche Krieg* had gained for him, Scheler was appointed professor at the University of Cologne. In August, he came down to Munich, and the two friends had a long talk. Scheler told Dietrich that, in the Sociological Institute at Cologne University, he had an "enchanting assistant", whose name was Maria Scheu. This news upset Dietrich deeply; he feared that this infatuation could be a threat to Scheler's marriage to Märit. He could not help but say to him: "Max, Max, be careful. You know how dangerous women are for you." At this, Scheler became infuriated and retorted, "You seem incapable of understanding that this friendship is something totally new and radically different, incomparable to all my previous experiences. My relationship with Maria is so pure that I dare not hold her hand. She is so unworldly, so mystically inclined, that my mission toward her is to unveil the beauty of the created world." He then pulled a letter out of his pocket and read it to his friend. Dietrich could not help but notice how "enchanted" Scheler was, and once again he began to fear for him.

A few days later, the two friends took a walk in the English Garden (the beautiful park of Munich), and suddenly, Scheler said, "You know, at times, I have the feeling that I am like a naughty child, always running away from God toward an abyss. God, in His infinite mercy, has always pulled me back and prevented me from falling into it. But I fear, I fear, that one day I shall run too far, and He will no longer rescue me."

These words shook Dietrich to the very depth of his being, and his prayers for his friend intensified. He had a premonition that this exceptionally talented man was heading for serious trouble.

In February 1920, Dietrich went to Rome for the second time. Once again, mention must be made of his love for the country of his birth, a love that his conversion had only deepened. Before, he had loved Italy. Now, he loved Catholic Italy. It was deeply marked by Catholic culture, Catholic tradition, and the Catholic ethos. He knew that many of the Italian people did not live up to the demands of their faith; but, in spite of deplorable weaknesses, the essence of the people remained marked by their Catholic tradition. They were "classical" in the sense that Dietrich was to give to this term in his book *Liturgy and Personality*.[27] They understood the importance of tradition; they valued marriage and the family. They enjoyed a soundness of views on the most important problems of human life. And, on the whole, they were not burdened by artificial problems and feelings. They were "human" in the good, and the not-so-good, sense of this term.

Now that the doors of Italy, closed during the long war, were opened again, Dietrich was always able to find valid reasons for crossing the Brenner and staying in that country where he felt so totally at home. Until 1937, he went to Italy every single year, usually more than once, and spent his vacations there.

The ostensible reason for Dietrich's trip to Rome in 1920 was a distressing matter of family business. Because Adolf von Hildebrand was a Swiss citizen, his properties in Italy (five houses, four in Florence and one at Forte dei Marmi on the western Italian seashore) had been protected from

---

[27] *Liturgy and Personality* (New York: Longmans, Green, 1940; Manchester, N.H.: Sophia Institute Press, 1986, 1993), pp. 147–61.

expropriation. But at the very end of the war, they were all confiscated by the Italian government. The reason for this change of policy was that a Swiss citizen had been caught spying for Germany in Italy. The Italian government then decided that Swiss citizens who held dual citizenship—both Swiss and German—were to be treated as enemy aliens.

Lisl's husband, Christopher Brewster, the American-turned-Italian-citizen, hated Germany. As soon as he was informed of this new regulation, he rushed to the Italian administration in Florence, and informed them that his father-in-law's properties were no longer under the protection of the law. (Had he said nothing, it is most likely that Adolf von Hildebrand would have kept all his properties. Given the sloppiness of the Italian bureaucracy and its tendency to procrastinate, it is unlikely that they would have made a move before the armistice, which was only a few weeks away.) The very next day, San Francesco, the three houses on the campo, and the von Hildebrand villa in Forte dei Marmi were seized.

Adolf von Hildebrand decided to appeal the government's confiscation of his property and sent his son to Italy to oversee the suit. As soon as Dietrich arrived in Rome, he hired a lawyer to defend his father's interests. The suit dragged on for several years, but all legal efforts proved to be of no avail.[28]

On the way to Rome, Dietrich met Lisl in Florence, and she accompanied him to the Eternal City. It was the first time that they had seen each other since Dietrich's conversion. Now both were members of the Holy Church, and their deep affection for each other was much deepened, having its

[28] Later these houses were put up for sale by the state. Lisl Brewster and Vivi Baltus, who were Italian and Belgian citizens, respectively, received their share back. Christopher Brewster bought San Francesco (which today is still in the hands of his heirs) and two of the houses on the campo at a very low price. Georges Baltus, Vivi's husband, bought one house on the campo and the von Hildebrands' villa at Forte dei Marmi.

roots in their love for Christ and His Church. They took a train down to Rome. The train was considerably delayed, and the travelers were becoming restless and impatient. But the brother and sister, totally absorbed in spiritual exchange, looked so radiant and happy that a fellow traveler remarked: "For lovers, time is never long."

Thanks to Lisl's spiritual director, Msgr. Faberi, she and Dietrich obtained the great privilege of having a private audience with the Pontiff, Benedict XV. For Dietrich it was an overwhelming experience. His faith was so deep, his love for the Church as the Bride of Christ so ardent, and his belief that the Holy Father truly represented Christ on this earth so rooted in his soul, that the thought of seeing him in person moved him to the very depth of his being. The night before the audience, he dreamed of the privilege he was about to receive and woke up sobbing. He saw the Roman Catholic Church with the eyes of faith, and he suffered much because of the secularistic and sociological view that many Catholics adopt toward her.

Benedict XV received the two converts in his library and was pleasantly surprised to find out that Italian had been their first language. But whereas Lisl was perfectly at ease with the Pontiff (for nothing ever intimidated her), her brother was so overwhelmed that he was speechless. Every thought that came to his mind struck him as insignificant, unworthy of the venerable person he was addressing. The Holy Father turned to Lisl and asked her to speak in his stead. "Your brother strikes me as a bit timid", he said. Lisl then enthusiastically told the Holy Father that her brother had written a beautiful article entitled "The New World of Christianity", and she praised it highly. Dietrich blushed that his first contribution to Catholic literature should be mentioned to the head of the Roman Catholic Church in such glowing terms. He was more at ease when, in 1921, on the occasion of the seven-hundredth anniversary of the foundation of the Third Order of Saint Francis, he had another audience with the Pontiff, this time accompanied by Gretchen, Siegfried Hamburger, and the dear friend Giulia Citerio (German by birth but married to an Italian) whose ardent faith had played an important role in his conversion. It was on this occasion that he gave a talk in the church of Dodici Santi Apostoli in Rome. Later it was published in a book on Saint Francis and translated into Italian by Giulia Citerio.[29]

In the autumn of 1920, a great event for the von Hildebrand family took place when Walter Braunfels' opera *Die Vögel* (based on Aristophanes' comedy *The Birds*) had its premiere in Munich. Its performance was directed by Bruno Walter.[30] The success was resounding. Bruno Walter truly understood the poetry and charm of this composition. The singers, particularly the soprano Ivogun, were outstanding, and the public was so enthusiastic that conductor, singers, and composer took many curtain calls. For Dietrich it was a very special joy. He had great admiration for his brother-in-law's talent, and it was the first time that it had received full recognition. He had wit-

[29] Dietrich von Hildebrand, "Der Geist unserer Zeit und das 700jährige Jubiläum des Dritten Ordens", in *Der Geist des hl. Franziskus und der Dritte Orden* (Munich: Theatiner-Verlag, 1921), pp. 1–7. The Italian translation appeared in *Lo Spirito di San Francesco e il Terz'Ordine Francescano* (Munich: Theatiner-Verlag, 1921), pp. 1–7. An English translation was published as *The Image of Christ* (Steubenville, Ohio: Franciscan University Press, 1993).

[30] Referring to this musical event, Bruno Walter writes in his biography, *Theme and Variations* (New York: Alfred A. Knopf, 1946), p. 235: "The most interesting production of my Munich period took place in the year 1920. It was Walter Braunfels' *Die Vögel*. Those who were privileged to hear Karl Erb's song of the nightingale from the treetop, and those who were cheered by the grotesque scenes and moved by the romantic ones, will surely remember with gratitude the poetic and ingenious transformation of Aristophanes' comedy into an opera. The composer was the son of the translator of Spanish dramas, Ludwig Braunfels, and the son-in-law of the sculptor Adolf Hildebrand."

nessed "an artistic birth", the moment when a great work is discovered and enters the public arena. Adolf von Hildebrand was not well enough to attend, but he rejoiced upon hearing that the performance had been so successful.[31]

Die Vögel was performed several times, but on one occasion Bruno Walter was unable to conduct and asked Walter Braunfels to take the baton. It happened that that very evening, another of Braunfels' works, *Variations on Berlioz*, was going to be performed at another concert hall for the first time, and the composer begged his brother-in-law Dietrich (known to be a marvelous *Klatscher*, someone who applauds with gusto) to attend the concert. When Dietrich was enthusiastic about a work, it was well nigh impossible for it to be a failure; his enthusiasm carried the public with him. Needless to say, even though he would have preferred to go to the opera, he agreed do his brother-in-law this favor.

Walter's new composition was also well received until suddenly, to everyone's amazement, a tall blond man stood up and shouted, "I protest against this Jewish music." [32] The denunciation triggered a tumult, and the man was ejected from the concert hall.

That was among the early overt manifestations of the hate campaign Hitler had started against the Jews, whom he blamed for the German defeat in 1918. It was the first time that Dietrich himself had come across anti-Semitism in Munich, and never before had he encountered such a shocking expression of it. It must be remembered, however, that Munich had been undergoing months of political unrest. In

[31] Walter Braunfels' *Die Vögel* is available on a CD recording that was a bestseller during 1998.

[32] Braunfels' father was Jewish. From a Nazi point of view, he was Jewish and therefore "contaminated". However, from a Jewish point of view, he was a *goy* (Gentile), as it is the mother who determines whether or not a child is a Jew.

November 1918, the Socialist Kurt Eisner had led a revolt in Munich. Further Communist uprisings took place in February and March of 1919, and on April 4 a Communist republic was established in Bavaria. It was overthrown on May 1. Eisner and several others at the forefront of these disturbances were of Jewish ancestry, and this fact was grist for Hitler's mill that he was using to further his political aims.

Dietrich was both outraged and upset by the incident at the concert hall. Before the First World War, "politicization" of the concert hall would have been inconceivable. However, both the Nazis and the Communists knew that propaganda through art could be a powerful political tool, and they spoke of "bourgeois art" or "proletarian art" as one way of infiltrating every layer of society with their poisonous ideology. This tactic went so far that the Nazis, once in power, introduced a distinction between "Aryan mathematics" and "Jewish mathematics"! This combination of stupidity and viciousness was too much for Dietrich von Hildebrand. From the outset of the Nazi movement, he had perceived not only its inanity (for the racist principles on which Nazism was based were obviously without foundation), but also its insidious malignity. The Nazi movement was thoroughly perverse, and it incorporated an anti-Christian ethos, which he opposed with his every skill. It was not a question of "right" or "left". It was a question of truth versus error; goodness versus crime and corruption.

After leaving the concert hall that night, Dietrich rushed over to confront the perpetrator of the scandal and told him that he should be ashamed of his behavior. He did not mince his words. Then Dietrich went home, deeply shaken, with a foreboding of worse to come. That such a thing could happen in Munich proved that a terrible disease had penetrated German society, and he knew it was his mission to alert his fellow citizens to the danger.

PART TWO

Every religious writer, or speaker, or teacher, who absents
himself from danger and is not present where it is, and
where the Evil has its stronghold, is a deceiver. . . .

—Søren Aabye Kierkegaard

Criminal actions offend God quite independently of
whether the victim is a Jew, a socialist, or a bishop.
Innocent blood cries to heaven.

—Dietrich von Hildebrand

S. A. Kierkegaard, *The Point of View for My Work as an Author* (New York:
Harper and Row, 1962), p. 59. Dietrich von Hildebrand did not know Kierkegaard's *Point of View* when he wrote the similar passage given above, but he
certainly lived up to the Danish philosopher's clarion call.

CHAPTER 4

Lengthening Shadows
1921–1933

Dietrich von Hildebrand turned thirty-two in October 1921. The years stretching between 1921 and 1933 were ones of constant activity, during which he enjoyed growing success as a professor, writer, and lecturer. Apart from his teaching at the university and his intense social life, Dietrich traveled extensively for both professional and personal reasons; he undertook these trips with his customary enthusiasm and his eagerness to gain enriching experiences. It was in many ways a remarkably happy and productive period in the philosopher's life.

And yet, as the 1920s progressed, it became clear to him that the then-gathering political forces would eventually threaten not only the beautiful existence he was enjoying in Munich but all of Germany, and possibly Europe itself. The lingering bitterness over the German defeat in the First World War and the disastrous effect on the German economy of war reparations had created a situation ripe for the emergence of the National Socialist movement, with its vicious policies of racial intolerance and military vengeance. The incident in the concert hall in the autumn of 1920 was merely the first rumble in a storm that was eventually to sweep across Europe, forcing Dietrich and his family to leave beloved Munich for the dangerous adventure of "waging war" with voice and pen on Hitlerism.

In 1921, Dietrich witnessed the death of both his parents. On January 18, 1921, he had the deep sorrow of losing his father. This great artist, whose life had been so happy, who had received so many talents, whose vital strength and temperament were such that he always radiated joy and optimism, had mellowed with age. God was slowly preparing him for the Calvary of the last months of his life, when, affected by a stroke, he not only lost his vitality but suffered from an awareness that his mind was clouding.[1] The story of this slow, unrelenting decline, which darkened the last months of his life, is not a theme of this book. But one incident that took place shortly before Adolf von Hildebrand's death illustrates the tragedy of human mortality. Because he and his wife were both ailing, their children decided that they should no longer sleep in the same room. It was indispensable for Irene's health to separate them, because Adolf's restlessness prevented her from sleeping. The separation upset Adolf deeply, but they told him that Irene had had to go to the hospital for treatment. Adolf was beside himself and kept calling for her. His love for her manifested itself with an intensity that was deeply moving. So, one day, his children, shaken by his despair, told him that she had returned from the hospital and that he could see her. His joy was overwhelming. He could not get dressed fast enough. Somehow he had imagined that as soon as he saw her dear face again, his mind would clear. He literally ran to her

[1] See Isolde Kurz, *Der Meister von San Francesco* (Tübingen: Rainer, Wunderlich Verlag, n.d.), pp. 8off.

bedroom, and he did experience a moment of rapture when he saw her—but, after a while, he understood that the increasing darkness into which his mind was sinking had not been alleviated. One day, he uttered the tragic words *"Adolf geht fort"* (Adolf is going away), referring to himself in the third person, as children do.

The death of his father shook Dietrich very deeply. He recognized with luminous clarity who his father was—a man of unusual nobility, of great goodness and generosity, always ready to help others, a man who possessed a matchless objectivity, who never experienced any difficulty in admiring artistic accomplishments even in people who considered themselves his rivals. In spite of all the honors that were bestowed upon him, he remained modest. Shortly before the outset of World War I, he had completed writing a magazine article critical of Auguste Rodin's works. When the war broke out, he wrote to the editor of the magazine, requesting him to refrain from publishing it, for he did not want to deprecate a French artist when France and Germany were at war. To do so would have given the impression that his criticism was tainted by political opportunism.

To Dietrich's great sorrow (though he fully realized that no one knows what takes place between the soul and its Creator at the awesome moment of death), Adolf never found the fullness of faith; but he was a deeply reverent man, reverent toward life and the mysteries of nature. It would not have crossed his mind to practice artificial birth control. He was deeply moved by the sight of a newborn. To interfere with the secrets of nature would have been abhorrent to him. He appreciated the gift of life and always looked at the positive side of things.

Dietrich now fully recognized the privilege that it was for him to be able to call such a man "father". He became keenly aware of the immense debt of gratitude he owed him and kept him in his daily prayers.

After the funeral, a celebration in honor of Adolf was held in Munich. It was attended by Archbishop Faulhaber,[2] who soon afterward was named cardinal and was later to become famous during the Second World War for his courageous stand against Nazism. When Dietrich thanked the archbishop for the honor he was bestowing on his family, His Excellency replied graciously that it was a matter of obligation to him to be present on such an occasion, as a sign of the great esteem he had for both Adolf and his son.

In September 1921, Dietrich's mother followed her husband to the grave. Dietrich was in the Rhineland for a talk when he received a telegram that she was close to death. He immediately canceled his lecture in Bonn and rushed back to Munich.[3]

---

[2] Michael von Faulhaber (1869–1952), consecrated archbishop of Munich and Freising in 1917, was named cardinal in 1921.

[3] To his amazement, Dietrich later found out through his friend Prelate Münch that the talk he had had to cancel in Bonn had been reviewed in a local newspaper. The gist of the review was as follows: "Von Hildebrand's talk was outstanding and brilliantly delivered, as expected, but it was clearly tainted by a certain gnosticism. Von Hildebrand belongs to the group of Germans who have been so deeply affected by the defeat of 1918 that they have become isolated. Their faces are pale and drawn, their blood circulates but slowly in their veins. They have clearly lost all vitality"—and so forth. The whole pretense of a "review" was so grotesque that Dietrich immediately wrote a letter of protest. Not only had he not given the talk, but all the ideas attributed to him were radically antithetical to his views. He hated gnosticism, and the German defeat had definitely not sapped his vitality. His letter was in fact published in the very newspaper that had originally printed the supposed review, but the editors added a note saying that the public would have been too disappointed had the talk of such an illustrious thinker been omitted in their report of the conference at which von Hildebrand was scheduled to speak. Hence it was a "legitimate journalistic license". This incident gives one an insight into the value of much of what is reported in and by the press. In light of it, Kierkegaard's remarks

Upon arriving in Stuttgart, Dietrich heard that Erzberger[4] had been assassinated. (He had also been in Stuttgart in June 1914 when Franz Ferdinand had been assassinated.) The political situation in Germany had become so unstable that assassinations were the fashion of the day. First Erzberger, then, in 1922, Rathenau.[5] The next victim was Ebert.[6]

When Dietrich, deeply shaken by all the sad news, arrived in Munich, he found his mother very weak but still conscious and resigned to God's will. She said to him, "I do not know whether God is calling me now, but I am equally ready to live or to die." To lose her was for Dietrich another great source of grief—she who had loved him so deeply and so ardently, who had given him such a happy youth, who was such a warm, lovable, and talented personality. As far as we know, her relationship to God remained weak, but it is to be hoped that the mother of six children who became such ardent Roman Catholics will, through God's mercy, receive some credit from a merciful Lord. In losing her, Dietrich fully recognized what he owed her and how tragic it was that their relationship since 1911 had no longer had the depth, the

---

about journalism gain their full import: "If I were a father and had a daughter who was seduced, I should not despair over her; I would hope for her salvation. But if I had a son who became a journalist, and continued to be one for five years, I would give him up" (*A Kierkegaard Anthology*, ed. Robert Bretall [Princeton, N.J.: Princeton University Press, 1951], p. 431).

[4] Matthias Erzberger (1875–1921), a German statesman, had been an opponent of German military policy and an advocate of peace without annexations in World War I. He was shot by former officers of the army.

[5] Walther Rathenau (1867–1922), German industrialist of Jewish extraction, had organized German war industries during World War I and had dealt with reparations as Minister of Reconstruction in 1921. He was assassinated by reactionaries soon after becoming foreign minister in 1922.

[6] Friedrich Ebert (1871–1925), German Social Democratic leader, was the first President of the German Reich (1919–1925). As President, he had suppressed the attempt of Hitler and Ludendorff to establish a dictatorship in Bavaria in the *Putsch* of 1923.

glow, and the intimacy that had formerly been theirs. He reproached himself bitterly for not having shown her a greater love now that, having become a Catholic, he should have been able to love her better and more deeply. Throughout the rest of his life, he kept her also in his daily prayers.

According to Irene von Hildebrand's last will, Dietrich and Zusi were granted the right to move into the von Hildebrand mansion. Neither of them inherited it, but they were entitled to inhabit it as long as they pleased, with the responsibility of paying the taxes on the property and covering all expenses related to it. If the house was ever sold, the payment was to be divided equally among the six heirs.

A few weeks after his mother's death, Dietrich, Gretchen, and Franzi (now aged nine) moved into the Hildebrand house at 23 Maria Theresia Strasse. They occupied the ground floor; Dietrich's third sister, Zusi, her husband, Fedja, and their children moved to the second floor. Fedja Georgii, being a sculptor, used his father-in-law's studio. This move enabled Dietrich soon to make of his parents' home a center of Catholic life in Munich.

Shortly afterward, an unfortunate episode clouded the friendship between Dietrich and Archbishop Faulhaber. Dietrich had made the acquaintance of a young Jesuit named Otto Karrer. They had become friends, and the young philosopher had great confidence in this priest, who seemed to exude an authentic supernatural spirit. For this reason, he asked him to prepare Adolf Reinach's sister, Pauline, for her baptism. Soon her sister-in-law, Anneliese Scheunemann, who had married Heinrich Reinach (Adolf's younger brother), followed suit. But one day, out of the blue, while Dietrich was practicing Gregorian Chant with a group of friends, a man named Scheller rushed in and broke the terrible news that Father

Karrer had left the Jesuit order and had entered a Protestant seminary in Erlangen. That someone for whom he had nurtured such deep respect and sympathy, and in whom he had placed such confidence, should have left the Church deeply disturbed Dietrich. He was beside himself with grief. Impulsive as he was, he said, "This is the last thing I would have expected from Father Karrer. Had I been told that Father Lippert [for whom he had a strong veneration] had left the order and the Church, I would not have been more amazed and shattered." Scheller hastened to repeat this remark to various people, and finally it reached Cardinal Faulhaber's ears, but by then it was distorted. Scheller reported that von Hildebrand's response had been, "Had this happened to Father Lippert, it would not have surprised me, but never would I have expected this from Father Karrer!" Quite understandably, the cardinal was shocked and informed Dietrich of his displeasure. But, much as Dietrich tried to explain, he could not convince His Eminence that his words had been totally distorted. From that moment on, Cardinal Faulhaber was more reserved toward him.

There is no doubt that, in his naïveté and impulsiveness, Dietrich lacked worldly prudence. He was so accurate when repeating the words of others that it never occurred to him that many people take liberties in reporting conversations. Moreover, he did not know that he was the subject of envy (he himself was never tempted to envy) and that many people were looking for an opportunity to "dethrone" a man they thought of as the cardinal's favorite.

Shortly after Father Karrer's desertion, Dietrich paid a visit to the nuncio, Msgr. Pacelli, whom he had briefly met with Scheler in 1917. Inevitably, the topic of Father Karrer's apostasy was raised, and the nuncio, who was as shaken by the news as Dietrich had been, said to him, "I can imagine that a Catholic may lose his faith, but I cannot conceive that he should decide to become a Protestant. Of course, it would be psychologically understandable had he fallen in love with a divorced Protestant woman and wanted to marry her, something the Church does not allow. But this does not seem to be the case. That Father Karrer should abandon the Roman Catholic Church, which possesses the fullness of revealed truth, in order to embrace a religion that has nothing to offer that is not part and parcel of Catholicism, is incomprehensible to me."

Not much later, Dietrich saw Father Erich Przywara, S.J., who was a great friend of Father Karrer's. Father Przywara told him, to his overwhelming joy, that he had gone to Erlangen in civilian clothes, had managed to see the ex-Father Karrer, and had succeeded in convincing the latter to leave with him that very day. Father Karrer was thus brought back to the Church. He had to do penance in Beuron for a year before he was again given permission to say Mass. He then became a secular priest, and later he devoted much time to the study of Cardinal Newman. Dietrich visited him in Lucerne in the early sixties.

In 1924, Dietrich and Gretchen decided to hold "afternoons" in the beautiful living room of the Maria Theresia Strasse,[7] a room that soon became famous in and around Munich. The purpose of these "afternoons" was to focus on a religious or philosophical question. A speaker gave a brief presentation that was then discussed at length by the guests. Everyone interested was welcome. The guest list was diverse, including high Church dignitaries, such as Msgr. Preysing;[8] leading

---

[7] See Kurz, *Der Meister von San Francesco*, p. 79, for a description of the living room in this house, which received so many illustrious guests.

[8] Konrad von Preysing (1880–1950) was the bishop of Berlin from 1935 and a leader of Catholic opposition to the ecclesiastical policy of the Nazi regime.

intellectuals of the day—artists, theologians, and philosophers (such as Prelate Grabmann, Father Przywara, and Father van Steenbergen); aristocrats, such as Archduchess Maria Josepha, mother of Emperor Charles of Austria, Infanta Maria de la Paz, wife of Prince Ludwig Ferdinand of Bavaria, and Count d'Ormesson; family members, friends, acquaintances, and ordinary working people. The number of those attending was at times one hundred and eighty. Holding these events meant a lot of work for Gretchen, but she proved to be a particularly gracious and talented hostess, loved by everyone. She truly was in her element and enjoyed these afternoons immensely. Not only was she doing that for which she was especially talented, but she became acquainted with many people worth knowing in the religious, intellectual, and artistic fields.

In addition to his duties as *Privat Dozent* at the University of Munich, Dietrich embarked in the early 1920s on a writing career devoted to philosophical subjects and timely questions. He proved to be extremely prolific. He had been a Catholic since 1914 and had been continually deepening his knowledge of the faith, reading extensively from Catholic literature. His first published article on a Catholic subject, "The New World of Christianity" (1920), was indicative of the bent his thought was taking and the harbinger of a series of works. It was soon followed by several articles on Saint Francis of Assisi. From that time on, Dietrich's greatest joy and special mission was to write about the transformation that the supernatural works in man's fallen nature. Throughout the decade, Dietrich kept up a steady flow of publications, often revising talks he had given into more polished articles or books.[9] Two of his more important works, *Purity*

[9] More detailed information about von Hildebrand's literary output during this period is in Adolf Preis's "Hildebrand-Bibliographie", *Aletheia* 5 (1992): 363–430.

and Virginity (1927) and *Marriage* (1929), had their origins in
talks delivered to meetings of the Katholische Akademikerverband (Association of Catholic Academicians), founded by
Prelate Franz Xavier Münch,[10] which sponsored Catholic
conferences throughout Germany. Prelate Münch was a talented and cultivated man, anxious to show that religious life,
far from denigrating human values, incorporated and transfigured them. Because the outlook of the Association was so
closely akin to Dietrich's, he took an active part in its pro-
grams.[11]

Max Scheler's greatest gift to Dietrich was to open up for
him the world of the supernatural; he had thereby made
available to his friend treasures that could only have originated from God Himself, for example, the mandate to love
one's enemies, which no human mind could have "invented".
No doubt, that sense of the supernatural was the crucial
factor that led to Dietrich's conversion. Now the unmerited
grace given him was blossoming in his soul and finding expression in his writings. Dietrich's friends often expressed the
wish that the entire Catholic clergy had been granted the
same sense for the inebriating taste of the supernatural. That
unmerited gift—for it was a pure gift—was the greatest source
of joy to Dietrich and, simultaneously, a source of sorrow
whenever he heard homilies lacking this sense. He met priests
and religious whose understanding of their faith was purely
conventional or purely traditional and, so to speak, crippled.
He was deeply saddened to know that many Christians tried
to "adapt" their faith to secular norms. He considered it his
mission to highlight, illumine, and revive the *sensus supra-*

---

[10] Münch (1883–1940), a theologian, had been general secretary of the
Verband since 1916.

[11] Von Hildebrand also served as president of the Katholische Akademikerverband foreign commission.

naturalis among German Catholics. All his books should be read with this factor in mind.[12]

As time went by, Dietrich was asked to lecture in various countries, including Czechoslovakia, Poland, Austria, Hungary, Italy, Spain, France, Belgium, Holland, Switzerland, and England. One trip, in 1929, deserves special mention. Dietrich had been invited to give conferences in Seville by the organization Pax Romana.[13] This invitation gave the passionate traveler a first taste of Spain, the homeland of Cervantes, whose *Don Quixote* had enchanted him since he was eleven years old. Unprejudiced as he was, eager to discover the genius and the flavor of each individual country, he enjoyed the trip immensely. He did not have occasion to go back to Spain until September 1940, when he traversed the country as a refugee fleeing from the clutches of Hitler. But what he saw of that great country sufficed to whet his appetite, and later, from 1954 to 1974, he visited Spain many times. Each time, he was more and more enchanted by its beauty, its sense of tradition and form, and its strong national characteristics. His lectures to the Pax Romana group in Seville in 1929 were

[12] Von Hildebrand's rejection of the philosophy of Father Pierre Teilhard de Chardin (1881–1955) is to be explained by the fact that the latter tended to blur the distinction between nature and supernature. The two thinkers met at Fordham University in the late 1940s, where Teilhard de Chardin was giving a talk. Much of what the Jesuit priest said was at loggerheads with von Hildebrand's concept of the supernatural, and he vigorously challenged the views of the famous French thinker. In the course of this discussion the latter exclaimed, "You are clearly a disciple of St. Augustine, who was responsible for this most unfortunate distinction made between nature and supernature." To be called a disciple of St. Augustine was to von Hildebrand the greatest compliment, but in Father Teilhard de Chardin's view it was otherwise. See *The Trojan Horse in the City of God* (Manchester, N.H.: Sophia Institute Press, 1993), appendix.

[13] Pax Romana was founded in Switzerland in 1921 as an international movement for Catholic students.

eventually to play a providential role in his escape from France eleven years later.

Because of his prolific intellectual activity, Dietrich needed a typist. He bought a typewriter and appointed a young man as his secretary. One day, the latter came to him visibly perturbed. Dietrich inquired into the cause of his agitation, and his secretary confessed that he had done something terrible. Dietrich immediately feared that the young man had sinned against the sixth commandment, and, having such a deep understanding of the mystery and sacredness of the sexual sphere, he was shaken at the thought. To his great relief, the young man "confessed" that, in need of money, he had pawned the typewriter! Dietrich's joy was such that he embraced the culprit and immediately gave him the money necessary to redeem the machine. This episode is typical of him. Even though the young man's action was reprehensible, the harm done could easily be repaired. Just as there is a positive hierarchy of virtues, there is a negative hierarchy of sins, and Dietrich appreciated that impurity is a graver sin than dishonesty, because the sexual sphere is not simply physical or biological but affects the human person very deeply. One can imagine the gratitude of the young man, who had expected bitter reproaches.

In addition to giving lectures to various Catholic groups, Dietrich frequently went to Italy to visit his sister Lisl, who was now the mistress of San Francesco. Not only did he wish to see family and friends, but he was still embroiled in the legal case his father had brought against the Italian government for confiscating his Italian properties. On one such visit, Dietrich resolved to combine that duty with a visit to Padre Pio.[14] Prelate Münch and another friend decided to join him.

---

[14] Blessed Padre Pio, born Francesco Forgione (1887–1968), was a Capuchin priest who received the stigmata in 1918. The donations he received when he

Dietrich had heard much about the saintly Capuchin who, like Saint Francis of Assisi, had received the stigmata, and he understandably longed to see someone who had the reputation of being a living saint. Although today San Giovanni Rotondo has become famous, even cursed by commercialism, in 1921 it was a small, insignificant, poor Italian village, and Padre Pio was little known. The travelers went to the one "hotel" of the place, pompously called La Bella Venezia, a dirty, miserable inn. In order to get to the second floor of the inn, one had to climb a ladder leaning against an outside wall. The proprietor, however, with the shamelessness some display toward tourists, charged them the price of a room at a first-class hotel in Rome. All this did not matter in the least to Dietrich, who considered it a privilege to have this chance to see Padre Pio, worth any inconvenience he might encounter. Fortunately, the day the group arrived, there were hardly any other visitors, and the three pilgrims could meet Padre Pio personally, go to confession to him, attend his Mass, and see the wounds that pierced his hands. The impression was overwhelming. Moreover, Padre Pio combined two traits that seem incompatible—a full presence, particularly evident in the way he greeted children, and a radical "other-worldliness". One felt powerfully that his gaze was continually fixed on things invisible. It was a great grace for the travelers, who departed San Giovanni moved and grateful.

Given his warm heart and Mediterranean sociability, friendship was very important in Dietrich's life, and the 1920s saw the flourishing of many new relationships. Two very different friendships stand out, one from the University of Munich, the other from the ranks of the Church.

---

became famous enabled him to build a hospital for the sick in San Giovanni Rotondo, near Foggia. In addition to priestly ministry, Padre Pio was also active in organizing prayer groups.

From the beginning of his teaching career, Dietrich had the joy of having several talented and devoted students. In 1923, however, he met a young man who immediately drew his attention. His name was Balduin Schwarz. He came from Hanover, and his brother, Reinhardt, was studying music with Walter Braunfels. Soon Dietrich established a personal relationship with him. They took walks together through the English Garden in Munich, and it was not long before Dietrich viewed Balduin as a spiritual son. Balduin was not only very intelligent, he also had an attractive and lovable personality, a great sense of humor, a profound love of music, and an openness to all cultural values. He was also a committed Catholic. In 1923, and again in 1938, he assisted Dietrich during his flight from the Nazis. Indeed, Balduin remained a great friend throughout Dietrich's life. He emigrated to the United States in 1941 with his wife, Leni, and their son, Stephan. They lived in an apartment house in New York, at 448 Central Park West, until 1964, when Balduin was appointed professor at the University of Salzburg.

Another notable friendship that Dietrich was privileged to make in the early 1920s was with Eugenio Pacelli,[15] who had earlier been named papal nuncio first in Munich and then in Berlin. At the time of their first brief meeting in 1917, accompanied by Max Scheler, Dietrich was struck by the sublimity, the sense of the supernatural, and the intelligence of this priest, who was destined to become a successor of Saint Peter as Pope Pius XII. Nuncio Pacelli, Dietrich thought, was truly a "Prince of the Church".

A few years after that first visit, the friendship that developed between the two men was to be a most enriching one for Dietrich during the early twenties. It was a special grace

---

[15] Eugenio Pacelli (1876–1958), Nuncio in Munich, then in Berlin, was Cardinal Secretary of State from 1930 to 1939, and Pope from 1939 to 1958.

for the young convert to be granted an intimate glance into the life of the Church, to meet someone who truly lived up to her divine teaching. Nuncio Pacelli combined all the charm of the Roman aristocrat—with his culture, his sense for tradition, his refinement, and his knowledge of languages—with a supernatural note that gave all these natural values their true worth.

It was a joy and a privilege for Dietrich and Gretchen to entertain this great Church prelate in their home in the Maria Theresia Strasse. There Nuncio Pacelli met Dietrich's brother-in-law Fedja Georgii (Zusi's husband), who was also to become Msgr. Pacelli's friend. (When Pacelli became pope, Fedja went in and out of the Vatican at will.) Nuncio Pacelli also made the acquaintance of Walter Braunfels, Bertele's husband, and once again a warm friendship developed.

To his delight, Dietrich discovered that Nuncio Pacelli shared his passion for music, especially for Wagner's opera *Tristan und Isolde*. Dietrich made it a point to be present at sitting sessions when Fedja worked on a bust of Nuncio Pacelli, while Walter played the piano to entertain their noble guest. *Tristan und Isolde* was often on the program, and Dietrich could read on Nuncio Pacelli's face how deeply moved he was by that sublime piece of music.

This friendship brought Dietrich more than one blessing. He wanted to shed light on the transformation of human life and human values through the "holy invasion" of the supernatural into man's earthly existence. He always placed love at the center of his life, regarding nothing—career, profession, research—to be more important than love and marriage. In reading Catholic literature and listening to homilies, however, Dietrich was struck by the fact that emphasis was usually on procreation, rarely if ever on the loving bond that should exist between the spouses.

In 1922, Prelate Münch invited Dietrich to give a talk on marriage at a conference the Association of Catholic Intellectuals was sponsoring in Ulm. The theme was close to his heart. His key insight was a distinction he introduced between the meaning of marriage—a union of love—and the purpose of marriage—procreation. He lamented the fact that the meaning of marriage had been much neglected in the past, if not in the official teaching of the Church, definitely in numerous homilies and then-current textbooks of Catholic moral teaching.

Conscious that he was breaking new ground, and anxious never to say anything that was not in perfect harmony with the teachings of the Church, Dietrich decided to expound his views to his friend Nuncio Pacelli. He often later recalled the pleasant long walks he had taken with him along the Isar River in Munich, discussing his ideas. To his delight, Msgr. Pacelli endorsed his views and encouraged him to publish them.[16]

Thanks to Pacelli's encouragement, he worked intensely on the text of his talk, which was a resounding success. Soon afterward, he enlarged and deepened his lecture and later published it under the title *Marriage*.[17]

*

[16] Von Hildebrand was clearly breaking new ground. He was soon followed by l'Abbé Violet in France. Deep as his views were, and great as his success was, nevertheless some narrow-minded Catholics considered his ideas to be "dangerous". I remember vividly the icy reception that Dietrich received in Salamanca in 1954, when, with a group of American students, he was visiting the Dominican convent in this beautiful city. When he mentioned his name, the prior looked at him with horror and said, "Are you this 'heretic' who has introduced the dangerous view that love is of essential importance in marriage?"

[17] *Die Ehe* (Munich: J. Müller; Verlag Ars Sacra, 1929); English trans., *Marriage* (Manchester, N.H.: Sophia Institute Press, 1983). Earlier, Nuncio Pacelli had written Dietrich a letter congratulating him on the publication of *Purity and Virginity* in 1927. It was one of many letters Dietrich received about this book, which also inspired many persons to enter religious life.

The decade that was to be so fruitful for some of Dietrich's friendships witnessed the end of one that he had cherished since he was a young man, namely, his friendship with Max Scheler. After the latter moved to Cologne to start teaching at the university, Dietrich had been alarmed by Max's growing infatuation with his assistant, Maria Scheu. This apprehension was confirmed when, soon after his father's death in 1921, Dietrich went to Cologne to give a talk at the Katholische Akademikerverband.

Märit Scheler fetched him at the station and greeted him warmly. She had invited him to stay at the Scheler home. It was only the second time that he had been the Schelers' guest since their marriage in 1912. During this visit, he learned that Maria Scheu had become the most important person in Max's life. Nevertheless, the relationship between Max and Märit remained friendly.

Scheler was expecting a visit from Wolfgang, his son by Amélie,[18] and had asked Dietrich to fetch the young man at the station. Dietrich, having met Wolfgang a few years earlier, would be able to recognize him, whereas his father would not. Of course, Dietrich agreed to this request. No doubt his presence at the Schelers' eased a difficult and tense situation. But in spite of Wolfgang's clearly neurotic traits, which he had inherited from his mother, Scheler found him "sweet".[19]

[18] As a boy, Wolfgang had been diagnosed as a psychopath. Dietrich had met him when he was working in Dr. Luxemburger's clinic during the war. Wolfgang was now about eighteen years of age, and Max had not seen him for years. Both he and Märit were apprehensive about this visit because Wolfgang had the reputation of being a kleptomaniac, pilfering whatever he could lay his hands on. Märit was concerned to protect her silverware from his grasp. According to Wilhelm Mader, Wolfgang, with his asocial tendencies, was—like many other disturbed persons—murdered by the Nazis in Oranienburg in the late thirties.

[19] Scheler once wrote that his son had inherited all the bad characteristics of both his father and mother, but none of their positive traits; see Wilhelm Mader, *Scheler*, p. 100.

Wolfgang stayed for only a few days, and then he was sent to a psychiatrist in Cleve, a Dr. Bergman, himself a member of the Association of Catholic Academicians.[20]

After giving his talk at the Katholische Akademikerverband, Dietrich was invited, with Max and Märit, by a Mrs. Koppel, to her house. There Dietrich made the acquaintance of Maria Scheu. The contrast between the people who had attended his talk at the Katholische Akademikerverband and Mrs. Koppel's guests, who had come to hear a talk given by Scheler, was striking. The latter were intellectual snobs, with a bohemian note of amorality that Dietrich found depressing. Some of the members of the Katholische Akademikerverband tended to be a bit "plain", but on the whole they were sound, believing, practicing Catholics. Even though Dietrich was not completely at ease with them, he much preferred them to the pretentious intellectuals enamored of *Schoengeistigkeit* ("affecting literary ways").

Scheler spoke at this gathering about metaphysical problems, and, as always, his talk was on a high level. His listeners, however, seemed more interested in brilliance of expression than in truth. All in all, this atmosphere was unpalatable to Dietrich, in spite of its intellectual high tone.

The political views of von Hildebrand and Scheler continued to diverge during the twenties. Italian fascism was aborning in 1922, and Scheler, returning from a trip to Nervi in northern Italy with both Märit and Maria Scheu, stopped in Munich. He told Dietrich how impressed he was by the dynamism of the new political movement. It had become a "historical reality" that fascinated Scheler. This political stance

[20] Dr. Bergman later told Dietrich that, one day, he and his wife had invited an important Dutch lady to their home; the young Scheler (who combined unpredictableness with arrogance) suddenly exclaimed, "Are all Dutch women as ugly as you are?" One can imagine the embarrassment of the hosts!

was to his friend a puzzle. To Dietrich, that something was "dynamic", "interesting", or "new" was totally irrelevant. From the start, he had strong reservations about Fascism. The questions of true or false, just or unjust, good or evil, remained primary concerns for Dietrich, and Fascism did not pass his test. Scheler, on the other hand, let himself be captivated by the dynamism of historical events. Again and again, it must be said how deeply these traits in Scheler saddened Dietrich. He had the premonition that not only was Scheler moving away from the Church, but that he was likely, to assuage his conscience, to turn against the Holy Bride of Christ, whose teachings condemned his "life-style".

Indeed, the tragedy of Scheler's life was coming to a head. In 1922, Dietrich received a letter from Scheler informing him that he wanted his marriage with Märit annulled and that he was taking the steps necessary to achieve this goal. The gist of the letter was as follows: "I can no longer stand to feel myself stained. I am continually being unfaithful to Märit, and I have been unfaithful to her from the very beginning of our marriage. In Maria I have found the woman who can save me. I want to live and die in the Holy Church in which I believe and which I love. I want to die a faithful Catholic. This is not possible as long as I remain married to Märit." He then went on to ask Dietrich, as the ex-fiancé of his wife, to further his case by cooperating with proceedings for the annulment of his marriage.

Dietrich had no choice. He refused to collaborate with Scheler's wishes; by now he knew so well how talented Scheler was at lying that he feared his moving words about his "attachment to the Church" were plainly a *captatio benevolentiae*, to win over his friend's assent. Dietrich did not hesitate. He took his pen and wrote Scheler a long letter telling him how heartbroken he was to hear that he wanted to terminate his marriage with Märit and that he could not possibly testify in his favor.

Soon after that, Scheler came to Munich, and once again the two friends discussed this crucial issue. Scheler still cared for Märit a great deal. He spoke lovingly about her and was clearly grieved at the thought that in divorcing her he would hurt her deeply. He firmly hoped that Märit would find someone else willing to marry her. A colleague of his was attracted to her, and Scheler had even encouraged Märit to accept his advances so that she would not be left alone. Dietrich begged his friend to pray ardently that his love for Märit might be revived, to which Scheler answered, "That is impossible, for I now love Maria. Such a prayer would militate against the very essence of love."

That was the last discussion Dietrich had with Max, who had played such an important role in his life. They still saw one another afterward, a few times, in Munich and in Cologne. Dietrich tried one more time to help his friend out of the morass into which he was falling, but Scheler would not listen. He accused Dietrich of lacking understanding for the "deep metaphysical significance" of his attachment to Maria— "because", said Scheler, "you are looking at the whole situation from the narrow point of view of the Church". A friendship between them was no longer possible; the chasm separating them had become too wide to bridge.

In the early twenties, Prelate Münch had told Dietrich that he had gone with Scheler to a place of pilgrimage called Kevelaer. The latter had told him that he wanted to pray there to find a solution to his marital problems. The shrine was very popular, and there always was a long line of faithful waiting to pray for a brief moment in front of the revered statue. When Scheler's turn came, he knelt for half an hour, absorbed in deep prayer. People waiting their turn were becoming irritated, for it was not proper for a single pilgrim to delay the flow for so long. Dr. Münch had been hopeful, however, that Scheler was opening his soul to God's will. To his bitter disappointment, when Scheler came out of the church, he told the prelate that, after praying ardently to the Mother of God, it had become crystal clear to him that he should marry Maria Scheu. Subjective wishes had triumphed.

In 1924, Scheler did marry Maria Scheu and thus broke with the Church. Sad to say, he then tried to sap Märit's faith by encouraging her to remarry outside the Church. Had Märit done so, Max's conscience would have been assuaged, knowing that his abandoned wife would be provided for. But Märit loved Scheler to the end of her life and refused to marry again.

From the moment of his marriage to Maria, a radical change took place in Scheler's writings. That great and brilliant mind, torn by insoluble personal problems, began to trample on the most profound insights he had had in the past. To his former friend, this was heartrending. Although Scheler remained brilliant to the end, this brilliance became shallow, and Dietrich saw it as but a tinkling cymbal, no longer capable of conveying the beauty of truth. He was convinced that only when intellectual brilliance is put at the service of truth does it deserve our admiration.

Scheler was bound to die young. His life-style was such that no human temperament could sustain it for long. He smoked between sixty and eighty cigarettes a day, and he drank heavily. In fact, he did everything possible to exhaust the vitality that had been his.

In May 1928, upon arriving in Frankfurt, where he had been offered a full professorship, Scheler had a stroke. He called Märit to his deathbed—Märit, whom he still loved in a corner of his torn heart and with whom he had continued to correspond. Deep down, he had not totally betrayed the great love he had had for her. Lying in his hospital bed, he told Märit he had some deep and important insights he wanted to write down—but death caught up with him.

When Dietrich received the news that Max Scheler was no longer in this world, he grieved deeply. But the main source of his sorrow was that Scheler, as far as he knew, did not find his way back to God and His Church. Their long-lasting friendship had "died" in 1922, when Max sought to have his marriage annulled. Understandably, Dietrich could now express his affection for this tragic man only in his daily prayers for one who had helped so many to find their way to the Church but who, because of his undisciplined heart, had himself strayed from the path of peace.

After Scheler's death, a Catholic priest, apparently unaware that Scheler had been excommunicated, gave him a Catholic burial. The ironic oversight—Scheler having helped so many people into the Church—seemed to be a felicitous misunderstanding. God alone was to judge him. An important chapter in Dietrich's life was closed forever.

When Dietrich was asked to write several articles about his friend, the task appealed to him, even though he knew it would be difficult. On the one hand, he wished to express his deep-felt gratitude for what Scheler had given him—primarily, for having opened up to him the glory of God's revelation entrusted to the Holy Bride of Christ, the Church. He also wanted to give testimony to Scheler's genius, to the uniqueness of a mind that was so incredibly rich and deep. On the other hand, Dietrich could not, as some of Scheler's admirers intended to do, sing a hymn to Scheler's glory without mentioning the tragic turn his philosophy had taken during the last years of his life: *Amicus Plato; magis amica veritas*

(I am Plato's friend; but a greater friend to truth). He felt obliged to point out the weaknesses in Scheler's philosophy and the deplorable turn his thought had taken when he left the Church and turned away from Christ and, finally, from God Himself. From that time on, Scheler trampled on the magnificent insights he had had in his younger years, a tragic expression of his bad conscience. The later Scheler totally betrayed the one Dietrich had loved so deeply and so faithfully. For him, the true Scheler had "died" years before his soul left his body. It was a case of a friendship that had been a light in his life and that had ended in complete disappointment. Dietrich worked intensely on these articles during the month of August 1928, while vacationing with Gretchen in Austria. They were published in the *Hochland* and in *Katholische Gedanke*.[21]

Much to Dietrich's regret, the "objectivity" of his articles on Scheler's work was deeply resented by Märit. She thought that, out of friendship, her ex-fiancé should have sung a glorious hymn of praise to her ex-husband. Her response led to a complete break between them.[22]

As nationalism and militarism continued to gain impetus in postwar Germany, Dietrich von Hildebrand responded to the moral call to speak against a movement that was not only

[21] Later all three articles were reprinted in *Zeitliches im Lichte des Ewigen* (Regensburg: Verlag Josef Habbel, 1932), and again in *Die Menschheit am Scheideweg* (Regensburg: Verlag Josef Habbel, 1954).

[22] Much later, in the 1960s, Märchen expressed the desire to reestablish a contact with her ex-fiancé. Dietrich received this information through Marguerite Solbrig, who had been a school friend of Märchen's. He did visit her in Heidelberg, where she was living in Mozartstrasse, and again a year or two afterward, in the home for elderly persons to which she had moved. Their meetings were cordial, and they recalled all the treasured memories they had shared for so many years. Dietrich was in Basel when he received the sad news of Märchen's death in June of 1971.

politically abominable but explicitly anti-Christian. His far-sightedness was bound to set him on a course of confrontation with the deadly Nazi regime led by Adolf Hitler.

Dietrich first attracted the attention of the National Socialist movement in 1921, when he accepted an invitation to attend a peace congress in Paris. The fact that a Frenchman, Marc Sangnier,[23] had invited a German (at a time when the French referred to Germans as *Boche*—a derogatory word for the Teutonic race) touched him. It was a truly Catholic, supranationalist act. Dietrich assumed rightly that Marc Sangnier understood, as he himself did, that the world war had shaken Europe to its foundations and that further conflicts on the continent might destroy Christian Europe altogether. He gladly went to Paris, but, once again, he got himself into trouble because of his anti-nationalist stand.

At the congress, Dietrich met a German journalist, Alfred Nobel, who was reporting on the event. A few days later, he was horrified to discover that a tactless and disparaging article had been published in a German daily criticizing Marc Sangnier for founding the review *Le Sillon*, which had been condemned by Rome.[24] The article triggered Dietrich's indignation. He considered any criticism of their generous

[23] Sangnier (1873–1950) was a French philosopher and socialist politician.

[24] The German bishops were monarchists at the time and strongly opposed to the Republican views expounded in *Le Sillon*. They sent negative reports to Rome and accused Marc Sangnier of spreading dangerous ideas. On the basis of this information, Pius X condemned *Le Sillon* and requested that the French thinker place his work under the supervision of the French bishops. Sangnier then decided to fold his organization. As soon as he received the papal letter— he who had invested much of his person and fortune in *Le Sillon*—he took up his pen and informed Rome that *Le Sillon* no longer existed. He added, "This is the most beautiful moment of my life, for I can now show the Church that I want to serve her as she wishes, not as I wish". He then founded La Jeune Démocratie, which, being a purely political movement, did not need to be placed under the authority of the bishops.

host, who was offering an olive branch to Germany, to be rude and inappropriate. Moreover, Sangnier's magnificent response to the papal censure was not even mentioned. The article was not signed, and that very day it was Dietrich's hard luck to meet Nobel and ask him if *he* knew the name of the *Esel* (ass) who had written the disparaging article. He was immediately apprised that the author was the very man he was addressing, and Nobel thus became his deadly enemy. Unfortunately, Dietrich soon gave Nobel an opportunity for revenge.

Even though most Frenchmen at the congress were friendly toward their German guests, a small minority resented that *Boches* had been invited, claiming that France had no reason to trust Germans. During one session, which had become stormy, Dietrich was called upon to intervene. He was asked point-blank to acknowledge that Germany was wholly responsible for the terrible armed conflict of 1914–1918. Dietrich answered that he would have no difficulty acknowledging the culpability of Germany if that country was convincingly proven guilty, but, without access to secret documents of the powers involved, he could not answer the question. A senator from Belgium (whose country had been terribly victimized during the war) then took the podium and asked him, "What do you think about the German invasion of Belgium on August 4, 1914?" Without a moment's hesitation, Dietrich answered, *"C'était un crime atroce"* (It was an atrocious crime). The French and Belgian members of the conference broke into a salvo of applause. Needless to say, the remark did not endear Dietrich to the German members of the congress who had nationalistic leanings, among them Alfred Nobel. Seizing the opportunity to take revenge, Nobel wrote an article for a German newspaper that totally distorted what Dietrich had said. The rest of the German press immediately picked up the report, and the scandal spread all over Germany.

When Dietrich returned to Munich, he found Gretchen deeply upset and distraught. She had seen the article accusing her husband of treason. She showed him a letter from the senate of the University of Munich requesting an explanation of his conduct. The letter said that if he could not satisfactorily justify himself he would lose his post as *Privat Dozent* at the university.

Dietrich calmly told Gretchen what had actually happened. He had never said that Germany was responsible for the war. He had said only that if historical documents were to prove that she was, he would have no difficulty acknowledging this fact and yielding to evidence. Concerning the invasion of Belgium, he did not have to apologize. What he had said was true. It was a crime.

He was able to give a satisfactory account of his behavior to university officials, and the scandal died down. The incident at the Paris peace congress was to have lasting repercussions, however, for the daring young man. In the wake of the news coverage that his remarks at the conference had triggered, he was to draw the hostile attention of those who held the opposite view, particularly members of the recently formed National Socialist (or *Nazi*) party. For example: Marguerite Solbrig, widow of his friend Hermann Solbrig, had worked in a hospital throughout the war. There she had taken care of a German soldier whose legs had had to be amputated as a result of battle injuries. Marguerite met this man again shortly after the Paris congress, and he tried to convince her that the National Socialist movement led by Adolf Hitler would be the salvation of Germany. He was bitter about the German defeat in 1918 and convinced that Hitler was the savior the German people needed. Marguerite answered,

"You should talk to Professor von Hildebrand about this. He will convince you how dangerous Hitler is." In reply, the man answered, "Dietrich von Hildebrand is a traitor. His name is on our list, and we shall properly dispose of him as soon as we grab power." Marguerite told Dietrich about this conversation, and that is how he found out in 1921 that he was on the Nazi blacklist.

Disturbing as the news must have been, it seemed unlikely to him that such a party could achieve any real success. But as the political situation in Germany continued to deteriorate (one political murder following another), and rampant inflation continued to sap the livelihood of ordinary German citizens, the Nazi party and its leader, Adolf Hitler, began to emerge as an important force on the chaotic German scene. Just how important was made evident by the famous Ludendorff-Hitler *Putsch* [25] of November 8, 1923, which took everyone by surprise.

On November 9, as usual, Dietrich went to an early Mass in the lovely baroque church of Sankt Georg, close to his home. Upon leaving, he met Prince Clemens (son of Prince Alfons, brother of Prince Ludwig Ferdinand), who asked him if he had heard what had happened the night before: in a beer hall, the Bürgerbräu Keller, the Bavarian government had been toppled. Ludendorff, the fanatical general of World War I and an archenemy of Christianity, who wanted to reinstate the old German pagan gods and whose views Dietrich detested, had been named president of Germany, with Hitler as chancellor. The prince's report sounded as if the whole of Munich was in Nazi hands and as if the army had offered no resistance. The immediate question was whether the Reichswehr would intervene and put down

[25] *Putsch* is the German equivalent of the French *coup d'état*.

the rebellion or whether the whole of Germany would be affected.

In horror and despair, Dietrich rushed home and informed Gretchen of what had happened. Knowing that his name was on the Nazi blacklist, he feared that his life was in danger. He immediately called his spiritual director, Father Alois Mager, O.S.B., who advised him to go to the university and meet his 9 o'clock class as usual. In the meantime, the Benedictine monk would determine the gravity of the situation, meet him after his class, and tell him what he thought was the best course of action. So far, only the right side of the Isar was in Nazi hands. Moreover, Dr. Kahr, the head of the Bavarian government who, the night before, had stepped down under Nazi pressure, had retracted his resignation.

Dietrich managed to pass the Isar bridge without difficulty; he arrived safely at the university and gave his class on metaphysics. There were fewer students than usual, and one could sense tension in the air. When he left the classroom, Father Mager was waiting for him at the door. He told him that the Nazis had put up posters saying that a people's tribunal had been set up. When someone opposed to the new regime was apprehended, the tribunal would pass judgment on his innocence or guilt. Anyone declared guilty was to be executed within the hour. "Consequently," Father Mager reasoned, "if you are caught, your fate is sealed. It would not help you if the *Putsch* collapsed soon afterward." He advised Dietrich to leave immediately for Württemberg, an adjacent province with its own local government.

Dietrich asked his student Balduin Schwarz to go to Maria Theresia Strasse to inform Gretchen of his plan of escape and to bring her and Franzi to the railway station, where they should take the first train leaving for Ulm in Württemberg. Father Mager urged Dietrich to avoid going to the main railway station, for fear that some sort of surveillance would already be in place and the Nazis would be able to identify him. He was advised to take a trolley car to Pasing, the first stop on the way to Augsburg-Ulm, board the train there, and meet Gretchen and Franzi on the train. The Benedictine monk offered to accompany him to Pasing, and a friend lent him money for his fare.

All went well. Dietrich met Gretchen and Franzi as planned. Arriving in Augsburg, the refugees heard that troops loyal to the government had engaged in a battle right in the center of Munich. In Ulm, they were informed that the *Putsch* had collapsed and that the instigators, Ludendorff and Hitler, were under lock and key. According to rumor, Hitler had been found hiding under the bed of one of his supporters, a Fraulein Erna Hanfstängl. Peace seemed to have been restored. Dietrich, Gretchen, and Franzi remained in Ulm until the next day and then returned to Munich. This was the third revolution that Dietrich had witnessed (the fall of the Bavarian monarchy, November 1918; the Communist revolution, May 1919) and it was not to be the last. For him personally it entailed the least dramatic of his escapes. It was merely a dress rehearsal for what was to come.

In the aftermath of the *Putsch*, Dietrich assumed that the Nazi threat was over. He was shocked and depressed when he found out that Ludendorff had been acquitted because of his "great deeds" for the German nation, that is, his resounding victory over the Russians at Tannenberg during the war. Hitler was sequestered in a comfortable jail in Landsberg, where he was writing his book *Mein Kampf*. He was freed a year later. Dietrich was outraged. Even so, he did not think that Hitler, considered by many to be a rather ridiculous figure, would make a comeback. The magazine *Simplicissimus* carried a cartoon of Hitler trying to sell his *Mein Kampf* for two Marks.

But in the years following the failed *Putsch*, Dietrich saw that the seeds of Nazism were germinating anew, and its detestable philosophy was resurfacing. It was gaining currency in what is called "public opinion". Traces of anti-Semitism continued, and "community" was emphasized more and more in public rhetoric at the expense of the individual. Dietrich had been too optimistic in assuming that Nazism had died when the *Putsch* collapsed. The evil was still there and had clearly left its mark on the spirit of the time. The dynamism of ideas that are "in the air" is such that most people are carried away by it, without even being conscious of how influenced they are by its siren song.

Few people had the inner strength to resist the power of the *Zeitgeist*. To Dietrich's great sorrow, this was true even of some Catholics. Karl Adam, the author of *The Spirit of Catholicism*, a work that rightly assured him the admiration of his co-believers, fell prey to the dynamism of nationalism. One day, commenting on the famous theological saying *Gratia supponit naturam* (Grace presupposes nature), he had the disastrous idea of adding to it the word *Germanicam*. The sentence then read: *Gratia supponit naturam Germanicam*. Unwittingly, Karl Adam was blowing the Nazi horn.[26]

Since his conversion, Dietrich had found it difficult to understand how people who have been privileged to receive the plenitude of revealed truth could be so tepid, so impressed by "public opinion", so infected by nationalism. To

---

[26] Years later, after Dietrich had left Germany and was staying in Florence, he received a new edition of the works of St. Thomas, published in 1933, a Church holy year. To his dismay he read, "Published during the German holy year"; and 1933 was the year in which Hitler had grabbed power in Germany! He wrote the publisher a letter of protest, and he was told in reply that as 1933 was a holy year for Catholics, it also was a holy year for German Catholics!

be a Catholic was, to his mind, to live in a continual state of gratitude for the unmerited gifts of faith, the sacraments, and the guidance of Holy Church. To be a Catholic meant to see "temporal events in the light of eternity". To be a Catholic meant to keep in mind a hierarchy of values—never to allow earthly concerns to overshadow the faith. He discovered more and more that, apart from some saintly personalities, many German Catholics, while scrupulously faithful to their Sunday obligations—a fact that impressed Nuncio Pacelli—often led mediocre lives, tainted by the philosophies of the day. How could one be a nationalist when the Church was so gloriously supranationalist? Dietrich himself felt much closer to a pious and faithful Italian or Frenchman than to a German whose religious views were either crippled or nonexistent.

Dietrich often gave expression to this grief, the intensity of which was to increase during the 1920s. Discovering how many otherwise good people had been infected by totalitarian views (which they did not recognize as such), he decided to write a new work in order to shed light on the Catholic view of the relationship between the individual and the community. It was to develop into an important work, one on which Siegfried Hamburger collaborated closely—*Metaphysics of Community*.[27] This book offered Germany an antidote to the poison spreading throughout the country, namely, the glorification of the state and the metaphysical denigration of the individual.

A couple of years after the book's publication (1930), Dietrich attended a conference at the Benedictine Abbey of Maria Laach, in the Rhineland, the proceedings of which demonstrated again the magnitude of the danger threatening

[27] *Metaphysik der Gemeinschaft* (Augsburg: Haas und Grabherr, 1930).

Germany. Once more, he was given an occasion to speak out as an opponent of the Nazi movement.

One of the main speakers was a Franciscan priest by the name of Thaddäus Soiron,[28] who was highly thought of by Prelate Münch. Father Soiron had the reputation of being good and reliable. Listening to the talk he delivered, however, Dietrich was both stunned and appalled. The content of his speech betrayed how much the Franciscan had been infected by the collectivist ideas of National Socialism. It was the tragic case of a man who had unconsciously been influenced by the *Zeitgeist* and had become blind to its incompatibility with orthodox Catholic doctrine. Father Soiron clearly gave precedence to the community over the individual, and his arguments were replete with philosophical errors and ambiguities. Nor was he the only speaker poisoned by Nazi philosophy.

The subject Dietrich von Hildebrand had chosen for his talk was "Individual and Community". It was the burning issue of the day, and he had already done much work on it in *Metaphysics of Community*. His lecture should have won the enthusiastic assent of any intelligent and awakened Catholic. It proved convincingly that any attempt to create community at the expense of the individual person was not only radically erroneous but would lead necessarily to a complete misunderstanding of the very nature of community. It pointed to the horror of both anti-personalism and totalitarianism and to the incompatibility of these ideologies with Roman Catholicism. It unmasked errors rampant in certain Hegelian formulations that placed the state above the individual, and forcefully argued that the opposite is true. Not only does the individual—rather than the community—deserve to be called

---

[28] Thaddäus Soiron (1881–1957) was a biblical scholar and noted homilist.

a "substance", in the fullest sense of the term, but only he has an immortal soul destined to an eternal union with God, whereas all human communities will one day disappear with the end of the world. On the other hand, Dietrich emphasized the dignity and value of a true community, thereby also condemning liberal individualism.

Against the background of the intellectual capitulation of Father Soiron's talk, Dietrich's speech had the effect of a bomb. It triggered both enthusiasm and violent opposition. Father Soiron accused Dietrich of defending a position at loggerheads with Catholic dogma, basing his faulty reasoning on the premise that all things reflect God, and because God is a Trinity, it follows that the community must be superior to the individual. A friend of Hedwig Conrad-Martius (one of Dietrich's fellow students from Göttingen) rebuffed him with the words, "But you seem to forget that, in God, the three Divine Persons form only one substance." A certain Mr. Schmidt, a pacifist and a federalist, was so jubilant over Dietrich's talk that he introduced a motion that copies of the text of the speech be duplicated and sent to all the members of the Reichstag.[29] This proposal was opposed by Father Soiron and his supporters. Someone then proposed that a committee be set up to subject Dietrich's talk to a critical examination. The committee—Father Soiron, a young Benedictine monk by the name of Father Damasus Winzen,[30] and two others—would suggest changes to make the talk acceptable to the majority. Dietrich, however, did not want his talk to be censured or "purged" by people who were clearly influenced by Nazi philosophy. He therefore suggested

[29] The Reichstag was the name given the German parliament after the unification of German states under Bismarck, from 1871 to 1945.

[30] Damasus Winzen, O.S.B. (b. 1901), emigrated to the United States in 1938 and founded the Abbey of Mount Savior in Elmira, New York.

that Mr. Schmidt's proposal be tabled—much to the relief of the opposition.[31]

The lamentable proceedings of this congress reached their climax when the industrialist Fritz Thyssen[32] took the floor and delivered a short address. He lashed out at Catholics who were either pacifists or enemies of "Fascism", carefully avoiding use of the words "National Socialism". The gist of his presentation was Nazi propaganda. The high point of this inane speech was reached when the famous tycoon concluded with the following words, "I find myself in good company, namely, with Saint Teresa of Ávila, who wrote, 'Be ready and arm yourself; the enemy is near.'" These words of the great Spanish mystic obviously referred to the necessity of warding off attacks of the devil. That Thyssen appropriated these words for military purposes bordered on the grotesque.[33]

---

[31] After Dietrich's lecture, the participants went to the refectory. He happened to sit next to a priest he did not know, who greeted him with the following words, "You seem to be a disciple of Spinoza." Dietrich was flabbergasted, for Spinoza's philosophy was one for which he had no sympathy whatsoever. "How so?" he asked him, greatly mystified. The priest answered, "In your talk, you said that communities were entities *sui generis*, an expression that is typically spinozistic." Dietrich could not help but laugh at the primitive nature of this remark. Thanks to his sense of humor, he saw the funny side of it. At the same time, this absurd allegation taught him once again how little some people are concerned about the question of truth and falsity. They are much more interested in putting a historical label on thinkers. It gives them the comfortable feeling of being both scholarly and well informed. Many years later, in the United States, a priest accused von Hildebrand of having "Kantian overtones" in his book *Transformation in Christ*, because he used the word "categorical". Professor Balduin Schwarz used the incident to take up his mentor's defense.

[32] Fritz Thyssen (1873–1951), director of the Thyssen Concern, supported the Nazi party from 1923 till 1939, when he broke with it and emigrated to Switzerland.

[33] When the congress was over, some industrialists employed by Thyssen drove Dietrich back to Cologne. In unison, they expressed their regret over their employer's contribution to the symposium. They saw clearly that he had made a fool of himself.

Significantly, German politician Franz von Papen[34] attended the congress. He played the role of the pious Catholic. While not hiding his Nazi sympathies, he tried to convince his coreligionists that National Socialism and Roman Catholicism were perfectly compatible. He no doubt deplored Dietrich's devastating condemnation of such a view at the conference. Shortly afterward, in June 1932, von Papen became chancellor of the Reich. A few years later, he was denouncing Dietrich von Hildebrand directly to Hitler himself.[35]

Von Papen's appointment in June was succeeded in July by an overwhelming Nazi victory at the polls, in which the party won 230 seats in Parliament out of 608. There was, however, a small ray of hope when, on November 6, 1932, the Nazis suffered a political setback: they lost 34 seats in the National Assembly. A political system like Nazism feeds on its dynamism, and any failure can jeopardize its chances of success. Von Papen had to step down. He was replaced by Kurt von Schleicher.[36] (Von Papen could not forgive von Schleicher for having replaced him; from then on he viewed him as a personal enemy.)[37]

[34] Franz von Papen (1879–1969), German politician, was Chancellor from June to December 1932. He supported Hitler and became Vice-Chancellor under him from 1933 to 1934; through sheer luck, he escaped the purge of June 30, 1934. In August 1934, he was appointed German Ambassador to Austria and worked for the annexation of Austria to the Third Reich.

[35] Lecturing in Frankfurt, Dietrich had made the acquaintance of Mrs. von Schnitzler, who knew Franz von Papen well—a man of mediocre talent. The latter once told her that upon coming home one night and seeing himself reflected in a mirror, he muttered: *"Franzchen* [the German diminutive for Franz], *Franzchen,* who ever would have thought that you would reach such heights."

[36] General von Schleicher (1882–1934) was chancellor only from December 3, 1932, to January 28, 1933.

[37] The general soon lost his life, in June 1934, a victim of the famous purge orchestrated by Hitler against "enemies of the Reich", i.e., in many cases, "friends" who had helped him to power and whom Hitler now considered a threat.

In light of the recent Nazi defeat, 1932 ended on a some-what hopeful note for Dietrich, but that brief period of hope was soon to be ended. Several events took place in January 1933 that convinced him he could no longer live in Germany.

On January 10, 1933, he was invited to give a talk at a pacifist congress in Munich. At first he declined, but Cardinal Faulhaber sent him a telegram urging him to accept, and he yielded to the cardinal's wishes.

The day promised to be exciting. The Nazis, opposed from the beginning to pacifism under any form, tried to sabotage the meeting by preventing anyone from entering the lecture hall. They had to be removed by the police.

Dietrich was the first speaker. He defended the thesis that, whereas idolization of the state was an ancient error that had blossomed in Sparta, nationalism was a new one that could be traced back to the French Revolution. Both errors, he argued, sprang from a dangerous tendency rooted in man's fallen nature. The greater part of his talk was dedicated to the Catholic conception of peace. He emphasized the importance of a supranational outlook and underlined the moral duty to fight both militarism and nationalism. To his dismay, however, he was followed by several speakers who clearly had Communist leanings and whose papers boiled down to an attack on the Catholic Church.

Dietrich found himself in a very painful situation. He had agreed to participate only to please Cardinal Faulhaber, and now he found himself with bedfellows who were viciously anti-Catholic, and Communist to boot. Communism was, in his eyes, as detestable as Nazism. At one point, he could take it no longer. He got up and declared that he would not tolerate this shameful attack on the Roman Catholic Church. He had not come to a pacifist congress to be subjected to Communist propaganda. He left the hall with a bitter taste in his mouth. It was deeply upsetting to him that he had had to brave Nazi opposition to share the floor with Communists whose philosophy was just as pernicious. He was convinced that, much as Nazism and Communism seemed to be opposed—one labeled "right" and the other "left"—the two systems were twin brothers in iniquity, displaying the same materialism, the same idolization of the state, the same totalitarianism, and the same atheism. He hated them both because he hated iniquity.

He went home very subdued. There he found Gretchen deeply shaken. While he was delivering his talk, the Nazis who had tried to disrupt the congress had telephoned her to say that it was scandalous that her husband should speak at a pacifist congress. They told her that they would soon settle accounts with him, a threat that she knew had to be taken seriously.

Later in the month, on January 27, Dietrich and Gretchen were invited to the home of a Mrs. Rickmers, together with a woman who was enthusiastic about the recently published *Liturgy and Personality*.[38] This book can be considered his song of gratitude for the sublime food that the Catholic liturgy had given him since his conversion in 1914. In this work, he expressed how his intelligence, his mind, and his heart had been enriched by the liturgy.[39] The conversation centered on the contents of the book for some time and then, inevitably, shifted to politics. To his utter amazement, Dietrich heard the woman who loved his *Liturgy and Personality* express her approval of Hitler. Once again, he was flabbergasted. How could one and the same person admire a work that was Catholic to the very core and simultaneously enthuse about a criminal?

---

[38] *Liturgie und Persönlichkeit* (Salzburg: Anton Pustet, 1932).

[39] The book was composed in only twenty-three days. Dietrich has written that "it was like a ripe fruit. All I had to do was to pluck it from the tree."

It was distressing to see the inroads Hitler made on public opinion. The final encroachment came on January 30, 1933, when President Hindenburg[40] made Hitler chancellor of Germany. When Hindenburg died the following August, Hitler seized for himself the offices of president and chancellor. Germany remained in his iron grip from then until 1945.

As soon as Hitler became chancellor, Dietrich understood that he had to leave the country, where he had by then struck very deep roots. He saw his options clearly. One was to remain in Germany, keep a low profile, refrain from expressing his horror of the Nazi regime, and wait until the tempest was over. This option he rejected. His conscience would not allow him to remain silent. He knew he could not control his tongue while brutality and immorality were becoming acceptable. He did not want his silence to be interpreted as tacit assent. A second option was to remain in Nazi Germany, follow the dictates of his conscience, and thunder against the evils perpetrated. But he knew that within days he would either be executed as a traitor or be sent to a concentration camp to perish. The only option remaining was to leave everything and face total poverty, fighting the Nazis from outside Germany through lectures and books, opening people's eyes to the threat menacing Christianity and the entire world.

Dietrich did not hesitate. He chose the third option—to be a beggar, but free.

When Dietrich decided to leave Germany, he was responding to his own particular situation, to a mission clearly addressed to him, namely, to denounce the philosophy of Nazism, in season and out. He knew he was called to raise his voice

[40] Paul von Hindenburg (1847–1934) was a German general, as well as twice President between 1925 and 1934.

when his soul was aflame with holy wrath. He hoped that by leaving Germany he would be able to continue his relentless fight against Hitler, alerting other nations to the crimes perpetrated daily by the Nazi regime.

Shortly after Adolf Hitler grabbed power, Dietrich, riding in a Munich trolley with a friend, started thundering against the new chancellor. Terrified, his friend begged him to desist. "Do you want to be thrown into a concentration camp?" she exclaimed. When he paid a last visit to the noble Fritz Beck,[41] a dear friend of his, Beck said to him, "It is inconceivable that you should stay in our unfortunate country. You must leave, and the sooner the better!" "Why don't you leave, too?" his friend retorted. Beck answered, "I have a mission here. The captain of a ship cannot leave it when it is in danger of sinking." Two great fighters were given different missions, and each followed his particular call, accepting all the dangers it would entail. Exactly fifteen months later, Beck paid with his life. He was murdered by the Nazis on June 30, 1934.

Never have I heard Dietrich censure those who, like Fritz Beck or Romano Guardini, chose to stay in Germany. It was clear to him that even though all men must submit to the same ethical and religious laws, the way of applying these laws can differ from individual to individual.

Even though he perceived clearly that he had to leave Germany, the decision was painful. He had built a special world in Munich. Most members of his family lived there. He had very many dear friends and a great following of enthusiastic and devoted students. He and his wife had hosted "afternoons" that had acquainted them with the leading Catholic intellectual and artistic personalities of the day, and

---

[41] Fritz Beck (1889–1934) had at one time been private secretary to F. W. Foerster, and later founded and directed a remarkable students' organization in Munich.

they had participated extensively in the city's stimulating cultural life. He lived in a beautiful home, in a magnificent city embellished with the masterful sculptural works of his father. All this he would have to give up. At the age of forty-three, he was to find himself without a home, without a profession, and penniless. (According to Nazi regulations, no one was allowed to take more than one hundred Reichsmarks across the border.)

But Dietrich, hating iniquity, saw clearly that God was calling him to sacrifice all those good things rather than to condone evil. For years to come, his motto was *Deus providebit* (God will provide, Gen 22:8). And so, on Sunday, March 12, 1933, six weeks after Hitler became chancellor, Dietrich stepped into voluntary political exile. He sadly said goodbye to his family, his friends, his lovely home (he actually went through the house to say goodbye to each room), and Munich. With a couple of suitcases, he and his wife took a train to Florence. For the first time in his life, he crossed the Brenner, going southward, with a heavy heart.

The travelers went immediately to San Francesco, now the property of Dietrich's beloved sister Lisl Brewster. Kind and generous, Lisl received her brother and sister-in-law with her usual warmth. The house was huge, and she put at their disposal two large rooms.

Shortly before leaving Munich, Dietrich had received an invitation that honored him greatly—to be the speaker representing Germany at a celebration taking place in the *Auditorium Magnum* of the Sorbonne, in April 1933, on the occasion of the elevation of Albert the Great to the dignity of Doctor of the Church. Because Dietrich had left Germany and vowed never to return so long as Hitler remained in power, it seemed to him that he had to decline this honor. He wrote a letter to the attaché of the German Embassy in Paris informing him of his situation, stating that he could not represent the current government of Germany. The home country of Albert the Great was being honored, and it was because Dietrich was German that he had been invited; moreover, the German ambassador in Paris was to preside at the festivity. Dietrich therefore suggested that another German replace him. To his great surprise, the attaché wrote back that the invitation was still valid and that he was expected to deliver an address. He even hinted that this lecture might open for him a possibility of being called to a professorship in Paris. The theme given him was "The Spiritual Unity of Europe and How It Is to Be Recovered", a theme he had very much at heart.

Dietrich also received a letter from Étienne Gilson, urging him to send him his talk as soon as possible so that he could translate it into French. He warned him, however, that he should carefully avoid making any reference to National Socialism, for fear of placing the German ambassador in a very difficult situation. Moreover, Gilson insisted, he should avoid mentioning that the spiritual unity of Europe could be achieved only through Holy Church, as the minister of culture, M. de Monzie, was a Freemason. All this did not ease the speaker's task, but he worked intensely on his manuscript with the always welcome help of Hamburger, who was in Florence at the time. He obediently avoided mentioning National Socialism but strongly condemned "nationalism"; and even though he drew a picture of the role played by the Roman Catholic Church in the spiritual unity of Europe, he purposely omitted saying that she would have to play a crucial role in reestablishing this unity. All in all, he was pleased with his lecture.

He had also been invited to give talks in Holland (Leyden and Utrecht), and he decided to combine the two sets of lectures. He first went to Belgium to visit his brother-in-law

Georges Baltus. From there he went to Holland. One day, he asked his host whether he did not feel closer to Flemish Belgians (who were Catholic) than to the Protestant Dutch. Whereupon his interlocutor answered by emphasizing the important cultural differences existing between the two countries: whereas Holland, he said, was a typical Renaissance country, open to adventure and conquest, Belgium had kept much of its medieval character. To Dietrich, it was an interesting and challenging remark.

At the university he made the acquaintance of the famous Dutch intellectual Johan Huizinga; Dietrich found him to be an impressive personality who deserved the reputation that his various publications had won him in Europe.

His lecture was well received. Thanks to Dietrich's openness to new and enriching experiences, he very much enjoyed his stay in Holland, whose culture and individuality are so strongly stamped in its architecture, life-style, and cleanliness, a country so close to Belgium and yet so very different. As always, he profited much from this brief trip.

Arriving in Paris, he tried to reach his nephew Wolfgang Braunfels, who was studying the history of art in the French capital. He was shocked and worried to hear that because of very serious troubles in his family, Wolfgang had had to rush back to Cologne.

He paid a visit to the embassy attaché, an engaging man who completely shared Dietrich's political views. The attaché told Dietrich that he was hoping that Gilson could secure for him a professorship at the Sorbonne or the Collège de France; there was, he said, a clear tendency to establish a rapprochement, a closer bond between Germany and France. The celebration honoring Albert the Great was proof of it. It was illustrated further by the fact that the German ambassador had been asked to preside at the celebration and, finally, that a German had been invited to deliver the key talk. It was to be hoped, said the attaché, that this would give the guest speaker a chance of joining a French university. Dietrich could not share this hope. After all, how could he possibly create a bond between a Germany whose government he detested and France? If he were offered a professorship as a sign of protest against Hitler's government, the situation would be vastly different. But there was no hope of that. Finally, he had no idea how Gilson, a historian and a Thomist, stood toward phenomenology.

F. W. Foerster, whose very name was anathema to the Nazis, was living in Paris at the time. Given his close link to his former mentor, Dietrich (probably prompted by the attaché) asked Foerster through their common friend, Comte d'Harcourt, not to greet him publicly. The limelight was on Dietrich, and anything that he said or did was bound to have repercussions; in addition, the reputation of the German ambassador had to be protected.

As would be expected, Dietrich also paid the ambassador a visit; he found him to be a cultivated man who received him with great friendliness. But he struck him as despondent and clearly worried about the situation in Germany. Although he expressed himself carefully, one could sense that he nurtured no illusion about the nature of Nazism.

Dietrich was also the guest of Gilson. He made the acquaintance of his attractive wife and a daughter, a lovely young woman of whom her father was very proud. Gilson handed Dietrich his manuscript, which he had translated into French, but suggested that he should replace a reference to Berlioz as being the greatest French composer with Debussy—which Dietrich declined to do. Gilson was a great admirer of Mozart but, unfortunately, not so receptive to Beethoven's music, and he had no understanding whatever

for Wagner. Every time Dietrich touched upon a philosophical theme, Gilson would immediately refer to some passage in
Saint Thomas, but he clearly was not anxious to pursue the
discussion any further. That was a bit of a disappointment.

The next day, Dietrich was invited to a dinner given by the
German ambassador. To his joy, he was seated next to his
friend the Comte d'Harcourt. It was Lent, and Dietrich could
not help but be impressed by the count's abstinence. The
meal was excellent, but d'Harcourt, while observing all pro-
priety, clearly denied himself.

Dinner was followed by a musical performance given by
young German singers studying at the Cologne Conservatory. After the concert, Dietrich went over to them and asked
whether some change had taken place at the conservatory.
"Don't you know?" they answered. "Your brother-in-law
was deposed by the Nazis because of his 'impure blood'."
Dietrich was horrified. Only a few weeks after Hitler had
grabbed power, this "ethnic cleansing" was already at work.[42]

The celebration honoring Saint Albert the Great began
with a solemn Mass at the cathedral of Notre Dame,
celebrated by a Dominican, with a choir also made up of
Dominicans, as was proper to honor a great Dominican saint.
The Mass was both solemn and beautiful, and the beauty of
Notre Dame was an ideal site for it.

Upon exiting the cathedral, Dietrich met the provincial of
the German Dominicans. After he praised highly the beauty
of the liturgical ceremony, the monk said in blunt reply: "In
Germany we too can sing beautifully." This was a surprising

---

[42] Walter Braunfels, whose father was Jewish (his mother was "Aryan"), then
bought a piece of property in southern Germany, on the Bodensee, very close
to the lovely town of Überlingen, not far from the Swiss border. There he and
his family lived through the war. As soon as Konrad Adenauer became mayor
of Cologne, he reappointed him to his position at the Cologne Conservatory.
Walter died in Cologne in March of 1954.

remark to make, as Dietrich had made no comparison between the two countries, nor had he spoken disparagingly of Germany. The provincial acted as if Dietrich's praise entailed an implicit criticism of his compatriots. But it was simply a "value response", to use Dietrich's terminology, and he suspected that the monk's remark was prompted by nationalism. Moreover, Dietrich doubted whether the German Dominicans were up to the level of the French branch of the order; the latter were well known for the spirituality of their culture.

The Mass was followed by a sumptuous meal given in the Dominican convent on the Rue St. Honoré. As guest of honor, Dietrich was seated next to titular Bishop Baudrillart, who had a visceral dislike of anything German. Because of the sensitive situation in which he found himself, it was impossible for Dietrich to speak disparagingly of Hitler, a theme that so disturbed his heart. His Excellency did his best to hide his dislike of Germany, but the juxtaposition of the two men was, of course, very awkward.

Upon leaving the dining hall, Dietrich once again came across the provincial of the German Dominicans. Dietrich could not help but praise the magnificent meal they had been served. To this the provincial retorted, "In Germany, we also can cook." This remark strained Dietrich's patience. He could not control his tongue and replied: "When it comes to culinary art, France is definitely superior to Germany"— for it was now clear that the German monk was indeed a nationalist.[43]

That same evening, the celebration in honor of Albert the Great took place in the Pantheon of the Sorbonne. Gilson, the first speaker, was well known for both his scholarship and

[43] Von Hildebrand always made a sharp distinction between "patriotism" (a legitimate love for one's country) and "nationalism" (an illegitimate feeling—an expression of a person's inflated ego).

his wit. He sketched a striking picture of the anti-nationalist spirit of the University of Paris at the time of Albert the Great. Its halls were honored by men such as Roger Bacon and Alexander of Hales (English), Albert the Great (German), and Bonaventure and Thomas (Italians). Gilson spoke longer than expected, and when Dietrich came to the podium the celebration was running short of time. Gilson informed the speaker that his talk had to be shortened—a most unpleasant thing for a speaker to do. For this reason, his speech did not have the success that he had hoped for it; it was a disappointing moment, but Dietrich was not the sort of person who lets himself be depressed by such contingencies.

While Dietrich was on the lecture tours in Belgium, Holland, and France, horrendous events took place in Germany. On April 1, there was a boycott imposed against the Jews. The French Cardinal Verdier responded beautifully to this shocking event and ordered his clergy in Paris to pray especially for these persecuted people. This act was particularly striking because the German bishops, who had earlier put a sentence of excommunication upon members of the Nazi party, had lifted the penalty shortly after Hitler came to power. To Dietrich, that reversal was a very bitter thing to witness. Church leaders are called to be watchmen, and the bishops should have been the first to sound the alarm and warn their sheep of the religious, moral, and human danger that the Nazi philosophy presented. It should have been so luminously clear that one could not honestly call oneself a Roman Catholic and at the same time accept the anti-Christian, materialistic, atheistic philosophy of Nazism. Woe to the religious leader who does not warn his sheep that the wolf is at the door! On the other hand, Dietrich knew that God never promised that the Church would always be led by holy and outstanding leaders; Christ promised only that "the gates of hell" shall not prevail. Nevertheless, Dietrich's sorrow was deep upon witnessing how cowardly and blind those appointed to be guardians had become. The number of people who fell victims to Nazi brutality and were dragged into concentration camps increased daily—one of them being Gerlich.[44]

At this time, Dietrich also paid a visit to Marc Sangnier, the one who had invited him to the pacifist congress of 1921. Inevitably, they started discussing the dreadful situation in Germany, and Marc Sangnier could not help asking, "Is it enough for someone to seize power, in order for him to gain recognition from Church authorities?" Alas, how many German Catholics did not live up to the demands of their faith during this period.

The last evening that he spent in Paris, Dietrich was invited to dinner by the attaché. Both the German provincial of the Dominicans and the prior of the Dominicans in Berlin were also guests. A very unpleasant discussion began when the provincial proclaimed that there was no reason to oppose Hitler because his emphasis on both the concept of authority and on the nation was definitely something deserving applause. He added, "It is worth noting how often Hitler mentions God's name." Dietrich could not help but respond: "Hitler is so stupid that when he speaks of God, he does not know what he is talking about." The poor host was obviously placed in the center of a tense moment. But the provincial insisted upon pursuing the theme, claiming further that "Catholics should play a leading role in the National Socialism movement and thereby give it a Catholic stamp." This

---

[44] Born in 1883, Fritz Gerlich was murdered by the Nazis in 1934. He had edited the magazine *The Straight Path*. Having converted to Roman Catholicism through the German mystic Therese von Konnersreuth, he understood it to be his mission to blast National Socialism. He paid with his life.

assertion was strongly contested by Dietrich, who retorted: "National Socialism and Catholicism are essentially at loggerheads and can never be reconciled. Moreover, it is sheer illusion to believe that Catholics could have any sort of positive influence on a movement that is evil to its very core."

The stand taken by the Dominican monks spoke volumes about the danger to which Roman Catholics in Germany were exposed: blinded to the viciousness of National Socialism through propaganda, stupidity, or wishful thinking, they were exposed to the danger of absorbing more and more of the Nazi poison without even noticing it.

After the meal, the prior had the regrettable idea of starting to sing the "Horst Wessel Lied".[45] Dietrich was beside himself and declared, "I must leave in twenty minutes. If you insist upon singing this, I shall leave this very moment." The prior desisted.

The attaché certainly did not have an easy guest. Nevertheless, he accompanied the *enfant terrible* to his hotel and expressed his deep regret about the stand the two Dominicans had taken. He agreed with Dietrich entirely, but explained that had he said a word in his defense, he would have lost his position (and possibly his head). It was with mixed feelings that Dietrich went back to Florence.

Dietrich and Gretchen stayed in Florence from March 1933 until the end of October. It was difficult for both of them, though Florence was, as always, beautiful and enchanting. A few weeks after their arrival, the famous *Maggio musicale* was in full swing; they could hear the music from San Francesco.

---

[45] The "Horst Wessel Lied" was a Nazi anthem (along with "Deutschland über alles"). The words and music were composed by a pastor's son who became a fanatical Nazi and was assassinated by the Communists. Clever Nazi propaganda made him a martyr.

Dietrich's heart, however, could not enjoy the beloved place of his youth. Much as he and Gretchen loved Florence, it was not home. The situation in Germany was a nightmare. The future was totally insecure. Dietrich knew that worse was to come, and he marveled that most people were living as if events were following their normal course. His acquaintances in Florence labeled him a pessimist, someone whose situation was difficult and who understandably painted the future in the darkest possible colors. But the situation could certainly not be as bad as Dietrich pictured it. Alas, his so-called pessimism about the situation in Germany proved to be plain realism.

Discouraged by this state of affairs, Dietrich decided to turn to "the consolation of philosophy" (the title of Boethius' best-known work) and to fulfill a promise he had given a publisher named Steinbüchel to write a book on epistemology. Once again in a short span of time, he wrote *The Nature of Philosophical Questions and Knowledge*, one of his more important philosophical writings. Because of the political situation, the book was not published in Germany until after World War II.[46]

It was typical of Dietrich that in this time of worry and sorrow he turned to philosophical inquiries. He worked with his friend and collaborator Siegfried Hamburger, who had been living in San Francesco for years, tutoring Lisl's talented daughter, Clotilde Brewster. The two friends spent many hours discussing philosophical questions. Their mutual understanding was truly extraordinary. The insight of one

---

[46] *Der Sinn philosophischen Fragens und Erkennens* (Bonn: Peter Hanstein, 1950). At that time, it was revised and some chapters were added. It was translated into English by von Hildebrand's devoted and talented student Dr. William Marra and published in 1960 under the title *What Is Philosophy?* (Milwaukee: Bruce Publishing Co., 1960; repr. London: Routledge, 1991).

immediately blossomed in the other and came back enriched and deepened. Such intellectual collaboration between two great minds is, I think, rare in the history of philosophy. Dietrich used to say, "If everybody were to praise a book of mine, and Hamburger was not pleased with it, I would totally rework it. If, on the other hand, Hamburger approved it, and everyone else was critical of it, I would not change a word."

Meanwhile, Dietrich received numerous visitors from Germany, whose reports on the situation in that unfortunate country confirmed his worst fears. Hitler now had an iron grip on the people of Germany. He used his power ruthlessly, and he ruled by fear. One sinister indication of the state of affairs was the form Dietrich received from the University of Munich, requesting him to indicate whether he was Aryan or Jewish. As a sign of protest against such a shameful inquiry, he wrote in "Jewish". (His paternal grandmother was, in fact, of Jewish extraction.)[47] By declaring himself Jewish, Dietrich was proudly asserting his solidarity with a persecuted people.

News from Germany illustrated dramatically the terrible turn that events were taking. There was, for example, the story of a schoolteacher by the name of Schemm who had been fired because of his drunkenness. He became an ardent member of the National Socialist party and was named *Kultusminister* in Bavaria. He gave a talk to university professors in Munich in which he pronounced: "From now on, in your scholarly work, you no longer need raise the question: Is this true? Your only concern should be: Is it in harmony with the spirit of National Socialism?" These words, uttered by a *Kultusminister*, speak volumes about the spirit of National

[47] This was Clementine Guttentag (1817–1879), whose parents had both come from Jewish families. She had died ten years before Dietrich's birth, had been raised a Protestant, and was totally liberal in her religious views.

Socialism, if the word "spirit" can apply at all! The Romanist Professor Vossler, playing upon Schemm's name, said wittily: "Ich bin beschemmt". (The German *Ich bin beschämt* means "I am ashamed.")

Deplorable as this spiritual and cultural decadence was, Dietrich was still more shaken by statements the German bishops made at Fulda in June 1933. Breaking with tradition, the bishops took a positive stand toward the Nazi government—praising its spirit of authority, its acknowledgement of the German nation, and so on—in a document that was bound to give German Catholics the impression that their spiritual leaders were endorsing National Socialism. The appendix to the Fulda document, challenging certain forms of racism, was much too weak to offset that impression. No word was said against the heresy of totalitarianism; no word of protest against the crimes that were being committed or against terrorism; no condemnation of the abominable philosophy of National Socialism. The same bishops who had previously excommunicated anyone belonging to the Nazi party were now making conciliatory statements. Dietrich was horrified: How could Catholic shepherds, responsible for protecting their flock from the wolves, fall so short of the mark as to mislead those entrusted to their care? To Dietrich this betrayal was a deep source of sorrow. He must have thought of the words of the prophet Ezekiel: "But if the watchman sees the sword coming and does not blow the trumpet, so that the people are not warned, and the sword comes, and takes any one of them; that man is taken away in his iniquity, but his blood I will require at the watchman's hand" (33:6). The failure of most German bishops to live up to their holy task was to Dietrich a special cross. He who had been given such an ardent love for Holy Church, he who understood so deeply the awesome greatness of the priestly vocation, was heartbroken to witness the behavior of those to whom so much had been entrusted.

Then, to add to his sorrow, he heard through Gretchen, who had gone back to Munich for a short visit, that a Göttingen acquaintance, a certain Dr. Jacobsohn, had committed suicide by throwing himself under a train. He was a noble and kind man for whom both Dietrich and Gretchen had a deep esteem. Only two years before, he and his son (a talented young man who studied under von Hildebrand) had visited their friends in Maria Theresia Strasse. Jacobsohn, like many Jews, had put down deep roots in Germany, and the thought that he and his children were no longer "full-fledged" German citizens drove him to despair. Gretchen was beside herself with grief and exclaimed, "If Jacobsohn were the only victim of Hitler's ruthlessness, this would be enough to condemn him as a criminal." The same fate awaited a Herr Block, a friend of Hamburger's, who came to Florence in 1933. Dietrich urged him to remain, but Block was unwilling to cut himself off from his roots. He returned to the country of his birth, and shortly afterward he too committed suicide.

Father Metzger (whom Dietrich had first met at the peace congress in Paris in 1921) also paid him a visit in San Francesco. Talking to him was a balm to Dietrich, for this priest was very clear about the anti-Christian character of Nazism. Dietrich warned him that his life would be in jeopardy if he returned to Germany, but Father Metzger felt that it was his duty to remain with his flock. Later, he paid the price of his heroism; he was murdered by the Nazis.

While some Germans were driven to despair and some chose heroic courage, others, such as the famous conductor Otto Klemperer, became embittered. Klemperer was Jewish, but he had converted to Catholicism. He was a handsome man, with a noble face, a sort of Maccabean type. He had a strong, dynamic, overpowering personality. He resented being forced to leave Germany because of his "impure blood". He hated Nazism, but Dietrich suspected that it was more because he had been victimized than because he fully grasped the horror of its philosophy. He lived in Fiesole in a magnificent villa overlooking the city, to which he invited his new friends. Soon afterward, Lisl Brewster-von Hildebrand invited Klemperer to San Francesco. He began to play on the piano a melody he had recently composed. It was basically a hate song, full of the spirit of revenge. Marguerite Solbrig, who was at San Francesco at the time, ventured to remark that that type of bitterness was incompatible with Christianity.[48]

Knowing how difficult it was for practicing Catholics in Germany to remain immune to the spirit of the time, Dietrich decided to write to the close friends he had left behind in Munich, warning them of the dangers to which they were being exposed daily. In this letter he wrote the profound words that appear in *The Memoirs* published in Germany:

> It is totally irrelevant whether—for political reasons—the Antichrist [read: Hitler] does not antagonize the Church at present and signs a concordat with the Vatican. The crucial question is the spirit that animates him—the erroneous teaching he spreads—the crimes he commits. Criminal actions offend God quite independently of whether the victim is a Jew, a socialist, or a bishop. Innocent blood cries to heaven. The absolute, unbridgeable antagonism existing between the Nazi philosophy

---

[48] Otto Klemperer later moved to Vienna, where he lived in an enchanting apartment in Schönbrunn. He often invited Dietrich and Gretchen, who both enjoyed the incredible beauty and culture of the place. He also frequently gave them tickets to the concerts he was directing.

and the Church is to be found in the former's racism, in its totalitarian system, in its anti-Christian ideology—and the evil character of these ideas is in no way diminished because Hitler happens to sign a concordat with the Vatican—a legal document he will trample upon as soon as he finds it convenient.

Each recipient of this precious letter immediately destroyed it. To keep it in one's possession was too great a danger.

It was a time of sorrow and anxiety. In addition to concern for family and friends in Germany, Dietrich and Gretchen spent many tense moments in the summer of 1933 awaiting the return of their son, Franzi, from a year abroad. Through Fritz Beck, Franzi had obtained a scholarship to study for one year in the United States at Williams College in Massachusetts. Endowed with an adventurous spirit, the young man was delighted. He left on a German ship in 1932. Unusually talented in languages, he had already acquired a remarkable mastery of English, and this opportunity enabled him to become truly bilingual.

In January 1933, when Hitler was appointed chancellor of the German Reich, the young German student was asked to comment on the local radio in Williamstown. Fully sharing his father's views, Franzi expressed his total rejection of the Führer in the most outspoken terms, thereby rendering himself vulnerable to Nazi blacklisting and arrest; for even at this time the Nazis were deploying well-trained spies in the United States.

Finding out about their son's public condemnation of Nazism, his parents, now in Florence, begged him not to take a German ship (on which he had a return ticket) back to Europe. If he did, he would have to land on German territory, and he might find himself subject to arrest. As they had no money to finance his return trip, they begged him to try to borrow the money for passage on a French or Italian liner. But Franzi was not only extremely courageous, he was a daredevil and, in contradistinction to his father, very sly. He was convinced that he could outmaneuver the German spy net. In spite of his parents' repeated admonitions, he took a German ship heading for northern Germany, having ascertained first that it would make a stop in the French port of Le Havre. While on board, he made the acquaintance of a female German student, whose political views he did not trust. She openly flirted with him and invited him to visit her parents in northern Germany. Franzi skillfully joined in the flirtation and accepted her invitation. Arriving in Le Havre, he pretended he was going to do some sight-seeing. Instead, he took the first train to Paris. From there he traveled to Florence, and before long he had arrived safely at San Francesco, to the joy of his anxious parents, who in the weeks before his arrival had found their only solace in prayer.

In July 1933, Dietrich received the visit of Klaus Dohrn,[49] his sister Nini's nephew by marriage. The young man had been working as a journalist in Rome and had an uncanny talent for politics. He came to Florence to discuss the political situation with Dietrich. Klaus shared Dietrich's hatred for Nazi ideology and, like him, saw that it was waging war on what was best and noblest in Germany. Hitler was the country's deadliest enemy. To love Germany and hate Hitlerism were two facets of the same thing. Both men agreed that a true German patriot had to do everything in his power

---

[49] Klaus Dohrn (1908–1979) was then a journalist. His mother, Hanneli Sattler-Dohrn, was Nini's sister-in-law. He, like von Hildebrand, fled Vienna in the wake of the annexation of Austria. He was for a while in a concentration camp in Spain, but eventually he emigrated to the United States.

to oppose this evil and liberate his country. They were over-joyed to see that at last one European politician recognized the gravity of the Nazi threat. He was Engelbert Dollfuss,[50] who, at the young age of forty, had become chancellor of Austria.

In the course of a long talk they had on the roof terrace of San Francesco, Dietrich and Klaus conceived a plan to found in Austria a weekly magazine dedicated to combating National Socialism—to unveil its dangerous and poisonous philosophy and to open people's eyes to the threat it constituted, not only for Germany, but for the whole of Europe, for Christianity, and possibly for the whole world.

The idea of having a chance to continue his fight against National Socialism, to put his talents at the service of a noble cause, and thereby to serve the Church enthused Dietrich. He decided to go to Vienna to obtain an audience with Chancellor Dollfuss, to expound his plans and win him over to the idea of supporting the weekly he had conceived. But Dietrich was penniless. Fortunately, a dear friend, Rosa Oldenburg, who was residing in Switzerland, volunteered to finance his trip. In August 1933, Dietrich was on his way to Vienna. He first arrived in Salzburg but, because the city had its *Hochschulwochen*, or summer academic courses,[51] precisely in August and several of the lecturers were well known to him, he decided to stay in nearby Hallein. This caution was not typical of him, but he had been advised that the Nazis liked to kidnap an enemy on foreign soil, gag him, put him in a car for a drive across the border, and then execute him.

---

[50] Engelbert Dollfuss (1892–1934) was named chancellor in May 1932.

[51] These courses were first offered in 1931. They were suspended during the war but were resumed afterward. Famous national and international speakers were invited, including Étienne Gilson, Jacques Maritain, Edith Stein, Alois Mager, O.S.B., Michael Cardinal Innitzer, and Rudolf Allers.

Salzburg was only a few miles from the German border, so it was a tempting hunting ground for the Nazi secret police.

Unfortunately, Dietrich combined his laudable caution on this occasion with a very imprudent decision. He called a man named Wilhelm Wolf,[52] whom he had met some time before in Salzburg at the home of his friends the Schuchters. Wolf had been introduced to him as an admirer of his books. Dietrich hardly knew him, but he naïvely assumed that Wolf, being an acquaintance of close friends of his, would naturally share their political views. He was to discover that he was greatly mistaken.

Dietrich made an appointment with Wolf at the railway restaurant in Salzburg, on his way to Vienna. He unfolded his plans, informing him that he was going to the Austrian capital in the hope of seeing Dollfuss and convincing him of the importance of founding an anti-Nazi magazine. He also mentioned that he was planning to see Kurt von Schuschnigg,[53] the minister of culture. Wolf immediately asked Dietrich to put in a good word for him with Schuschnigg. He told him that he had been maligned by Father Alois Mager because of a misunderstanding and that this could jeopardize his career. Without asking for further details and without checking the facts with Father Mager, whom he knew well as his former spiritual director, Dietrich—always eager to do someone a favor—promised to do so. He naïvely assumed that Wolf had truly been the victim of a misunderstanding.

Dietrich's first visit to Vienna was a fiasco. After several unsuccessful attempts to see Dollfuss, he tried one more time.

[52] Wilhelm Wolf (1897–1939) was an official in the Austrian Ministry of Education; he belonged to the "Catholic Nationalists" and occupied an important post when the Nazis took over in 1938.

[53] Kurt von Schuschnigg (1897–1977) was an Austrian politician who became Chancellor after the death of Dollfuss in July 1934; he held this post until March 1938, when he was arrested and imprisoned by the Nazis until 1945.

After a long wait, he was informed that the chancellor had had to leave urgently for Salzburg. Discouraged, Dietrich saw that his trip had not been planned wisely. Crestfallen, he went back to Florence via Salzburg, hoping that he could meet with Dollfuss in that city. This hope was not fulfilled, but Dietrich did not give up. He planned carefully for a return trip.

Father Mager knew a man named Gottfried Domanig, who had been a close friend of the chancellor's since their schooldays. Either Father Mager or another Benedictine monk, Dom Thomas Michels, who knew Gottfried Domanig's wife well, recommended Dietrich to him. This connection proved to be critical.

In October 1933, Dietrich once again boarded a train going to the Viennese capital, a flicker of hope in his heart that this time he would succeed. Through friends, he had made the acquaintance of a man named Breitenfeld and his lovely wife, Johanna (née Schönborn, a close relative of now-Cardinal Christoph Schönborn), who both shared his political views and concerns. They invited him to spend a few days with them at their residence close to Saalfelden and generously offered him the use of their apartment in Vienna while they were still vacationing. Their kindness and help, which extended over weeks, was God-sent and proved to be invaluable when Dietrich and his family moved to Austria at the end of the month.

Arriving in Vienna, Dietrich immediately called Gottfried Domanig, who invited him to his home. Dietrich had the pleasure of seeing again Domanig's wife, whom he had met years before in Rome. For a while she had been the secretary of another friend of Dietrich's—the historian Ludwig von Pastor[54]—when the latter was residing in Rome.

[54] Ludwig von Pastor, Austrian Ambassador to the Holy See, is best known as a historian of the papacy.

The meeting between Dietrich and Gottfried Domanig went extremely well. The latter was clearly impressed by the philosopher's personality, his clarity of vision, and the value of his plan. Domanig was confident that an interview with the chancellor could be arranged in the near future. After a few days of feverish suspense, Domanig called Dietrich to inform him that he was coming to fetch him the following Saturday to bring him to Dollfuss' home, not to his office in the Ballhaus. This news delighted Dietrich. It would give him the opportunity of a much more personal contact with the chancellor, and the informality would enable him to learn something of the man, not only of the statesman. He would receive an "inside" view of the situation.

With a beating heart, Dietrich went to what turned out to be a historical encounter. The chancellor received him with great friendliness and warmth and listened with full concentration to the plans that had matured in Dietrich's mind. Dietrich spoke with the conviction of someone who knew that he was fighting for a worthy cause. It was clear to him that Dollfuss had an unusually quick and sharp mind. He said to his visitor: "Today, political questions are no longer purely political; they center on questions of *Weltanschauung*. For me the fight against National Socialism is essentially a fight in defense of the Christian conception of the world. Whereas Hitler wants to revive the old Germanic paganism, I want to revive the Christian Middle Ages."

The chancellor immediately grasped the importance of the project his visitor was developing and intuited the powerful intellectual asset that Dietrich could be to him in his own fight against National Socialism. He promised the refugee not only the support of the Austrian government for his magazine but also a full professorship at the University of Vienna as soon as a vacancy occurred. His plan was to make an exchange of professors: those who were friendly to the Nazi philosophy should move to Germany, while professors in Germany who opposed Hitler's regime should be appointed in Austrian universities.

Dietrich von Hildebrand could not have expected more, and he left Dollfuss with his heart full of gratitude. Not only had the chancellor fully grasped the value of the plan he had expounded, but his personality had made a deep impression upon him. He exuded intelligence, warmth, and a human note steeped in a deep faith; he clearly perceived the threat that Nazism constituted for Christianity, and, in contradistinction to contemporary politicians, he saw that fighting Nazism was the *Kairos*, the call of the hour, and that this call was coming from God. Unfortunately, Dollfuss stood alone. Statesmen in the rest of Europe seemed to be in a state of political somnolence.

Elated by the success of this interview, Dietrich then made an unwise decision that revealed again his naïveté and his tendency to trust people without carefully checking their credentials. That was a result partly of his ideal background and partly of his instinctive dislike for mistrusting people. He hated "worldly prudence". He liked to show his hand and to be open with friends and acquaintances. He hated deviousness and the cult of secrecy that some people cultivate. He also was loquacious and had never mastered the art of controlling his tongue. But political life in Vienna at the time was undergoing a severe crisis, with rivalry, backbiting, and treachery rampant. In short, the city was a hotbed of intrigue. Dietrich's background and personality had ill-prepared him for that.

Dietrich decided to turn a second time to Wilhelm Wolf. Not only did he report in detail on his interview with the chancellor, but he asked Wolf for all sorts of practical advice concerning salaries and appointments. Common sense should have warned him that his talk with Dollfuss should be kept secret for a while. Besides, it was through Domanig that he had had the favor of seeing the chancellor, and he should have turned to him for advice. In hindsight, Dietrich often acknowledged to me that his action had bordered on madness.

Interestingly enough, Wolf had little reaction to the report, and he did not give the enthusiastic response to the plans for the magazine that Dietrich had anticipated. Dietrich being totally preoccupied with his new mission, however, it was only later, when Wolf showed his true colors, that he remembered how cool Wolf's response had been.[55]

Dietrich also paid a visit to Edmund Weber,[56] who told him that the chancellor had earmarked for six months a sum of money from an emergency fund to enable him to move to Vienna and establish himself there. Weber was to be the funnel through which Dietrich would receive the state money Dollfuss had promised to finance the magazine.

If Dietrich nurtured no suspicion of Wolf's antagonism to his plans when he spoke with him, he had immediate reason to reconsider, when, the very next day, he entered a café and was greeted by three men (whom he knew superficially; one of them was Eugen Kogon). They said, "We congratulate you on the success of your interview with Dollfuss." Dietrich

---

[55] Later that evening, going back to the Breitenfelds' lodging, von Hildebrand suddenly found that he had lost the keys to their apartment. Crestfallen and upset, he called them to apologize; but, instead of being irritated, they promised they would send immediate help. Soon afterward, a Father Frödl, a Jesuit and a friend of the Breitenfelds, proved to be an expert locksmith and managed to open the door, and he let the absent-minded professor in.

[56] Edmund Weber (1900–1949), a journalist, became the director of official communications in the press office of the Austrian federal government in April 1933.

was dumbfounded. How could these men (whose political stand he did not trust) know about his visit to Dollfuss? In answer to his query, one of them answered sardonically, "I happen to know everything that takes place in Vienna." The answer to Dietrich's query was easy—Wilhelm Wolf.[57] But even this fact did not yet open his eyes. Later he was to find out that the man in whom he had confided, the man he had warmly recommended to Schuschnigg, was a Nazi at heart. He had let the fox into the chicken coop.

So, after seven months of uncertainty, during which Dietrich had witnessed with despair a Germany buckling under Hitler's dictatorship, he stood before the opportunity he had desired. He was about to move to Vienna to start a weekly magazine that would systematically denounce and unmask the Nazi philosophy and be a trumpet call to all Christian governments to unite in fighting evil. He knew this task would be fraught with difficulty and frustration and that it could bring danger for himself and his family. He was convinced, however, that he was responding to a divine call to which he must give his whole-hearted assent. His conscience would not allow him to follow the advice of Prelate Münch, who urged him to move to Sicily and write his *Ethics*, safely away from the perils of the dangerous political sphere. He was convinced that his call was to go to Vienna, enter the fray, and wage an intellectual war on the abomination called National Socialism. Resolved on this course, Dietrich von Hildebrand returned to Florence and began preparations for his departure for the Austrian capital.

---

[57] See footnote 52, page 253.

CHAPTER 5

Vienna
1933–1938

At the end of October 1933, Dietrich, Gretchen, and Franzi moved to Vienna. Much as Dietrich von Hildebrand loved the Austrian capital, a city of music, charm, and beauty, the fifty-four months he was to spend there were, from many points of view, a time of severe trial.

He and his family were for a while the guests of the kind and generous Breitenfelds, who offered them hospitality until they found adequate housing. They did find a lovely apartment facing the Stefan's Dom, into which they moved in December 1933.

The magazine was christened *Der Christliche Ständestaat* (The Christian corporative state). This name was not Dietrich's choice. He wanted a title that referred explicitly to his anti-Nazi stand, but he had to yield to the pressure of Friedrich Funder, the editor-in-chief of the magazine *Reichspost*. Dietrich had met Funder during his first visit to Vienna in August 1933. When Dietrich told him that he was hoping to move to the Austrian capital, Funder had applauded. He had published in the August 1933 issue of

Reichspost an article that Dietrich had written in Florence entitled "The Great Hour for Austria", which was, in a way, a synopsis of his future plans.[1]

The first problem to be tackled with Edmund Weber was the question of salary. Weber offered Dietrich a salary of 600 schillings a month. Typically, Dietrich reminded Weber that he had already been promised money from an emergency fund for six months. Should he be given a salary while he was receiving the emergency fund? Weber was clearly surprised at his guilelessness. "But you are heading the magazine and deserve remuneration", he said. Then von Hildebrand urged Weber to endorse the appointment of Klaus Dohrn, who had collaborated with him on the plan for the magazine, as his assistant. He requested for Dohrn a salary of 500 schillings, a large sum for a beginner in the journalistic field. Weber was both reluctant and puzzled, reluctant because he thought it was wiser for the promotion of the magazine to appoint an Austrian citizen to the post and puzzled because he thought that the salary requested was much too high for an unknown young journalist. Weber made it clear that he disapproved of the arrangement. Dietrich knew, however, that the word "parsimony" had no place in Klaus' vocabulary and that he would not be able to manage on a lower salary. In an attempt to resolve the impasse, and to Weber's amazement, Dietrich then suggested that Klaus be given 600 schillings and that he himself take a salary of 500 schillings. Weber now understood that he was not dealing with a "child of this world". With a sigh, he granted his request. Dietrich also convinced Weber that he needed Marguerite Solbrig as his secretary. Marguerite was Jewish, although as a child she had been baptized Protestant, and she had entered the Catholic Church in 1919.

[1] Dietrich von Hildebrand, "Österreichs große Stunde", *Reichspost*, no. 231 (August 20, 1933): 1ff.

Dietrich knew that if Marguerite remained in Germany, she was doomed to a concentration camp. Her life was clearly in danger. He convinced her to move to Vienna, where she arrived early in 1934. Her coming proved to be a blessing for both Dietrich and for *Der Christliche Ständestaat*. With her he had someone whom he could trust unconditionally and who fully understood the importance of his mission.

The first weeks in Vienna were terribly hectic. Dietrich had to organize the publication of the magazine, no easy task. He also had to appoint employees, rent a place of business, and find a printer. Moreover, he had to supervise the work being done in the apartment he had found before he could move into it with his family. (Despite its loveliness, the apartment had no toilet.) He was not the sort of person for whom this type of activity is easy, but he knew he had to do it. He was carrying on a mission God had entrusted to him, and he was driven by a sense of duty. Still, the obstacles were formidable. He was no organizer. He had to rely on collaborators whose efficiency and trustworthiness were often far from what he had a right to expect. Several of them lacked the selfless dedication required for that kind of work. More than once, his directives were not obeyed, and yet he was officially in charge and responsible for the publication of the weekly. Because of his warmth and his unconventionality, he was incapable of asserting his authority, and his subordinates, aware of this weakness, often abused his kindness. Not all of them viewed their work at *Der Christliche Ständestaat* as a moral and religious calling. To some, it was a political concern; to others, a way of earning a living.

Every month, Dietrich had to wait in line at the office of Edmund Weber. This was not only humiliating; it cost him much time and energy that could have been put to better purposes. But he accepted everything as the price he had to pay to accomplish what he considered his mission. In spite of all the many difficulties, the first number of the magazine was published in early December 1933.

A remarkable feature of *Der Christliche Ständestaat* was that it attacked both Nazism and Communism simultaneously. That was necessary—many people had become Nazis because they opposed Communism, and others had become Communists because they hated Nazism. The confusion was great, and it was crucial to show that these two ideologies were in fact equally poisonous and that they stemmed from the same roots: atheism, anti-Christianity, the triumph of brutal force, totalitarianism, and contempt for the dignity and the rights of the individual.[2]

In this herculean, thankless task, Dietrich was helped by the boundless devotion of Marguerite Solbrig. More than once, she saved the week's publication of *Der Christliche Ständestaat* through her dedication, courage, selflessness, and perseverance. One of her more laborious tasks was to get Klaus Dohrn (a "professional" bohemian) to write his brilliant articles and submit them on time for publication. More than once, she actually pulled him out of bed to get him to do so.

The response to the magazine was more hostile than Dietrich had anticipated. Many people considered him a pessimistic refugee, a prophet of doom whose warnings disturbed the joyful life of the Viennese capital. He was an unwelcome Cassandra, a party-spoiler. Some had caught the "Nazi virus" and had opposed him from the very beginning. Some considered Nazism an expression of the "world spirit" and were convinced that to run counter to this historical

---

[2] See the articles in the *Der Christliche Ständestaat* and Rudolf Ebneth, *Die Österreichishe Wochenschrift "Der Christliche Ständestaat"* (Mainz: Matthias Grünewald Verlag, 1976), p. 83.

current was both useless and meaningless. Finally, there was a rampant anti-Semitism in several Austrian circles that did not take kindly to von Hildebrand's relentless opposition to anti-Semitism as anti-Christian. A shocking instance occurred when, invited to give a talk at a seminary, Dietrich thundered against anti-Semitism, stressing its total incompatibility with the authentic face of the Catholic Church. To his deep dismay, several seminarians simply left the room. He was never invited to speak there again.[3]

Dietrich von Hildebrand made no compromises. He did not water down his message. He spread the truth, in season and out of season. While acclaimed by the many who were warm supporters of his work, he was hated by others. The anti-clerical, lapsed Catholics, the pro-Nazis, the Communists, the anti-Semites, all labeled him a dangerous man whose activities ought to be curbed. He received numerous anonymous letters, some merely abusive, others threatening, even to suggesting that he should be hanged "on his own intestines".

In addition to his heading *Der Christliche Ständestaat*, Dietrich led an active social life. Not only had he and Gretchen resumed holding the "afternoons" that they had given in Munich, but they were also frequently invited out. Dietrich regarded all this social activity as important for his mission as an anti-Nazi apostle, for it enabled him to meet as many people as possible so as better to spread his message.

If this were not enough activity already, during his years in Vienna Dietrich kept up an extensive schedule of traveling to

---

[3] Léon Bloy: "Anti-Semitism, a completely modern invention, is the most terrible slap that our Lord received in His face during His Passion, which is still going on; it is the most bloody and unforgivable slap because He receives it on the face of His mother and by the hands of Christians": in *Das Mysterium Israels*, ed. Jacques und Raïssa Maritain (Otto Mueller Verlag), p. 301.

give lectures, as he had in the 1920s. He often used these lectures as opportunities to reiterate his opposition to National Socialism. In December 1933, soon after he was settled in Vienna, he was invited to speak at the University of Louvain in Belgium and at the Institut Catholique in Paris. In Belgium, he hoped to be able to pay a visit to the empress Zita,[4] who was residing in Steenockerzeel, outside Brussels. Before acting on these plans, however, he discussed them with Weber. After all, he was in a semi-official position, and he wanted to make sure that the Dollfuss administration had no objection to this visit. Weber gave him permission to pay his respects to the empress.

He had been invited to Belgium by a Professor De Bruyne, who was teaching at the University of Ghent, but he gave his talks at the Catholic University of Louvain. There Dietrich made the acquaintance of the rector of the university, Msgr. Ladeuze, and of the faculty. His theme was the nature of a priori knowledge, which was the very backbone of phenomenology, and his talks were well received. He did not miss his chance to attack Nazism, proclaiming it a joy and a blessing to lecture in a university that was still truth-centered, and adding that, unfortunately, this was no longer the case in German universities. This final remark was little appreciated by some young Dominicans who were studying in Louvain, and they hastened to write a negative critique of his talk. But Msgr. Noël, a professor at the Institut Supérieur de Philosophie, warmly thanked the speaker and hinted that he, too, deplored the political situation in Germany.

After leaving Louvain, Dietrich paid a visit to Empress Zita. He was received by Count Trauttmansdorff and Count

---

[4] Empress Zita (1892–1989), Princess of Bourbon and Parma, was the consort of the last Habsburg (Hapsburg) emperor, Charles; they were driven out of Austria in 1918.

Czernin, secretaries to the empress. She was a most impressive personality, with the noble bearing of a queen, exhibiting dignity, moral strength, and yet a winning gentleness. She embodied the great tradition and culture of European aristocracy at its best. Dietrich had always been an ardent admirer of Emperor Charles,[5] whom he considered a saintly man, and he gave expression to this veneration. Young Archduke Otto (who was twenty-one) also came into the room.[6] They discussed the political situation: it was clear that Empress Zita radically opposed Nazism. She favored Dollfuss' political views, but as an archmonarchist and a member of the deposed Habsburg dynasty, she could not share her visitor's enthusiasm for his leadership.

It was a strange situation for Dietrich von Hildebrand. On the one hand, he was indeed himself an ardent monarchist and considered the demise of the Habsburgs a terrible blow not only for Catholic Austria but for Europe. On the other hand, he had a deep admiration for Dollfuss, who singlehandedly was fighting the Nazi Goliath. The theme of the hour had to be collaboration with him, inasmuch as the Habsburgs had been stripped of all political power.

Deeply impressed by this visit, Dietrich proceeded to Paris for his talk at the Institut Catholique. He immediately got in touch with his friend Count Robert d'Harcourt, who had often been his guest in Munich and whom he had not seen since March 11, 1933, when the French aristocrat had come to the Maria Theresia Strasse to say goodbye to Dietrich and Gretchen, just a few hours before their departure. To his joy, he also saw F. W. Foerster, who was then residing in Paris. He

[5] See note 4, above. Having succeeded Franz Josef, who died in 1916, Charles was forced to resign in 1918. He died in exile, in Funchal, Madeira, in 1922.

[6] Otto, the eldest child of Charles and Zita, was born in 1912.

also met the renowned Russian philosopher Nicolay Berdyayev,[7] a man with a facial tic that from time to time caused his features to contract into terrible grimaces. Dietrich's lecture, devoted to the incompatibility between Christianity and National Socialism, met a warm response. Msgr. Baudrillart,[8] rector of the Institut, who was known to be very anti-Boche, had not advertised the lecture at all. As a result, Dietrich spoke in front of a small audience. Overcoming his antipathy for everything German, Msgr. Baudrillart addressed a few friendly words to the speaker.

Dietrich also saw the great Thomist philosopher Jacques Maritain,[9] who invited him to Meudon, where he made the acquaintance of Maritain's wife, Raïssa, and her sister, Vera. Dietrich had not seen Maritain since 1928 in Constance, where they had met for the first time at a conference, and he was again impressed by his spirituality and his deep religiosity. After dinner, Maritain took his guest to his private chapel, where both men prayed for a few moments. He gave Dietrich a copy of his book *Les Degrés du savoir* and asked him whether Dollfuss, whom Maritain admired, would appreciate a copy. Dietrich assured him that the Austrian chancellor would be delighted. He then left Paris so that he could arrive back in Vienna for the Christmas vigil.

The year 1934 proved to be as eventful as 1933 had been, with Dietrich editing *Der Christliche Ständestaat*, lecturing,

[7] Nicolay Aleksandrovich Berdyayev (1874–1948) was a Russian Orthodox philosopher of religion. Later, in Vienna, von Hildebrand heard him give an outstanding lecture, being particularly struck by the following remark: "Whereas the whole of creation is anthropocentric, man, the king of the material universe, is called upon to be theocentric"—a profound and very pertinent thought at a time when man was claiming metaphysical independence from his Creator.

[8] Alfred Cardinal Baudrillart (1859–1942), French theologian and historian, had been a professor at the Institut since 1883. He was named cardinal in 1935.

[9] Jacques Maritain (1882–1973), French Thomist philosopher, became a convert to Catholicism in 1906.

and continuing to observe with alarm the political scene. During the year, Dietrich received a visit from Eduard Pant,[10] a senator from Oberschlesien, a territory that had become a Polish possession after World War I. Senator Pant was fighting for the rights of German minorities in Poland. At the same time, with unusual clearsightedness, he was radically opposed to National Socialism, even though it claimed to be a defender of the oppressed German minority in Poland. Pant managed to be a faithful Polish citizen while simultaneously fighting for the rights of the German minority. From the moment they met, he and von Hildebrand discovered they were kindred spirits. They were united not only by their common faith but also by their condemnation of National Socialism.

Senator Pant extended an invitation to Dietrich to give talks in Kattowitz, which he accepted. In April 1934, he boarded a train going to Bohemia. The train, however, was made up of cars going either to Poland or to Germany. Over and over again, Dietrich anxiously made inquiries to ascertain that he was in the right car. The idea of finding himself inadvertently on German soil was terrifying to him. The talks he gave in Kattowitz were successful, and Dietrich and Senator Pant developed a lasting friendship.

Senator Pant frequently came to Vienna, and one day he told Dietrich that when he was a young man he had dated Hitler's half-sister Angela,[11] who had married Leo Raubal, by whom she had two daughters, one of them named Geli. It was a well-known fact that Hitler was infatuated with his

---

[10] Eduard Pant (1887–1938) was the publisher of the weekly *Der Deutsche in Polen*, which was an organ of the Deutsche Christliche Volkspartei, a political party that represented ethnic Germans living in Poland.

[11] Angela Raubal (1883–1949), Hitler's half-sister, married Leo Raubal in 1903.

niece and had invited her to share his apartment in Munich. One day, in 1931, it was announced that Geli had committed suicide. There were rumors that Hitler and his cronies had had a hand in her death, but nothing could be proven.

In the course of one of his visits to Vienna, Senator Pant called on his former sweetheart. They decided to go to the cemetery where Geli was buried. Coming to the tomb, Senator Pant ventured to say to the bereaved mother, "It is inconceivable that a lovely young girl chose to take her own life." Angela Raubal burst into hysterical tears, and, though she was choked by sobs, Senator Pant heard her say, "It is in no way true that she took her own life. She was murdered. . . . Adolf . . . Göring. . . ." But it was impossible for the stunned senator to understand the rest of her sentence.

In 1934 Austria began to experience socialist political unrest. In February, out of a clear blue sky, the socialists, led by a Dr. Otto Bauer, mounted a revolution in Vienna (the fourth Dietrich had witnessed). Having access to a cache of weapons, they began shooting in the streets. Dollfuss did everything in his power to negotiate with the rebels. He promised them total immunity and begged them to stop shooting, for the good of the country. They would not listen to reason, however. What was Dollfuss to do? As head of state, he had to guarantee the safety of the citizens. He could not possibly allow the meaningless killing to go on. There were socialist snipers on roofs and at windows, and no one venturing onto the streets was safe. Very much against his will, Dollfuss called in the army to suppress the rebels, and within a couple of days calm was restored. Dr. Bauer fled the country. Inevitably, however, there had been casualties on both sides. At a religious memorial service held in the Michael church, Dietrich was deeply moved by the words spoken by the chancellor,

preaching peace and reconciliation and offering his prayers
for all those who had lost their lives, whether soldiers or
socialists. Dollfuss then declared a general amnesty.

Whatever grievances the workers who fomented the revolution had, they should have realized that, at a time when the
one great threat was National Socialism, any unrest in Austria
was bound to weaken the government and play into Hitler's
hand. There was nothing Hitler wished for more than unrest
in Austria. It would offer him a "legitimate" pretext to invade
this small and virtually defenseless country. For that reason,
many socialists had been opposed to the rebellion, but their
preference had been defeated by a single vote.

The consequences of the revolt's suppression were serious
for Dollfuss. The press hastened to label him a "murderer".
Jacques Maritain, who two months earlier had expressed to
Dietrich his admiration for the chancellor, was now outraged
by his handling of the crisis. The chancellor was labeled a
nasty dictator, one who trampled ruthlessly on the workers.
Maritain organized a protest in Paris and collected signatures.
(Interestingly, Gabriel Marcel[12] refused to sign the document.)
Today history textbooks and encyclopedias present Dollfuss
as an undemocratic, autocratic, ruthless chief of state. It is to
be hoped that, in time, historians will restore his reputation
by shedding light on the abysmal difference between totalitarianism and authoritarianism. In the first case, the rights of
the individual are ruthlessly trampled upon. He is considered
a slave to a Leviathan called the State, to whom he belongs
body and soul. An authoritarian government, on the other
hand, is limited strictly to the political sphere. In times of
emergency, heads of state are granted extraordinary powers

[12] Gabriel Marcel (1889–1973), French philosopher, dramatist, and critic,
converted to Catholicism in 1929. He shared many of von Hildebrand's political convictions.

that allow them to make the quick decisions that the slow
democratic process of arguments and counterarguments ren-
der impossible. It is true that Dollfuss headed an authoritarian
government. But, as he confided to his close friend Gottfried
Domanig, he considered it his tragic fate that, although at
heart a democrat, he had to play the role of a "dictator". A
peace-loving man, he had been forced to call in the army to
put down a revolt. Someone with a historical mission (and
Dollfuss had one) is often forced into a role totally opposed to
his basic position and deepest aspirations.

In a book dedicated to Georges Bernanos,[13] I found an
article drawing a parallel between this famous French writer,
well known for the strong political positions he adopted, and
Jeanne d'Arc, the sweet, gentle maid of Domremy who heard
the call to wage war—*bouter les Anglais hors de la France*—to
lead fierce battles and witness fearful bloodshed, in order to
fulfill a mission that she would never have chosen and that
cost her her life. Analogously, Dollfuss was a man of peace
who was called upon to fight. He found himself in a dramatic
situation that justified the stance he took, and he knew that
by taking such a stance he was opening himself to unfair
criticism. Someday history may acknowledge that it was Dollfuss' greatness to have perceived "the call of the hour" with
clarity, opposing the abomination of National Socialism at a
time when most politicians were suffering from an acute case
of moral blindness. That was the great political theme he was
called upon to address, and it prevented him from turning his
attention to other themes that he had very much at heart.
After all, he was the only political figure in Europe at the time
who was fully clear-sighted, and for that he paid with his life.
Hitler had no reason to order the murder of a Chamberlain—

---

[13] *Georges Bernanos*, ed. Albert Beguin (Neuchâtel: La Baconnière, 1949).

that well-intentioned but pathetically blind politician who swallowed wholesale the lies that Hitler served up to him in Munich in 1938.

This is what Chesterton had to say about this episode in the Austrian chancellor's life: "Against this heathen horde Engelbert Dollfuss, a small man of poor and peasant ancestry, stood up by the ancient instinct of such ancestry, resolved to save the remnant of the Roman civilization of Germany." Referring to the socialist revolution, he wrote:

> I will say only this. That any judgment on it is worthless, which does not face the fundamental fact; that it was dealing with Mutiny in time of War. It is obvious but inadequate to say that Dollfuss was fighting upon two fronts. He was an Austrian patriot, a Catholic very considerate of the claims of the proletariat, who found himself attacked from behind by the Communists, at the very moment when he was defending his own country against tyrants who had oppressed everybody, including the Communists. . . . Nothing would be more typical of the traditions from remote times, than the tale of a dwarf who led armies that defeated the stupid giants of the German forests. But whether or no he will be remembered on earth will matter to him very little; for though the swine who trod over him forbade him even a priest, we know upon what Name he called when he died.[14]

The short-lived socialist revolt considerably weakened Dollfuss' position. Unwittingly, the socialists had played into Hitler's hand. They had undermined the Austrian chancellor's

[14] "The Death of Dollfuss", *The End of the Armistice* (1940), reprinted in *The Collected Works of G. K. Chesterton*, vol. 5 (San Francisco: Ignatius Press, 1987), pp. 574–75.

popularity, thereby encouraging the Nazis' imperialist designs on Austria. Dollfuss was doomed. He had already once escaped an attempt to assassinate him, in October 1933. It was clear his enemies were going to make another try.

But another unfortunate episode must here be mentioned. It was decided that capital punishment, which had been abolished in Austria, should be reintroduced in the hope of deterring the series of criminal assaults—clearly instigated by the Nazis—that were proliferating there. This measure seemed to be a reasonable response. But when Weber told Dietrich that he hoped that the first culprit caught would be a Communist and not a Nazi, Dietrich became upset. Weber clearly feared that if the first victim of this new law were a National Socialist, the result would be an uproar in Germany and an increase in the political tension between the two countries. To Dietrich this argument was in no way convincing. He was certain that Hitler's hatred for the Austrian chancellor was such that whatever Dollfuss did or did not do would be subject to relentless criticism. Totalitarian states have their agenda, and it is naïve to assume that their conduct is dictated by the actions of their adversaries. They ruthlessly pursue their own course.

Tragically, the first criminal caught was neither a Nazi nor a Communist but an arsonist. Animated by revenge, he had burned down a barn. Obviously, such a deed, though deplorable, did not deserve capital punishment. But the Austrian courts seemed pleased to find a culprit who was not a Nazi and on whom the new law could be applied. Dollfuss was unhappy about the sentence, but he thought it was his duty to let it be carried out. He prayed ardently for the condemned man, but he decided not to commute his sentence of execution. Dietrich was beside himself: this outrageous injustice was deeply upsetting to him. Moreover, apart from the moral question, Dollfuss was making a serious mistake. The day on which that unfortunate man lost his life, Dietrich and Gretchen were spending the evening with Mataja and Oberst Bam, both of whom were likewise horrified at the arsonist's fate. He was no doubt guilty, but there was a shocking disproportion between his offense and his punishment. Neither the host nor his guests could condone a *raison d'état* to justify an injustice. It was a sad evening.

The deadly hatred that the Nazis had for Dollfuss did not abate, and finally, on July 25, 1934, they acted. Early that morning, Dietrich had paid his usual monthly visit to Weber. The latter had told him how pleased the chancellor was with his work and that, as a token of appreciation, he was giving him an extra sum of money to enable Dietrich and Gretchen to take a well-deserved vacation. Elated to know that a man for whom he had such profound esteem was pleased with *Christliche Ständestaat*, Dietrich rushed home to share the good news with Gretchen. More than the welcome sum of money, Dollfuss' appreciation was a comfort and a balm to him.

Shortly afterward, he received a phone call from Father John Österreicher, a convert from Judaism, who had founded a remarkable organization for the conversion of Jews, the Pauluswerk. (Margarete Solbrig, the daughter of Hermann and Marguerite, was Father Österreicher's secretary.) He told Dietrich that he had just heard on the radio that Dollfuss had resigned and that the new chancellor was Anton Rintelen,[15] who had publicly supported Nazism. Dietrich was thunderstruck and exclaimed, "This is impossible. I just saw Weber, and he would have told me had anything of the sort taken place." Soon afterward, Father Österreicher called again, saying, "There seems to be unrest in the city. Something is going on."

---

[15] Anton Rintelen (1876–1946) was an Austrian jurist and politician.

July 25 turned out to be a tragic day. Dietrich turned on the radio, and in a short while a terrible announcement came through. Dollfuss was being held prisoner in his office at the Ballhausplatz. No one knew for sure what was happening. Dietrich wrote: "I knelt down at my desk and begged God to save Dollfuss. I broke into sobs at the thought that this noble fighter against the anti-Christ, this lovable, kind, and deeply pious man, had fallen into the hands of criminals." Dietrich foresaw that, even if Dollfuss survived, it was likely that he would be forced to compromise his position. How terrible to think that he had fallen into the hands of his deadly enemy and that nothing could be done to liberate him.

By 7 P.M. the Austrian chancellor was dead, and the public was finally informed of what had taken place. Just a few minutes before the official change of guards was scheduled to take place at noon, Nazis wearing state guard uniforms had invaded the chancellor's office, and, as he tried to escape, they shot him. Dollfuss collapsed on the floor, where he stayed for hours, bleeding to death. He begged his assassins to send for a priest and a doctor; they ignored both requests. His whole staff was taken prisoner. Two guards took care of him, putting a bandage on his wound. Dollfuss thanked them with the words, "Children, you are so kind to me. Why are the others so different? My one aim was to work for peace. We never attacked anyone. We had to defend ourselves. May God forgive them." He was allowed to speak briefly to Major Fey. He begged him to ask Mussolini to take care of his wife and two children. (In 1934, the Italian dictator had not yet fallen into Hitler's clutches.)[16]

---

[16] At that time, Mussolini's fate as Hitler's ally had not yet been sealed. As related by John Toland, Mussolini described Nazism as a "revolution of the old Germanic tribes in the primeval forest against the Latin civilization of Rome" and called Hitler "the murderer of Dollfuss": *Adolf Hitler* (Garden City, N.Y.: Doubleday, 1976), p. 355.

Dollfuss died as a Christian—while praying. The most far-sighted politician of that tumultuous epoch had fallen victim to the ruthless brutality of the Nazis.

Dietrich von Hildebrand's sorrow was profound. For once, he had met a politician whom he could admire. Dollfuss had understood the menace that Nazism constituted not only for Germany and Austria but for the world, and he was murdered by his relentless enemy, Adolf Hitler. Even though Dietrich's primary concern was the tragic end of Dollfuss and the fate of Austria, he also recognized the consequences of this event for himself. Who would be the next chancellor? Would he understand the importance of Dietrich's own mission to fight Nazism and oppose its ever-growing infiltration in Austria? Would he continue to support *Der Christliche Ständestaat*?

Shortly after the assassination of Dollfuss, Dietrich was asked by the Salzburg publisher Pustet to write a book about the chancellor. Dietrich locked himself in his study and, in twelve days, completed a biography of this great statesman. The published work was critically acclaimed and translated into Spanish, but it was soon forgotten.[17] In his book *Modern Times*, the historian Paul Johnson grants Dollfuss only a few lines and does not even mention that he was assassinated by the Nazis—a surprising omission.[18] When the cronies of one head of state assassinate another head of state, that is a traditional *casus belli*; it certainly deserves to be mentioned.

Pressed by Father Österreicher, who was convinced that Kurt von Schuschnigg[19] would be a better chancellor than his

[17] Dietrich von Hildebrand, *Engelbert Dollfuß: Ein katholischer Staatsmann* (Salzburg: Anton Pustet, 1934).

[18] Paul Johnson, *Modern Times: The World from the Twenties to the Eighties* (New York: Harper and Row, 1983), pp. 322–23.

[19] Kurt von Schuschnigg (1897–1977) was federal chancellor of Austria from 1934 to 1938.

rival, Prince Ernst von Starhemberg,[20] Dietrich paid a visit to President Wilhelm Miklas[21] and urged him to appoint von Schuschnigg. This task was intensely distasteful to Dietrich, who thought it tactless for him to interfere in Austria's internal political decisions. But when Father Österreicher wanted something, he proved to have an iron will and could be fiercely tenacious. He left von Hildebrand no peace, and he appealed to his conscience, knowing that that was the best way of convincing him to see the Austrian president. Dietrich reluctantly yielded to the priest's pressure. Wilhelm Miklas (whom Dietrich had met previously) was very friendly. He told Dietrich that even though it was too soon after Dollfuss' tragic death to choose his successor, he too was inclined to think that von Schuschnigg was a better choice.

Kurt von Schuschnigg did become chancellor. He was a good, friendly man, with impeccable aristocratic manners. He was quite young, in his late thirties. From the very first moment, however, Dietrich von Hildebrand and Klaus Dohrn sensed that he had neither the vision nor the personality and clear-sightedness of Dollfuss. He was *Grossdeutsch* in his outlook and nurtured the thought that the cultural bond existing between Germany and Austria was so deep that he could create a climate of "peaceful coexistence". In his political naïveté, he had convinced himself that one can live peacefully with the devil if one treats him courteously and does not irritate him unnecessarily. He opted for a political program of "good will" toward his fierce neighbor.[22]

[20] Prince Ernst Rüdiger von Starhemberg (1899–1956) was vice-chancellor under Dollfuss and Schuschnigg from 1934 to 1936.

[21] Wilhelm Miklas (1872–1956) was president of the Austrian Republic from 1928 to 1938.

[22] Von Hildebrand saw Schuschnigg later in 1948, at Fordham University, where the former chancellor of Austria had been invited to give a talk. The

Soon after von Schuschnigg became chancellor, Dietrich was informed that the Austrian government would no longer finance *Der Christliche Ständestaat*. At that date, only about half of the money originally promised by Dollfuss had been received. The very moment that Dollfuss died, Weber's attitude toward Dietrich changed radically. He who had been extremely friendly toward him, knowing that Dietrich was a *persona grata* with Dollfuss, now, sensing that the political winds had turned and that the new chancellor considered Dietrich's work a nuisance, became extremely reserved and made it clear that he wanted to keep his distance.[23]

No longer supported by the government, *Der Christliche Ständestaat* was facing a bleak future. That it managed to survive until the *Anschluß* (the German annexation of Austria) borders on the miraculous. Financially, it always was on the brink of bankruptcy. For more than forty-four months, Dietrich was forced to solicit contributions for the publication of the paper just to cover daily expenses and to pay salaries, which often could not be paid on time.

There never was someone less talented for fund-raising and more helpless in financial matters. San Francesco was no nursery for business people. Gottfried Kunwald, a noble Jewish lawyer, once told Dietrich, "You are a child of light, and not a child of the world; one must come to your help"; and he did help him more than once with his wise advice. Dietrich was trusting and naïve, always giving people more credit than they deserved, and more than once he was either cheated or found himself in hopelessly tangled situations. He was so

---

seven years he had spent in a concentration camp had opened his eyes to the essence of Nazism, and he humbly acknowledged to von Hildebrand that his assessment of the situation from 1934 to 1938 had been seriously flawed.

[23] Many are those who have had a similar experience; Polonius is a type whom one can meet in daily life and whom one meets very often in politics.

ingenuous concerning business practices that, once, assuming his act to be one of friendliness, he countersigned a document lending a large sum of money to a staff member of *Der Christliche Ständestaat*. He did not understand that if the money were not paid back on time, he himself would be held responsible. The staff member had claimed that he was a talented fund-raiser who, if he were given a sum of money, could pull the magazine out of its financial difficulties. As any businessman could have foreseen, results were not as promised, and Dietrich could have found himself in serious troubles. The *Anschluß* put an end to that worry.

The challenge of seeking support for *Der Christliche Ständestaat* became still more difficult in the wake of an incident that occurred in the autumn of 1934. Dietrich received and accepted an invitation to give a lecture at the Sacred Heart University in Milan. Not only did he greet with pleasure every opportunity to go to *il dolce paese dove suona il si* (the sweet country where the "si" [yes] resounds, as Dante put it), but this occasion would give him another chance to speak out against Nazism in Italy. During his talk, he showed how empty the philosophy of National Socialism was, highlighting at the same time the arbitrary and artificial foundations of racism.

After his lecture, he was interviewed by the press. Unworldly and childlike as he was, he volunteered the information that his paternal grandmother was Jewish. It never occurred to him that this show of solidarity with a persecuted people could have dire consequences for his fight against anti-Semitism in Austria. This information, eagerly disseminated by the press, soon found its way to the Viennese news media. No sooner had he returned to Austria than he heard himself labeled "The Jew Hildebrand". In and of itself, this would not have disturbed him in the least; his feeling of deep solidarity with the Jewish people was sincere. But being labeled put him in a vulnerable position. His radical rejection of anti-Semitism was now seen as simply a man fighting *pro domo*. Friedrich Funder, who had so warmly greeted Dietrich's coming to Vienna in 1933, now turned against "this Jew".[24]

As Dietrich's situation at *Der Christliche Ständestaat* worsened in the wake of the Dollfuss assassination, he needed all the more the full professorship at the University of Vienna that Dollfuss had promised him. Now that Schuschnigg was chancellor, it was incumbent on him to fulfill this promise. However, as soon as von Hildebrand's name was mentioned in this connection, it triggered a state of turmoil in the university. Many intellectuals had been more or less infected by the Nazi virus, and these did everything in their power to prevent a "fanatical" anti-Nazi from spreading his dangerous ideas. Moreover, Dietrich von Hildebrand was known to be an ardent Catholic and a daily communicant. Such piety was no recommendation in intellectual and scientific circles.

Schuschnigg found himself in a predicament. On the one hand, he was bound by a promise. On the other, he did not want to make enemies of the university professors. As a compromise, he forced an elderly member of the faculty, a certain Professor Gomperz, to take his retirement, claiming

---

[24] That von Hildebrand himself was the victim of anti-Semitic abuse is illustrated by the text of an anonymous postcard, produced by Ludendorff Buchhandlung in Munich, that was sent to the editorial offices of *Der Christliche Ständestaat*: "Nothing characterizes your attitude toward 'Christian morality' better than the fact that that old swindler Matajas, . . . who stashed away the money he got by fraud under foreign names, is your collaborator. And he has the nerve to write about the gospel! His lines drip with religiosity. Yeah, you are all the same, you bums! You know exactly why you all 'battle' together! Vaugoins, Matajas, Seifert, Schmitz, Kimmels, Poukars, and the rest are all bums and low-down religious collaborators of the Jew Hildebrandt [sic]! A fine direction!"

that financial constraints made the step necessary. Having fabricated this excuse, Schuschnigg could then in good conscience tell von Hildebrand that it was impossible to give him a full professorship at the present time but that he could count on it as soon as it became financially feasible. Those were empty words. A few months later, Schuschnigg appointed another full professor of philosophy, Alois Dempf, who unknowingly stepped into the position that rightfully belonged to von Hildebrand. The latter consoled himself with the thought that at least Dempf was not a Nazi. In the meantime, Schuschnigg did appoint von Hildebrand an *aussergewöhnlicher* professor, a position of less honor and financial remuneration than a full professorship.

The denial of the full professorship to von Hildebrand put him in an increasingly difficult financial position. The salary of an *aussergewöhnlicher* professor was a mere pittance, on which he could not live. Fortunately, God had given von Hildebrand a great gift. He never allowed himself to be crushed by financial concerns. Because he was fulfilling a mission, he trusted that God would help him. Humanly speaking, however, his situation was very precarious.

In order to be appointed at the university, even *aussergewöhnlicher* professors were required to make a series of calls to dignitaries in the city. One of them was to the cardinal of Vienna, Theodor Innitzer.[25] As Dietrich entered the episcopal palace, His Eminence greeted him with great friendliness. "Dear Professor," he said, "I am so happy to hear that you will soon be able to take a post at our university. You can well imagine how I rejoice over this. There are so very, very few committed Catholics teaching there." He then named two of them, adding that there was a third, a Herr Eibl, but that the

[25] Theodor Innitzer (1875–1955) was consecrated archbishop of Vienna in 1932 and was named cardinal the year following.

latter was a fool who kept making novenas for the Nazi victory in Austria! Dietrich von Hildebrand left with the feeling that the cardinal was both a friend and an ally.

Cardinal Innitzer, though kind and well-meaning, was in truth a spineless man, one of those numerous people who yield to pressure, who hate to say "no", and who usually take the side of the latest visitor. Immediately after his interview with von Hildebrand, the Cardinal received the visit of none other than Wilhelm Wolf, the same man in whom the naïve von Hildebrand had confided several times, thinking him to be an anti-Nazi. Wolf cleverly hid his true colors until Hitler had invaded Austria.

While von Hildebrand had recommended Wolf to Schuschnigg in August 1933 because he asked for his help, Wolf now repaid that kindness in his own way. He told the cardinal that the majority of professors were strongly opposed to Professor von Hildebrand's appointment. He brought His Eminence a long list of names of those who viewed the candidacy of this "troublemaker" as a grave source of problems that would disrupt the peace the university was enjoying. He added that von Hildebrand was known to create havoc wherever he went. His hope was that the cardinal would add his illustrious name to the list of those wishing to block the appointment. The gist of his message was that Dietrich von Hildebrand was a fanatic, and fanaticism had no place in a respectable university. Without more ado, His Eminence took his pen and signed the petition! Shakespeare could have written, "Bishop, frailty is thy name." Despite this petition, however, Schuschnigg persisted in giving Dietrich the lesser professorship. Dietrich was to begin his teaching duties in February 1935 (he had not taught for twenty-three months).

In Germany and Austria it is customary for a newly-appointed professor to give an inaugural public lecture. Von

Hildebrand's was scheduled for January 1935. He had formed the bad habit of arriving at the university at the last minute, rushing up the long staircase, and arriving breathless at the lecture room. Accordingly, on the day scheduled for his public lecture at the University of Vienna, Dietrich arrived late, and he said to himself that it might be better to go straight to the lecture hall with hat and coat on. "If I go to my office," he reasoned, "I will be further delayed." Rushing up the stairs, he met a young girl who was going down: "You are going to Professor von Hildebrand's lecture?" she asked. Indeed, he was. "Don't even try to get in. It is packed", she advised. He was pleasantly surprised and assumed this to be a sign of interest.

Because of the girl's remark, he decided to go first to his office and take off his coat. There he found the dean of faculty, Dietrich von Kralich, pale as a ghost, who greeted him with the words, "Dear Professor, you cannot give your lecture. There is a fierce demonstration going on against you. It might lead to bloodshed." To this Dietrich replied calmly, "Dear Dean, I must give my talk, and I shall give it. You understand that if I give in today, those who oppose me will repeat the show, and I shall never be able to teach at the university." The dean then consulted with Hans Pernter, a high official in the department of education, who took von Hildebrand's side and declared that the lecture had to be given at any price. Soon afterward, Baron Karl von Stein, the legal adviser of the university, joined the discussion. Together with the police, he was responsible for peace and order at the university. Dietrich knew him well as one who shared his views on Nazism. In no time, Stein took matters in hand: "You will give your lecture", he told Dietrich von Hildebrand. "I have just called out forty-eight armed policemen, who will take care of the troublemakers and remove them from the lecture hall." Shortly afterward, the public who had been waiting, wondering what had happened to the speaker, were informed that only philosophy majors and those who had received personal invitations would be permitted to attend the lecture, which was going to be given in another auditorium. It took some time to sort everyone out, but when the process had been completed the forty-eight policemen, armed to the teeth, came to the dean's office to collect von Hildebrand. Escorted by this impressive force, Dietrich entered the hall to which the lecture had been reassigned and received a standing ovation. He gave his lecture, the topic of which was purely philosophical. As a matter of principle, he never discussed politics on university grounds. It was his conviction that a professor should not use his post as a platform for political propaganda. After a few minutes, some students in the audience, disillusioned that the speaker was giving them no occasion to protest, got up and left the room, banging the door behind them.

This event made news on the Austrian radio that very evening. Later, Dietrich found out that the demonstration had been planned by his would-be colleagues. They had encouraged their own students from various faculties to come with clubs and cudgels to beat up the unwanted professor.

Needless to say, the thirty-odd months von Hildebrand taught at the University of Vienna were not pleasant. Whenever he entered the faculty room, the pro-Nazi professors would ostentatiously turn their backs or refuse to shake hands with him. There was, however, one exception. Professor Moritz Schlick always treated Dietrich courteously. He was a logical positivist, and his philosophical position was radically antithetical to von Hildebrand's. But Schlick was also an anti-Nazi, and, during those fateful years, that was the key issue. It was one of those interesting cases in which there is a clear dichotomy between a person's character and his ideas. It was ironic that a man with whom von Hildebrand could not have discussed philosophical problems for two minutes without clashing was the one who appreciated the work he was doing to curb the threat of Nazism in Austria.

Then, tragedy. On June 22, 1936, Schlick was murdered at the university. One of his students was dating a young man who was clearly mentally disturbed. She once told Professor Schlick that this man wanted to marry her, and she asked for his advice. The latter had no choice but to say that he could not encourage her to do so. The disturbed young man got wind of this and shortly afterward shot Schlick, who died instantly.

Dietrich was much upset by this terrible event. A little while later, Schlick's son came to see him and asked him to defend his father in *Der Christliche Ständestaat*. The magazine *Schönere Zukunft* had published a hostile article on Schlick, stating that his death was the expression of the people's spontaneous protest against his "typically Jewish anti-metaphysical position". Although Schlick himself was not Jewish, the article went on, he had nevertheless adopted allegedly Jewish views and was therefore a representative of the Jewish spirit. The article concluded by saying that his being shot was, therefore, not a murder but an elementary protest against his destructive anti-metaphysical philosophy.

Without a moment's hesitation, von Hildebrand took up pen to compose the dead man's defense. First he showed that the murder had been committed for purely personal reasons and had absolutely nothing to do with any intellectual protest. He showed further that there was no connection whatsoever between Schlick's philosophy and his death. Moreover, he convincingly proved how inane it was to claim that the Jewish spirit is essentially anti-metaphysical. He referred to thinkers such as Maimonides, Spinoza, Bergson, and Husserl, who give the lie to this claim. Finally, he showed how revolting it was to use the tragic murder of an Aryan as a stepping-stone to further anti-Jewish propaganda. He was happy he could make this modest contribution to the memory of a man who was a decent human being, whatever the flaws in his philosophy.

Throughout von Hildebrand's years in Vienna, he drew more and more hostile attention to himself as a result of his journalistic and academic activities. It became clear to him that the Nazis were bound to monitor his activities and would be looking for an opportunity to assassinate him. The threat to his safety, however, never deterred him from his continual public denunciations of National Socialism. His suspicions were confirmed when, early in 1935, he received a letter from the Austrian chief of secret police, Hofrat Ludwig Weiser, requesting that he pay him a visit. But Dietrich already had plans to go to Rome to see Nuncio Pacelli, who by then had been named a cardinal and appointed Vatican Secretary of State. A Jewish businessman by the name of Wilhelm Berliner, head of the large Phoenix Insurance Company, financed his trip; he wanted information on the official position of the Church concerning Nazism.

After the usual greetings, von Hildebrand began to discuss the Nazi question with Cardinal Pacelli. He said, "Is your Eminence aware that [a historic] moment has taken place in Germany, the like of which happens only every three hundred or four hundred years, a moment in which (possibly) millions of Protestants and Socialists would have found their way to the Church, if all the bishops in Germany—without any compromise—had opposed National Socialism with the words *Non possumus*, if they had built a wall against National Socialism and had denounced all its crimes, if they had pronounced a total 'anathema against Nazismus'?"

To which Pacelli answered: "Indeed, but martyrdom is something that the Church cannot command. It must be freely chosen." The cardinal then said that there could be no possible reconciliation between Christianity and racism; they were like "fire and water". The interview gave von Hildebrand great satisfaction. He was confident that Cardinal Pacelli was fully aware of the gravity of the situation in Germany.

Another important visit that Dietrich made while in Rome was to Prelate Kaas.[26] More than once, *Der Christliche Ständestaat* had taken a critical position toward this man and had expressed its satisfaction upon hearing that he was being sent to South America. To pay him a visit was no pleasure, but apparently Prelate Kaas had expressed a wish to see Dietrich von Hildebrand. It was clear that this priest had been much offended by the criticisms leveled at him, for, as Dietrich stepped through the door, and even before the two men greeted each other, the priest said: "You have done me wrong; I have no share of responsibility in the position adopted by the Center party." He began to defend himself vigorously, while putting all the blame on Chancellor Brüning (chancellor of Germany from 1930 to 1932) and claiming that he himself was an outspoken enemy of National Socialism. Nevertheless, it is to be noted that Prelate Kaas had sent Hitler a telegram of congratulations on his birthday on April 20, 1933. The whole tenor of the discussion was highly unpleasant. On the one hand, Dietrich remained unconvinced; on the other, he was not in a position to judge whether the accusations Prelate Kaas threw at Brüning were justified or not. But the priest's attitude reminded von Hildebrand of the French saying: *Qui s'excuse, s'accuse* (he who excuses himself, accuses himself).

[26] Kaas was a member of the Reich, president of the Center Party from 1928 to 1933.

It was only when Dietrich came back from this trip that he remembered the request from Dr. Weiser, and he decided to comply with it. In appearance and looks, Weiser resembled Sherlock Holmes as he is usually pictured. He had an intelligent face, sharp features, and a calm, controlled expression. He was very friendly, and he asked Dietrich how he was feeling. As Dietrich informed him that he was well, the chief of the secret police immediately started *in medias res*: "You see, dear Professor, for the head of the secret police, a political murder is always a very unpleasant affair." Dietrich immediately took the hint and retorted that for him it would be very painful too. Weiser then proceeded to say: "We have our secret sources of information, and we know that the Nazi underground is planning to assassinate you." He then lectured Dietrich on how he could and should protect himself. He was told that he should never receive an unknown visitor when alone—and this at a time when he was continually seeing refugees coming from Germany. Weiser elaborated: "Your so-called visitor is likely to put a chloroform mask on your face and then stab you in the heart. When your wife comes home, she will find a corpse. Also, do not ever enter a car unless you know the driver well. Take your name off your front door and out of the telephone book. Never make appointments by telephone." Dietrich had been doing exactly the opposite on every count.

As Dietrich was well informed about Nazi techniques, he was not surprised by Herr Weiser's description of the Nazis' plans for his assassination. He had known from the beginning that the Nazis were murderers who could justify any immorality that served their aim. All the same, it was not pleasant news. One thing, however, stands out. Dietrich von Hildebrand was not at all the sort of man who brags that nothing scares him. He refused to take meaningless physical risks. He had no trace of *hubris*. To him, human life was something infinitely precious. Why jeopardize it through silly bravado? God had given him remarkable moral courage, however. As a child he had opposed the ethical views of his father and sisters. He never feared standing alone against a howling mob. In Vienna, he was fulfilling a divine call, and he thought: *Deus providebit* (God will provide). This was to be his motto for many years to come. Of course, he felt bound to share with Gretchen the unpleasant information he had received, and from that moment on she lived in a constant state of anguish (her blood pressure became alarmingly high) and always accompanied him to the university, even though her presence would hardly have been much of a protection or a deterrent to the Nazis!

In May 1935, Dietrich accepted an invitation to give talks in Budapest. When he stepped out of the train at the Hungarian capital, he was greeted by the gentleman who had invited him and by a man he did not know, who told the traveler that he was a detective. His name was Del Monaco. He accompanied the visitor to his hotel, but, before allowing him to enter the room assigned to him, he entered himself, checked carefully under the bed and in the closet, and then told him that he could safely come in. Dietrich was baffled by this behavior, but he became genuinely upset when Mr. Del Monaco told him that he was going to lock him in his room and return at 9 o'clock the next morning to get him. Dietrich had found out that there was an early Mass in the nearby church and expressed his desire to attend, but the detective told him that he started work at 9 o'clock and that Dietrich would have to wait for him to come.

That was all very strange indeed, but this scenario continued throughout his visit. The detective accompanied him everywhere, always showing the same concern and the same care. One day, when Dietrich was being driven by his friend to a famous Benedictine abbey, the detective noticed that a car was following them closely. He told the chauffeur to stop. He then stopped the other car and checked on the driver and his passengers. He came back with the information that they were ordinary tourists and that they could proceed safely. Much as von Hildebrand enjoyed the beauty of Hungary, its strong national atmosphere, and its special talent for festivity, he found it very peculiar that Mr. Del Monaco did not leave him alone even for a moment.

When Dietrich returned to Vienna, he told Gretchen about this mysterious adventure, and she confessed that she herself was the key to the episode. Worried about Dietrich on this trip because it was a typical Nazi trick to kidnap people while they were traveling, she had written a letter to Chancellor Schuschnigg, telling him that according to the head of the secret police her husband's life was in danger. She suspected, of course, that the chancellor's life was also threatened, but he had his bodyguard, while her husband had no protection whatsoever. Schuschnigg must have been moved by her plea, and he had made arrangements with a member of the Hungarian secret police to follow von Hildebrand step by step. That was typical of Gretchen. Shy and reluctant by nature to step into the limelight, she could overcome her inhibitions when she feared for the life of someone she loved.

And so the years in Austria wore on, under the constant burden of activity and danger. The political situation continued to deteriorate, and it became more and more questionable whether the country could avoid a Nazi invasion. Despite the crushing tensions weighing on him during this period, von Hildebrand managed to write one of his more enduring works, *Transformation in Christ,* an exploration of the radical change that takes place in a person through grace.[27] The serene tone of the book belies the anxious circumstances in which it was composed. The book was published under the pseudonym Peter Ott. Had Dietrich von Hildebrand been identified as the author, the book could not have been sold in Germany—the main market for the Swiss publisher.

By early 1938, it was clear that the stalemate between Nazi Germany and Austria could not hold for long. On February 12, 1938, Schuschnigg accepted Hitler's invitation to meet him in his Bavarian mountain "retreat" in Berchtesgaden. Schuschnigg recognized later that this meeting had been a piece of "political blackmail".[28] But in his naïveté, in his desire to achieve "peaceful coexistence" at any price, the Austrian chancellor still hoped against hope to achieve some positive results. He did not want his conscience to be burdened by the thought that he had turned down any opening that might lead to peace.

From the very first moment, Hitler played the bully, intimidating his well-mannered, aristocratic adversary. Knowing that Schuschnigg was a chain-smoker, Hitler prohibited him from touching a cigarette during their colloquies. Schuschnigg was so addicted to tobacco that he could not function well when prevented from satisfying this craving.[29]

---

[27] English trans. *Transformation in Christ: On the Christian Attitude of Mind* (New York: Longmans, Green, 1948). During the summers of 1936 and 1937, a group of close German friends, who had missed him terribly since his departure from Munich, financed his trip to Italy. They rented San Francesco, and Dietrich gave the group a series of lectures, which were published later in Switzerland, by Benziger, under the title *Umgestaltung in Christus*.

[28] See Kurt Schuschnigg, *Austrian Requiem*, trans. Franz von Hildebrand (New York: G. P. Putnam's Sons, 1946), p. 198.

[29] See W. F. Foerster, *Erlebte Weltgeschichte 1869–1953* (Nürnberg: Glock und Lutz, 1953). According to Foerster, the Austrian Chancellor was living in a cloud of smoke that symbolized the fog in which he lived and made him reject any warning of danger (p. 215).

The Führer set before Schuschnigg a whole series of conditions for not invading Austria, one of which was that the chancellor "curb the journalistic activities of Dietrich von Hildebrand", an objective the Nazis had been seeking for years.[30] Schuschnigg signed this agreement, knowing it was not worth the paper on which it was written.

The Austrian chancellor's meeting with Hitler, as recounted in his memoirs, makes it indisputably clear that, by 1938, the Nazi forces had identified Dietrich von Hildebrand as the most outspoken opponent of National Socialism and were seeking to silence him by whatever means possible. I have in my possession a copy of a letter designated *Top Secret* and dated April 30, 1937, which the German ambassador in Vienna, Franz von Papen,[31] wrote to Hitler. In this letter von Papen refers to Dietrich von Hildebrand as the leading enemy of National Socialism; this letter echoes an oral statement that von Papen had made to Father Alois Mager, in which he called von Hildebrand "the most dangerous enemy of National Socialism". Other documents from the time place von Hildebrand near the top of the list—immediately after members of the government—of persons to be arrested in the event of a German invasion of Austria.

Schuschnigg decided to call a plebiscite, giving the citizens of Austria a chance to decide whether they wanted to remain Austrians or to become part of the German Reich. As soon as Hitler learned of this move, he became frantic; he had reason to fear that the outcome would not favor him. He wanted the plebiscite canceled and ordered some of his cronies, using sound trucks, to proclaim in Graz that the

---

[30] See documents from 1935 onward in Rudolf Ebneth's *Die Österreichishe Wochenschrift*, pp. 252ff., especially the chapter "*Der Christliche Ständestaat*". This book is a crucial document but does contain some inaccuracies.

[31] See note 34, p. 231, above.

plebiscite had been called off. Hitler knew only too well that the plebiscite results could be a resounding defeat for National Socialism. The pro-Nazis in Austria were only a minority, though a very vocal one. Hitler then decided that the moment had come to invade his helpless neighbor. To prevent the plebiscite, scheduled for Sunday, March 13, 1938, from taking place, he scheduled the invasion to occur first.

Dietrich, knowing of the threat to his life, had been watching for signs of a German invasion. During this period, he was lecturing frequently in Salzburg. In view of the precarious political situation, he made an agreement with his closest friends in Salzburg to warn him as soon as they noticed any unusual military activity at the frontier. Such activity would be a clear sign that the invasion of Austria was imminent. The code expression to be used in the event of impending invasion was: "If Anna wants to see her grandmother before it is too late, she should leave immediately."

On Shrove Tuesday, March 1, 1938, a Nazi sympathizer living in Salzburg told his wife (a fervent Catholic) that "von Hildebrand is doomed". He had been informed that the Nazis were getting ready to eliminate their troublesome enemy. As soon as his wife received this dreadful information, she ran to a priest who was a close friend of Dietrich's and related to him what she had just heard. This priest immediately called Vienna and transmitted the coded message. Not knowing what to make of it, because the news media had not mentioned anything about an impending invasion, Dietrich nevertheless decided to flee. A friend, Hellmut Laun (a recent convert), had an old car, and Dietrich asked him late in the evening to drive him and Gretchen to the Czech border, so that they could catch the last train going into Czechoslovakia. This trip, undertaken at night, during the winter, on a badly lit, unknown road, was something of a nightmare. The car

kept breaking down, and when the kind driver and his passengers finally did arrive at the border, the last train had left.
They had no choice but to spend the night at an inn. Dietrich
could not close an eyelid. The inn was situated on the main
road, trucks kept rolling noisily by, and he imagined they
were filled with regiments of soldiers. The next morning,
Wednesday, he bought a newspaper. Everything seemed to be
normal; there was no report of an invasion. So he and
Gretchen took a train back to Vienna,[32] thinking it had been
a false alarm.

A few days later, however, on Friday, March 11, Hitler's
forces invaded Austria.

---

[32] The incident is recounted by Hellmut Laun, *How I Met God*, trans. David
Smith (Chicago: Franciscan Herald Press, 1985), pp. 137–39.

CHAPTER 6

The *Anschluß* and Flight
1938–1940

Within hours of the German invasion of Austria, the face of Vienna changed radically. All sorts of sinister characters roamed through the streets, wearing the swastika in the lapel of their coats. Dietrich von Hildebrand knew that time was up. He still hoped to sell his furniture, books, and works of art to an American citizen, George Shuster, later president of Hunter College, who happened to be in Vienna at the time; unfortunately, he ran out of time. He then decided to take a train leaving for Pressburg, on the border between Austria and Czechoslovakia. Knowing that he was being watched by the Gestapo, he left his apartment on foot, with just his hat, coat, and cane, so that it would seem he was taking a walk. He had told Gretchen to pack up a few things, take a taxi, and meet him at the railway station. But the city was in a state of panic. There were no taxis to be found. Accompanied by his nephew, Michael Braunfels, and a young friend, Gilbert Schuchter, Dietrich walked to the Opera before finding one. Michael Braunfels found another taxi and went back with it to the Habsburger Gasse to fetch his aunt. At the train station,

Dietrich procured the tickets and, with a beating heart, waited for the arrival of his wife, having firmly decided that he would not leave without her. Finally, she arrived with a suitcase she had packed in haste. They just caught the train, the last one leaving Austria before the Nazis took over Vienna. It was crowded, mostly with Jews, who knew that remaining in Austria would cost them their lives. Arriving at the Czech border, the passengers were informed by an officer going through the various compartments that no Austrian citizen was permitted to leave the country. Despair was written on the passengers' faces. They knew that this order sealed their doom.

When he received his professorship in Vienna, Dietrich had automatically become an Austrian citizen, but he had never applied for an Austrian passport. He and Gretchen had their Swiss passport with them, a most valuable inheritance from Bruno Hildebrand's accomplishments in Switzerland some ninety years earlier. When the guard came to the von Hildebrands, they showed him the precious document. In a Swiss passport, the place of birth is not indicated. All that is mentioned is the Canton to which one belongs. In von Hildebrand's case it was Zürich. Below, there was written only "Professor". The guard—a member of the old Austrian guard, which within hours would be replaced by Nazi guards—looked at it and, seeing it was in order, let them stay on the train. All the Austrian passengers had to get off.

The train remained in the station for some time, during which Dietrich and Gretchen ardently thanked God that their Swiss passport had saved them from being detained in Austria. Then slowly, terribly slowly, the train started moving. When it had traversed half of the bridge separating the two countries, the guard said, "We are now on Czech soil." The von Hildebrands were saved. Franzi, however, was not with them. He was skiing at the time, and his parents had to leave Vienna without him. A terrible anxiety assailed them. Would Franzi fall into Nazi hands? A few hours later, all the Austrian border points had an arrest warrant for Dietrich and his wife, accompanied by their photographs and all pertinent information.

Early the next morning, Dietrich called his home in Vienna. The maid answered the phone, but she immediately made him understand that she was not alone. At two o'clock in the morning, several Gestapo officers had come to his apartment to arrest him. Interestingly enough, there was a huge fireplace in the living room, and Dietrich had always said jokingly, "This is a good place for me to hide, in case the Nazis come to get me." But the Nazis had left nothing to chance, and they knew the layout of the apartment perfectly. The fireplace was the first place that they checked.

Within days, all of von Hildebrand's earthly possessions— his furniture, paintings, manuscripts, and books—were taken to the Dorotheum in Vienna and sold at public auction. Von Hildebrand's anti-Nazi magazine was immediately seized and closed by the Gestapo. The last number of *Der Christlische Ständestaat* had appeared in Vienna on March 6, 1938. The next number, ready before the *Anschluß*, appeared only in Prague shortly after this fateful day.

From Czechoslovakia, Dietrich and Gretchen went to Budapest, where he had friends and acquaintances. They then proceeded through Yugoslavia and Trieste in northern Italy directly to Switzerland,[1] where they settled in Fribourg, sometime in the third or fourth week of March 1938. They were to remain in peaceful Switzerland for eleven months.

They had escaped from Hitler's claws, but on their way to

[1] They did not go to Florence at this time.

Switzerland, they were torn by the thought that Franzi might have fallen into his clutches. They had not been able to reach him and had no idea of his whereabouts. Dietrich and Gretchen lived through hours of heartrending anxiety until they arrived in Fribourg, where, to their unspeakable joy, they found Franzi safe and sound. He told his grateful parents that he too had had a miraculous escape. Off skiing when the *Anschluß* took place, he wisely did not go back to Vienna. Instead, he decided to take a train going west, to Switzerland. When he arrived at Buchs (at the Swiss border), all the passengers had to leave the train for customs. By then, the old Austrian guards had already been replaced by Nazi guards, who had a list of all their enemies. They had a warrant of arrest for Dietrich and Margarete von Hildebrand, with photographs and all pertinent information. On the way to Buchs, Franzi had prepared himself for any emergency. His Swiss passport indicated only the Canton from which he came. He had to have a ready answer to all the questions that could be put to him—the address where he lived, its exact location, possibly the names of his neighbors, and so on. Unlike his father, Franzi was good at that sort of thing. When he was ordered to step out of the train and was being interrogated, he thought he could handle the situation adequately. But, after checking his name, the guard suddenly pulled out a warrant of arrest for a certain Dietrich von Hildebrand, his wife, Margarete Laura, and their son Franz. "Do you know these people?" the guard shouted. Franzi was unprepared for this, but he played innocent and disclaimed knowing his parents. "But", the guard went on in a threatening voice, "you have the same name." "That may well be," said Franzi cooly, "but there are very many Hildebrands in Germany and Austria." Then, all of a sudden, he had a brilliant thought. "Look," he said, "the name is not the same. My name is

Hildebrand, not von Hildebrand." (The Swiss citizenship had been granted to Bruno Hildebrand many years before his son was knighted, so the Swiss passport did not carry the aristocratic "von".) The guard was visibly confused. Because there was a long line of people to be examined, he said sternly to Franzi, "I am not finished with you. Go into the waiting room. I shall come back to you as soon as these people have been examined." With a palpitating heart, Franzi ordered a cup of coffee. He fully appreciated how dangerous his situation was. He was sadly mulling over his fate when, all of a sudden, an Austrian employee, wearing the typical cap of railroad workers in Austria, addressed him with the words, "Do you want to take the train leaving for Switzerland?" "Indeed, I do", Franzi exclaimed. "Well, the train is just about to depart. I am going to let you go straight to the platform, otherwise you will not make it on time." And opening a locked door, he enabled Franzi to leave the waiting room without passing through the checkpoint. The conductor was about to give the sign for departure. Franzi opened the door of the closest car and jumped onto the train just as it started moving. He too was miraculously saved. When he sat down, his heart was pounding so violently that he could hardly breathe. One can only imagine the hymn of gratitude that sprang from his parents' hearts at their reunion.

Dietrich von Hildebrand had lost all his earthly possessions, but he, Gretchen, and Franzi had escaped Hitler's clutches, so gratitude was what was called for. Earthly losses were only earthly losses.

All of Dietrich von Hildebrand's forebodings, however, had been realized. The forces of evil were victorious. Christian Austria was now in the hands of the devil and was being brutally trampled upon by the boots of the *Schutzstaffel* elite guard—the SS. Hitler, like an octopus, was spreading his tentacles farther and farther. Would the Austrian Requiem awaken the European powers? No. The West, morally decadent as it was, closed its eyes. Soon Czechoslovakia was to suffer the same fate, and then Poland.

It was a period of intense trial and suffering, but God never abandons those who trust in Him. There were some lights shining in the darkness. One of these was a radiant Christian charity the von Hildebrands experienced. From March 1938 until they arrived on American soil on December 23, 1940, Dietrich and Gretchen were totally dependent upon the charity of others. They literally did not have a penny of their own. And yet, from the very first day, they found friends, acquaintances, and people unknown to them who had heard of their plight and came to their aid. Many a time, when I remarked to my husband that this life of total insecurity and political horror must have been terribly trying, he answered, "Yes, but I would not have missed it for anything in the world. To taste true Christian charity is an incomparable gift. It kept releasing in me floods of gratitude." Thus, in his poverty and insecurity, he tasted once again the unique gift of the supernatural, and in the very midst of his intense sorrow his soul experienced the joy of gratitude.[2]

In Fribourg, the von Hildebrands first stayed for a while at the house of Dietrich's disciple and close friend Balduin Schwarz, who was teaching in Fribourg at the time. (He was the student who had accompanied Gretchen and Franzi to the railway station on November 9, 1923, when they fled Munich in the wake of the Hitler-Ludendorff *Putsch*.) Because Balduin was being supported financially by his father, who was living in Hanover, he would have lost his source of income had it been known in Nazi Germany that he was

[2] See the section on gratitude in *The Art of Living* (Manchester, N.H.: Sophia Institute Press, 1994), pp. 103–39.

harboring a "traitor". As a result, the von Hildebrands had to look for another abode.

It was arranged that the refugees would be guests in a school at Haute Rive, situated a bit outside of Fribourg, where they were given free room and board. There they made the acquaintance of a young couple, Auguste Overney, a teacher at the school, and his wife, who made a point of helping them in every possible way. They had no hot water in the rooms they occupied, so Auguste, knowing that they got up early to go to Mass, would himself get up, heat water for them, and put it in a pitcher in front of their door. Auguste also had a small plot of land that he cultivated lovingly. The first fruits and flowers were given to Dietrich and Gretchen. There was a priest, l'Abbé Schervey, who one day came to visit Dietrich. He said, "Dear Professor, thank God you have a roof over your head and the amount of food necessary for sustenance, but you do not have a cent of pocket money. Do me a favor. I receive a stipend of two hundred francs per month. Please, do accept half of it out of friendship." Tears often came to von Hildebrand's eyes and those of his wife. They were tasting the sweetness of Christian charity, and this manna was to be their food for months to come, both in Switzerland and later in France.

When he was living in Austria, von Hildebrand had often been invited to lecture in Switzerland and France. That was how he had made the acquaintance of Msgr. Bruno de Solages, rector of the Catholic University of Toulouse, in southern France. Hearing that Dietrich von Hildebrand was now a refugee in Fribourg, Msgr. de Solages offered him a professorship in Toulouse. When France entered the war in September 1939, many of the priests teaching there had been called to military duty as chaplains, and substitutes were needed. Dietrich gratefully accepted the offer. The pay was very low (6,000 French francs a year, at that time about three hundred dollars), but he would experience the joy of teaching again. Moreover, ever since his childhood, when he was instructed in the culture of France by Mademoiselle Böhrer, he had had a special love for the charm and poetry of that great country. In February 1939, he and Gretchen moved to Fiac, a small village outside Toulouse.[3]

Once again, Providence cared for them. In Fiac, a French aristocrat, Comte de Rivals, put his castle at their disposal. He himself was living on his property in a smaller but more comfortable house, which had central heating. As the month of February was still quite chilly, he invited the von Hildebrands to be his guests until the first signs of spring made their appearance, that is, until late in March. Once again, the von Hildebrands met with nothing but kindness and generosity.

Dietrich took up his teaching duties, and twice a week he took a bus to Toulouse. He also started working on a book, *The Hour of Judgment*, a fierce condemnation of National Socialism and totalitarianism, and on another one (as yet unpublished) on justice. The first book was ready for publication when, in May 1940, the Germans invaded Paris. The galleys were immediately destroyed. No trace of this work remains.

Life in a small French village had its charm. Everything was simple and traditional. Dietrich daily carried water from the well and brought it to Gretchen for washing and cooking.[4]

---

[3] In Fiac, late in February 1939, Dietrich and Gretchen had heard the great news that Cardinal Pacelli, whom they had the privilege of knowing so well, had been elected pope.

[4] I have met very few people in my life who submitted more easily to their state of creaturehood than did Dietrich. How often did he do the dishes singing Italian songs all the while. These "boring and easy chores" (as the French poet Verlaine calls them) were things belonging to man's earthly situation, and he did them with humble submission. He knew himself to be God's creature, and he accepted joyfully all the burdens that creaturehood implied.

In August 1939, Hitler and Stalin signed their mendacious non-aggression pact, an action that was to seal the fate of Poland. Dietrich was still in Fiac when he heard the horrible news, and he immediately foresaw its inevitable consequences. At the same time, however, he could not refrain from experiencing a certain feeling of jubilation. "This is the hour of truth", he exclaimed. He had long been saddened that some people became Communists because they hated Nazism and others Nazis because they rejected Communism; he therefore hoped this shameful treaty (which Hitler, true to custom, broke two years afterward) would finally open people's eyes. To him, it had been crystal clear from the beginning that Nazism and Communism were twin brothers, advocating the same materialistic, atheistic philosophy, the same abominable totalitarianism, the same total disrespect for the dignity and value of the individual, the same hatred of the Church.

The Nazi drama was not yet over. In 1939, after conquering Poland and slaughtering many of its citizens (the invasion took place on Friday, September 1, 1939), Hitler's armies took over Norway, then Denmark in April 1940. And the final blow came on Friday, May 10, 1940, when Nazi forces invaded Holland and Belgium, preparing to invade France within a matter of days. (The *Anschluß* had also taken place on a Friday.)

On May 4, 1940, Dietrich had gone to Marseilles to give a series of lectures. During this brief sojourn, he made the acquaintance of Father Perrin, who became a close friend of the philosopher Simone Weil.[5] He also had the joy of striking up a friendship with the provincial of the Dominicans, Father Perceval.[6] The Dominicans were the audience for most of his

[5] Simone Weil (1909–1943) was a French author and philosopher.

[6] Dietrich had previously made the acquaintance of Father Perceval when, in 1935 and 1936, he had spoken at conferences dedicated to social and political

talks, but he also gave a lecture on marriage in a local parish. The sons of Saint Dominic received him with great warmth and friendliness.

Dietrich returned to Toulouse on Friday, May 10. He saw posters all over town informing the population that Hitler had invaded Holland and Belgium. Even though he had anticipated this horrible development because he knew the Nazi agenda through and through, nevertheless he was stunned. From the very first day, he knew that France would not be able to resist the onslaught of the *Blitzkrieg*. He knew the quality of German militarism; he knew that Hitler had educated his people to honor brutal force. He knew the discipline and the training that young Germans had received. France was in no way up to the task of confronting the German army. Day after day, he heard on the radio that German troops were advancing rapidly southward. The *Blitzkrieg* was no slogan. It was a fearful reality. By May 20, the Germans had reached Abbeville in northeastern France. By May 24 they were attacking Boulogne and Calais, and by June 14 Paris had surrendered.

One day during those tense weeks, as Dietrich was having lunch with his colleagues at the Catholic Institute, he suddenly started sobbing. One of them kindly inquired whether he or someone in his family was sick. He answered in a broken voice, "No, but I have reasons to fear that France is lost." He was more upset about the collapse of France than his French colleagues were. He knew better than they what was in store for the country.

As soon as the Germans invaded France, Dietrich knew that he had to flee again or risk capture and execution by the Gestapo. From mid-May on, he made frantic efforts to find a

---

issues, arranged by Msgr. Bruno de Solages. All the other participants were French priests and monks; he was the only layman and only foreigner.

way out of France. He was especially concerned about Gretchen, whose blood pressure remained dangerously high. He had also to take care of Franzi, who had come down from Paris with his young Irish wife, Deirdre Mulcahy, and their baby daughter, Catherine, just ten months old. Two courses seemed to promise safety—either return to Switzerland, hoping that that country's neutrality would be respected, or travel to Portugal, from which country they could take a ship out of war-torn Europe to safety in either North or South America. Dietrich sought the help of the Swiss consul in Toulouse but received none whatsoever. Dietrich first asked him for a visa for Portugal, but he was told that there were no diplomatic relations between Switzerland and that country. Dietrich then asked the consul whether he could help him return to Switzerland. Once again, the answer was no. The total lack of interest shown by the consul made Dietrich suspect that the man's sympathies were with National Socialism. In the meantime, the Germans were rapidly advancing along the eastern border of France, blocking the possibility of exiting France to the east.

Dietrich next tried to get false French papers with the aid of Msgr. de Solages' brother, Bernard, a secular priest—again, without success. In early June a public announcement informed the people of France that private cars could no longer be driven, and that checkpoints had been put on all roads. Escape seemed impossible. Nevertheless, Dietrich kept up efforts to obtain the necessary exit papers from government officials. By the third week of June 1940, he succeeded in obtaining a French exit visa and a Portuguese visa. Both were useless, however, without a Spanish transit visa. He was informed that it was impossible to get one in Toulouse, and that it could be obtained only in Bayonne, in the southwestern corner of France.

On June 21, therefore, Dietrich decided to attempt the trip from Toulouse to Bayonne.[7] He managed to convince a taxi driver to take him, his family, and his friend Father Österreicher (who had fled to Toulouse in late May after the Germans entered Paris) to Bayonne. The first night, they could not go farther than Sauveterre de Bearn. The next morning, June 22, von Hildebrand and Father Österreicher took a quick side trip to Gurs, where they knew that Margarete Solbrig had been interned as a foreign alien.[8] They then went on to Bayonne, and Margarete met them there after her release from detainment on June 23.[9]

---

[7] Von Hildebrand's itinerary on his way out of Europe has been deciphered from brief notes that he composed and dictated to me shortly before his death in 1977. Corroborating evidence has been provided both by what he had related to me personally and by passports of the von Hildebrands in my possession.

[8] Margarete Solbrig (Mücki) was the daughter of von Hildebrand's childhood friend Hermann Solbrig and his wife, Marguerite, who had been von Hildebrand's secretary in Vienna. Mücki had been Father Österreicher's secretary.

[9] Siegfried Hamburger suffered the same fate as Margarete Solbrig. He too, being a German citizen, had been interned for a while. But as a result of an injury to his eardrums during World War I, he had become totally deaf. His selflessness and spiritual radiance always impressed those who met him—even the inmates of the internment camp, who often fought ruthlessly for a better bunker, a bit more food, a more comfortable spot. A young German Jew by the name of Ernst Wolf started writing notes to him, that being the only way he could communicate with the deaf man. He told Hamburger the story of his life. His father was a rich businessman. One day, entering his father's office, Ernst found a large check made out to the Nazi party. Horrified, he decided to leave home. He abandoned everything and attached himself to the Spanish Republican army to fight against Franco. When Franco won the civil war in 1939, Ernst went to France, where he was interned in 1940. Meeting Hamburger in the internment camp became for him the occasion for a human and spiritual revolution. He started questioning Siegfried, and gradually their exchanges turned to religion. With his usual tact and gentleness, Hamburger spoke about the gospel and opened for the spiritually starved Ernst the treasures of God's love. The latter's soul was touched by grace, and when he was discharged from the camp he was baptized and entered the Church. Through Hamburger, he

Only those who have experienced political upheavals can picture the state in which our refugees found Bayonne. A town of one hundred and fifty thousand inhabitants now had to shelter some three hundred thousand people. Refugees of every nationality were crowding into the place. It was almost impossible to go to cafés and restaurants. Hotels were full. But Providence never abandoned Dietrich and his family. A worker on the outskirts of the town took pity on them and on sweet little Catherine, so blissfully unaware of their dangerous situation, and allowed the family to stay overnight. While in the city, von Hildebrand found out that they could not obtain Spanish transit visas there but would have to go farther south, to the small town of Hendaye.

On Monday, June 24, the von Hildebrands took a taxi to Hendaye, picking up on the way a Mr. von Seckel, an Austrian tobacco magnate, and his girlfriend. Mr. von Seckel was on the verge of despair and wanted to take his own life. But Dietrich persuaded him to have confidence and promised to

---

then met Margarete Solbrig. It was love at first sight, and they became engaged. But as the tornado of the *Blitzkrieg* ravaged France, Ernst, as a German Jew, had no chance of escaping except by joining the Foreign Legion. His fiancée remained in France until there was some promise that Ernst would be discharged from the Foreign Legion and could meet her in Lisbon. Margarete— who had waited for months for this happy reunion—managed (with the help of Edmond Michelet) to leave France and head for the Portuguese Capital. But to her despair and dismay, Ernst was not on the ship coming from North Africa. She had no choice but to leave for the United States alone. Dietrich von Hildebrand, who was already in New York at the time, made desperate efforts to get Ernst an American visa, but all his efforts in that direction were in vain. The young Jew had fought on the communist side in Spain and was therefore regarded as an undesirable refugee. Dietrich then went to Washington several times to obtain a Cuban visa for Margarete's fiancé. In this he did succeed, but the Cuban government always set a time limit to its validity, and each visa expired by the time it finally reached Ernst. One sad day, in February 1943, Margarete received the dreadful news that her fiancé had died of a serious infection. She never married.

help him as much as he could. Mr. von Seckel, on the other hand, helped the refugees financially.

The situation in Hendaye was as chaotic and desperate as it had been in Bayonne. The Spanish consulate was assailed by hundreds of refugees, for whom getting a Spanish visa was a question of life or death. Von Hildebrand had a personal letter from the archbishop of Toulouse, Msgr. Saliège, urging the consul in the most moving terms to grant him and his family this precious seal. The crowd was informed, however, that only people with a diplomatic passport would be admitted inside. The police, in a state of great tension, were ruthlessly pushing back the refugees. Meanwhile, the news was spreading that the Germans were advancing rapidly along the French coast and could be expected in the very near future. Having failed to obtain the life-saving Spanish visa, Dietrich had no idea where to turn.

If ever one can speak of providential intervention, where God's loving hand clearly changes what seems to be an inevitable course of events, it was then. Accidentally, milling about Hendaye trying to figure out what to do next, Dietrich met the niece of the ex-premier of France, Edouard Herriot.[10] She informed him of the conditions of the armistice that had been signed between Marshal Pétain and Hitler.[11] Much of the southern part of France would remain unoccupied by the invading forces. However, the German troops were proceeding all the way down to Bayonne and were expected to reach that city within hours. South of Bayonne, French territory

[10] Edouard Herriot (1872–1957) was a French statesman; he was premier of France from 1924 to 1925, and again from June to December 1932.

[11] Henri Philippe Pétain (1856–1951), a French military professional, was premier of unoccupied (and then occupied) France from 1940 to 1944. After the war, he was tried, convicted, and sentenced to death for collaborating with the Nazis during the war; the sentence was commuted to life imprisonment by Charles de Gaulle.

would remain unoccupied. The eastern part of southern France would also remain free.

This piece of information was crucial. Dietrich decided that they should try to get back to Bayonne, and from there go to Pau or Lourdes, so as to reach unoccupied territory before the Nazis captured Bayonne. It was a race. The clock was ticking.

Traveling as fast as they could, the von Hildebrands headed in the direction of Bayonne. But when they had reached the city, the driver flatly refused to take them to Pau. The Germans were now "at the door", and he did not like the thought of being associated with refugees.

The situation again seemed hopeless. The von Hildebrands were in Bayonne, knowing that the invading forces would arrive within hours. They had no place to stay and no means of transport out of the city. They were left standing in the town square with their suitcases at their feet. To add to their misery, a heavy rain started to fall. Images flitted through Dietrich's mind of dramatic stories he had read as a child that paralleled the situation in which they now found themselves. There was no exit. Within hours the Germans would control the town, and the fate of this small group of refugees would be sealed. In such moments, one knows that deliverance can come only from the hands of God, and Dietrich and the others prayed ardently, hoping against hope.

God heard their prayers and intervened in a miraculous way. By then, it was getting dark. All of a sudden, Dietrich heard someone addressing his son in French, "Are you not Dietrich von Hildebrand's son?" "I am here, too", Dietrich exclaimed. The person whose voice he had heard turned out to be Père Duployer, a Dominican. Dietrich had met him previously in Fribourg, where Msgr. de Solages had for several years organized conferences to which Dietrich had been invited. To see a familiar face in such dramatic circumstances is itself a blessing. Father Duployer had joined Les Chasseurs Alpins ("The Alpine Hunters", a French infantry corps that patrolled the Alps on skis) and had arrived from Norway just one hour earlier. He told Dietrich that within hours he was scheduled to fly to Morocco with his regiment.

Dietrich explained to him his desperate situation, that he and his family were trapped in Bayonne, the Germans were expected any minute, and, having been labeled Hitler's number-one enemy in Vienna, he and his family were in danger of immediate arrest and execution. He begged Father Duployer to take them with him to Morocco. "But," the priest replied, "we are taking a military plane, reserved for the army. I simply cannot grant your request. Nevertheless," he suggested, "come to the Grand Hotel. I want you to meet my colonel. We shall then discuss what we can do for you."

Soon afterward, Dietrich, accompanied by Father Öster-reicher, went to their place of appointment and met the man in whose hands his fate now lay. Both priest and layman prayed continually and put their confidence in God. To Dietrich's amazement, the colonel greeted him warmly. "Dear Professor," he said, "I do not know you personally, but my wife heard your talks at the Pax Romana Congress in Seville in nineteen twenty-nine, and she raved about them." Dietrich found out that the Colonel knew his friend Msgr. de Solages well. They had frequently gone mountain climbing together. This coincidence filled Dietrich's heart with gratitude. A human contact was established, and that was all important.

Père Duployer then told his guests that the plans of his regiment had taken another course. They were not to fly to Morocco but to take buses to Pau, and they were to leave soon. After a brief deliberation, the colonel told Dietrich that he and Father Österreicher were welcome to accompany them to Pau. "But what about my wife?" Dietrich exclaimed. "I am sorry," said the colonel, "but a military transport cannot take women." Close to despair, Dietrich then exclaimed, "Do you expect me to leave her all alone, exposed to the greatest dangers, just to save my own life? It is out of the question." Another deliberation followed, and then an inspiration came to the colonel: "I think I have a solution", he said. "We could put you all in a bus marked with a Red Cross; that would take care of our problem."

Overwhelmed by gratitude, Dietrich rushed back to his family, and soon afterward they were on their way to Pau, which was to remain unoccupied until 1942. For the first time in days, they could eat without having their throats constricted with anguish. It was also their first good night. Many bad ones, however, were still to follow. During their short stay in Pau, Franzi, always on the lookout for news, went out to collect information and came back, pale as a ghost, with the terrible news that paragraph 17 of the armistice Pétain had signed contained a clause that all refugees in the unoccupied zone of France were to register with the local police, who were required to send a complete list of all foreigners to the occupying forces. Those sought by the Gestapo were subject to extradition. Once again, the von Hildebrands were in a trap. The French were likely to sympathize with the refugees, but there are always people who, for a paltry sum of money, are ready to betray others. Moreover, disobeying the order of paragraph 17 could mean retaliation. The Nazis could decide that, since the conditions of the armistice had not been respected, they were entitled to invade the whole of France.

In view of this new development, the von Hildebrands decided to go back to Toulouse. There they would be farther from the occupied zone and closer to friends and connections who might be able to help them. They arrived on June 27, 1940. Since all hotels and inns required their guests to register at the police station, the only chance of not being asked for papers was to look for a room in the slums of Toulouse. Von Hildebrand knew that in a city of this size he could easily find someone who, in return for being well paid for a room, would not ask any questions. He found what he was looking for—a smelly, dirty room in a basement; it had no toilet, no doorbell, and no daylight. The house, if it can be called that, was situated in a street that was clearly inhabited by the unreliable stratum of the population. The man willing to rent them the room asked no questions and gleefully pocketed the shameful amount of money that he requested for such accommodations. The contrast between this dwelling and San Francesco was tragicomic. It challenged Dietrich to live up to the example of Saint Paul, who could adapt himself to poverty as well as to riches (see Phil 4:12).

As a precaution, during their stay in Toulouse, the von Hildebrands remained in their hovel all day long. Only very early in the morning did they go out to attend Mass in the nearest church, take a watery cup of coffee in a cheap bar, and rush back "home". Whenever Dietrich saw a policeman, he would immediately turn in another direction. He knew then what it felt like to be a thief or a criminal sought by the police—always on the alert, always in a state of fear. Mr. von Seckel, who found other accommodations in the city, came every day to give vent to his despair, repeating that they were hopelessly lost. Such complaining did not help the morale of the other refugees. Msgr. de Solages did everything in his power to help his friends, but all his efforts proved to be in vain.

Dietrich and his family remained in Toulouse from late June to mid-July 1940. Although they had escaped the immediate danger they faced in Bayonne, Dietrich knew that he was still a hunted man, that at any moment his hiding place could be found out and he and his entourage would be arrested. The half-life he was leading in the shadows of Toulouse's slums could not go on forever. It was imperative that he find some way out. He kept praying that, again, divine Providence would intervene. Before long, his prayer was granted.

In 1939, von Hildebrand's friend Balduin Schwarz, with whom he had initially stayed when he fled to Fribourg, had left Switzerland and for a while was teaching in a school in Limoges. When the Germans invaded France, he had volunteered for the French army and served at the front. But as the German army was racing down France, his wife, Leni, and their little boy, Stephan, left Limoges and took a train to Toulouse. Thanks to Msgr. de Solages, they found out where the von Hildebrands were hiding and brought them an important piece of news. Balduin had received a letter from Professor Yves Simon, a French philosopher teaching at the University of Notre Dame in Indiana, urging him, if he or his family needed help, to turn to a friend of his who lived in Brive la Gaillarde. His name was Edmond Michelet. Simon praised his friend highly as a deeply devout Catholic and a man of incredible generosity. Leni was convinced that Michelet could help Dietrich and his family. The problem was that the mail was totally unreliable. Not only was it censored, but France was in a state of chaos, and one never knew whether letters would arrive at their destination.

Meanwhile, Mücki Solbrig, who had been interned in Gurs, was informed in early July that she was entitled to go back to the place that she came from, namely, Limoges. In order to do so, she had to go through Brive. As soon as Dietrich received this information, he did not hesitate and scribbled a hasty note to Edmond Michelet. "I do not know you", he wrote, "but my life is in danger. Is there anything you can do to help me? Miss Solbrig will explain the rest." He gave this message to Mücki, who gave it personally to Edmond Michelet when she traveled through Brive to Limoges.

It is almost two hundred miles from Toulouse to Brive. To travel such a distance in July 1940 was extremely difficult. Humanly speaking, it was madness to expect a total stranger to pay attention to von Hildebrand's plea. But once again, he put all his hope in God.

The days of early July dragged on. The dirt, the smell, the heat, the darkness, and the insecurity were nearly unbearable. But some five days after Mücki left, on or about July 12, 1940, von Hildebrand heard a knock on the door. His heart beating wildly, he went to open it, thinking that the police had found his hiding place and had come to threaten him for having failed to register as required.

A man he did not know stood before him, wearing a Basque beret. He brusquely asked him, "Am I talking to Dietrich von Hildebrand?" With a trembling voice, von Hildebrand answered, "Yes." The man then said, "I am Edmond Michelet from Brive." Unable to trust his eyes, von Hildebrand embraced his visitor. There is a French maxim, attributed to Napoleon: "Impossible is not French." It truly applies in this case. One could just as well say, "Impossible is not Catholic", for Michelet was an ardent Catholic who served God in serving his neighbor.

There was no time for talk: "I have a car waiting for you", he said. "Please join me immediately." In a few moments, Dietrich and Gretchen had packed their few belongings and joined the man who turned out to be their savior. Father Österreicher was invited to accompany them, too.

Michelet had left nothing to chance. The car he had brought had a Red Cross sign painted on it. There was also a nurse, a veteran of World War I, who for this occasion had put on her old and somewhat tight uniform. This was a necessary precaution because there were police at all check-points, and traveling was a risky affair. Once in the car, Michelet informed his guests that he was a wholesale grocer by profession, that he was married and had seven children, and that he was responsible for supplying Brive with victuals. For this reason, he had access to some gas, which was strictly rationed at the time. He had gotten out of Brive by offering a tankful of gas to a captain he knew who was eager to get some. In return, he had asked the captain to give him an official permit to go to Toulouse to pick up some sick people, a bargain to which the captain had agreed. Michelet was planning to provide Dietrich, his family, friends, and ac-quaintances with false French identification papers. Then they could go down to Marseilles and try their luck at getting visas there. Michelet was incredibly busy. Not only did he have to provide for a whole town, but his house was full of refugees coming from northern France and the Low Countries. Nevertheless, he managed to find a room at his brother's house, where von Hildebrand and his wife were received with a Christian kindness that, once again, brought tears to their eyes. After eight days, they were each given the famous "green card" (*carte d'identité*), with false names. Ironically, von Hilde-brand had become Jules Richard, a name that ill-fitted a penniless man, for *Richard* in French means "very rich man". With these precious papers in their pockets, the von Hildebrands could now enjoy the beauty of Brive, its cathe-dral, and its lovely squares. The horizon, nevertheless, re-mained clouded. It was still not clear whether they would ever be able to escape from France, for a new regulation had been passed requiring all exit visas to be sent to the French government in Vichy, which in turn had to send them to Wiesbaden, Germany, for final approval. In addition to obtaining a Spanish transit visa, the von Hildebrands now had to find a way to obtain another exit visa from France (for the one they had obtained before the armistice was no longer valid), without alerting the Vichy officials (and then the German Nazi authorities) of their departure.

The Michelet family made a deep impression on the von Hildebrands. They found it difficult to find words adequate to express their gratitude to these extraordinary people. They were exemplary Christians who risked their lives to help foreigners and total strangers. Their fervent prayers went up to God, through whose providence they had met with help from these heroic individuals. In spite of the tremendous difficulty of the situation, there was love and peace in the Michelet household. Madame Michelet seemed to be fully worthy of her extraordinary husband. It was she who forged the prefect's signature on their green cards, aware of the risks. (Her youngest child at the time was only four years old. In his book on his father,[12] Claude Michelet relates that Edmond paid a visit to the prefect of Brive la Gaillarde and invented a reason that forced the prefect to leave his office for a short period. Michelet then used the seals that were needed to produce fake *cartes d'identité*.)

The von Hildebrands and Father Österreicher stayed in Brive for about ten days. On or around July 22, 1940, they left Brive and took a train back to Toulouse. When the guard came to check on the passengers, all they had to do was to show the "green card", and they were left in peace. When they arrived in Toulouse, they rushed to give Franzi, his wife,

---

[12] *Edmond Michelet, Mon Père* (Paris: Presses de la Cité, 1971), p. 8.

Mr. von Seckel, and his friend the documents the Michelets had obtained for them. During their absence, Franzi had had a terrible scare. A policeman had caught him and insisted that he should register immediately. Thanks to Msgr. de Solages, who had interceded with the police commissioner, Franzi was given a brief respite. Now, with his false papers, he was safe.

After one night in Toulouse, again hunting the visas that would enable them to escape France, the whole von Hildebrand entourage moved south to Marseilles. The very day of their departure, July 24, the Nazis were "visiting" Toulouse. Just to see the abhorred Nazi uniforms made them all shudder. They arrived in Marseilles on July 25 at 8 A.M. Michelet was waiting for them, to make sure that everything was working smoothly. He stayed only for a few hours. Now that he had achieved what he intended to do for his protégés, he could rush back to Brive, where other urgent duties awaited him.[13]

The von Hildebrands immediately went to the Dominican convent on Avenue Rostand, where Dietrich had given talks in early May. They were received like old friends. With loving efficiency the Dominicans found living quarters for

[13] After having helped innumerable people, Michelet was arrested by the Gestapo in 1943 (the whole of France having been occupied in 1942) and sent to Dachau. There he continued his work of charity, helping other prisoners in every possible way. In 1945 an epidemic of typhus broke out in the camp, and Michelet nursed his companions until being infected with the disease himself. The liberating forces found him taking care of the sick. He was the last one to leave the camp, having refused to go until all his countrymen had been repatriated. Finally, he returned to France, where his wife and seven children anxiously awaited him. In 1946, Michelet was named minister of the Army by Charles de Gaulle. Later, when de Gaulle once again became head of state, he reappointed Michelet. Michelet, who was one of the very few men de Gaulle trusted and admired, died in 1970. There are rumors that the process for his beatification has been initiated.

them. First they were the guests of a generous young family on the outskirts of Marseilles. There, they celebrated the feast of Saint Anne on July 26. Soon, they were transferred to a beautiful apartment in Marseilles itself, one that a rich lady who was leaving for the summer had put at the disposal of refugees. It was large enough to accommodate not only all the von Hildebrands but Mr. von Seckel and his friend as well. Once again, their hearts overflowed with gratitude. In spite of all this, their situation remained precarious, but the fragrance of supernatural charity was so gratifying that all they could do was to thank God and thank their benefactors.

August commenced, for the refugees a month rich in fruitless efforts, disappointments, and anxieties. The question remained: How were they to obtain the exit visa they needed to get to Portugal, without alerting the Nazi officials?

While in Marseilles in August 1940, von Hildebrand, through the Dominicans, made the acquaintance of the Brazilian consul, a devout Catholic, who gave them Brazilian visas. Through him also, von Hildebrand was able to obtain the Spanish transit visa he had long been seeking, as well as a Portuguese visa. All these seals, however, were useless without French exit visas.

For a while, it seemed that Dietrich would have to find a way out of France that would not require a French exit visa. He left no stone unturned seeking an avenue of escape. One day, he heard that there was a foreign ship anchored at some distance from the shore of Marseilles and that it was going to the United States. With Mr. von Seckel, he hired a small boat, which took them out to the ship. They tried to convince the captain to take them as passengers without an exit visa. But the captain refused to grant their request.

Another hope arose on the horizon when Dietrich found

out that an employee of the prefecture of Marseilles had arranged a way of escape through the Pyrénées. The employee collaborated with a Spanish customs officer at the border and had succeeded in guiding several people to Spain. He requested the sum of 80,000 francs per person, however—400,000 francs for the whole von Hildebrand family. Of course, Dietrich von Hildebrand did not have the money. But a priest whom he had previously met, hearing about his plight, came to see him and said, "I am not rich, but I have inherited a house from my parents. Please, allow me to take a mortgage on that house and give you the money you need for your escape. Do me the favor of accepting my offer." Dietrich von Hildebrand broke down in tears when he heard this proposal. He was overwhelmed by the charity he had tasted daily since March 11, 1938, twenty-nine months earlier. This offer was so generous that he felt he could not accept it. Moreover, if the Nazis ever found out that this priest had helped an enemy escape, he could be sent to a concentration camp. Von Hildebrand raised this objection, but the priest rebuffed it, saying, "Do you truly think that to risk my life in order to help a friend would be a valid reason for my not doing it?" That was Catholicism at its truest. Indeed, there are people who live the saying of Christ, "There is no greater love than to give one's life for a friend." Nevertheless, Dietrich felt that he could not accept this noble offer.

Not long after, he heard that the escape route through the Pyrénées to Spain had been discovered by the Nazis, and that the last batch of refugees, including their guide, had been arrested.[14]

---

[14] The tragic thing was that when people safely reached Portugal, they would tell their friends and acquaintances about their escape route. Lisbon was full of Nazi spies who carefully collected such information and relayed it to their superiors in France.

The days in Marseilles were passing quickly, and the anxiety of the von Hildebrands mounted as they contemplated what would happen if the Germans decided to occupy the whole of France. By this time Dietrich had seemingly explored every legal and illegal method of getting out of France and was now running out of options. Finally, early in September 1940, a priest whom he had met informed him that his brother-in-law was working in the prefecture in Perpignan and that he might be able to help him and his family. This brother-in-law had been caught delivering illegal French exit visas and had been fired, but he would not officially leave his position until Monday, September 9. The priest said that he might be able to come up with the needed documents if Dietrich applied to him immediately. Armed with a letter of recommendation from the priest, Dietrich and his family rushed to this man's office on Friday, September 6. The employee requested the passports of all of von Hildebrand's entourage, promising he would return them on Monday, September 9. Von Hildebrand handed them over, with a trembling heart.

The weekend was long and full of anxiety for the refugees. Dietrich had taken an enormous risk in entrusting their passports to a stranger, and one who was already in a compromised position. What if the man was caught again and all their passports were seized? Even after so many close calls, von Hildebrand knew he might be facing the end game in his efforts to elude the Nazis. There was no way of predicting whether the risk would be worth it. He and his friends would simply have to wait. Prayer alone sustained them.

One can imagine the refugees' relief when they received back the passports on Monday, September 9, carefully stamped with the French exit visas. After their months of failed efforts to amass the necessary documents, the way was clear. Within hours, von Hildebrand and his family, Mr. von Seckel and his friend, and Father Österreicher took a train for the Spanish border. They left France at Cerbère and entered Spain at Port Bou. They spent one night in Barcelona and then went straight to Madrid, where Dietrich paid a brief visit to the papal nuncio, Gaetano Cicognani.[15] He was disappointed that he could not visit the Prado museum because it was closed that day. The party then went to Lisbon, entering Portugal on Friday, September 13, 1940. At that point, the von Hildebrand entourage disbanded. Von Seckel and his friend took ship for the New World, as did Father Österreicher, who sailed directly to New York.

Arriving with his family in the Portuguese capital, Dietrich found out that the American Rockefeller Foundation had been desperately trying to locate him. He had in fact covered his traces so well that their efforts had been in vain. He was informed that his friend Jacques Maritain had managed to put him on the list of one hundred professors whose lives were in danger because of their "impure blood". Dietrich's name, along with that of his friend Balduin Schwarz (whose wife was Jewish), was added to the list because Maritain knew that von Hildebrand had fought against Nazism in Vienna and that he was sought by the Gestapo. The Rockefeller Foundation would cover the costs of the trip to the United States.

Dietrich, Gretchen, Franzi, Deirdre, and little Catherine waited in Portugal until the middle of October 1940 to obtain the necessary visas that would enable them to depart for the United States. On October 15, Dietrich and his wife obtained an American immigration visa; and on November 13, the whole von Hildebrand family embarked on the *Serpa Pinto*, a Portuguese ship, on its way to Rio de Janeiro via

[15] Gaetano Cicognani (1881–1962) was papal nuncio to Spain from 1938 to approximately 1953.

Dakar. They arrived in the Brazilian capital, where, once again, they were received with kindness, thanks to a Benedictine friend of von Hildebrand's, Otto von Württemberg. They also went to São Paolo and visited their dear friends Heinrich Reinach and his wife, who had wisely left Germany a few years earlier because of the Nazi racist laws.

On December 13, 1940, Dietrich von Hildebrand and his wife embarked on a ship heading for New York. (Unable to obtain an American immigration visa, Franzi and Deirdre stayed behind in Brazil until they were able to get visitor visas to the United States in February 1941.) To their surprise, their great friend of yore, Friedrich Wilhelm Foerster, and his family were on the same ship. They arrived in New York on Monday, December 23, 1940. Father Österreicher was at the pier to greet them. As soon as his voice could reach them, he shouted the good news that Dietrich von Hildebrand had been appointed to a professorship at Fordham University, the Jesuit university in New York.

God, in His goodness, had saved him.